MORGAN
the
MAGNIFICENT

MORGAN
THE MAGNIFICENT

The Life of
J. PIERPONT MORGAN
(1837-1913)

By

JOHN K. WINKLER
Author of *John D., A Portrait in Oils*

NEW YORK · THE VANGUARD PRESS

BM848W

BT 2630

TO

H.

A Practicing Friend

CONTENTS

CHAPTER ONE

THE MAN

PERHAPS ONCE IN A HUNDRED YEARS IS BORN A MIND capable of entering a sphere of higher mathematics closed to ordinary mortals. A direct and synthetic mind that cuts across lots and flies straight to conclusions, intuitively and by processes unknown to itself.

Such a mind we call genius.

Such was the mind of John Pierpont Morgan.

By sheer mental magic, Morgan solved the most complicated problems. He was a mathematical marvel. This quality in itself destined the direction of great affairs. But no single faculty placed this astonishing American upon his lofty pedestal as the greatest banker, the greatest organizer, the greatest master of capital of his time.

Morgan had vision and surpassing imagination. Add to these incredible audacity, sublime self-confidence, unqualified courage, amazing virility of mind and body, and a personality that can only be described as overwhelming. Small wonder, then, that this man, part poet, part pirate, grew (in the estimation of himself and others) almost into a God; and, as a God, ruled for a generation the pitiless, predatory world of cash.

Morgan was a colossal adventurer in the realm of reality. He took what he wanted. His code was his own.

[3]

He did things that today could not be defended in law or morals. But, for his time and generation, he played the game and played it fairly. He preferred the strong rather than the weak as antagonists. Of course, when it suited his purpose, he bowled over both.

Eventually he became a sort of super-government. Often, indeed, he took unto himself or events forced upon him the function of Government itself. In the panic of 1907 he was dictator of the United States in all save formal title; and there were other occasions when his tremendous power had to be called upon to repair the ineptitude of the lawmakers.

In the early years of the century, Morgan unquestionably was tending toward almost exclusive control of the cash and credit of America. His enormous transportation and industrial combinations had swept into his hands a large part of the country's available capital. He became a symbol. He was Wealth, Power, Gold.

Wall Street paid him homage that was almost comic. Everyone scrambled to get into his stock pools. Staid, conservative men of affairs went into transports of bliss when Morgan placed their names upon his subscription lists. At the lifting of a Morgan finger awe fell upon the financial community. It was odd, almost grotesque, that one man's personality could play so large a part in a country consecrated to the idea of popular infallibility.

Morgan's power was not confined to America. The great of the earth fawned before him. Kings and Emperors vied to do him honor. It seemed that nothing could stop him. But something did.

[4]

A Safe Man in the White House was shot by an assassin, and a bold, intelligent, ambitious young political captain became President. That event spelled the doom of Morgan's plan, if plan he had, to organize the basic industries of the country into enormous aggregations of capital such as the United States Steel Corporation. The Steel Corporation was Morgan's masterpiece—an industrial empire that only he could have fashioned.

Theodore Roosevelt, the new President, was dowered with an energy as abnormal as Morgan's own. Roosevelt was, in Henry Adams' expressive phrase, "pure act." Also, he was fearless and quick to respond to the public will. The public—that portion of it which was not seeking eagerly to enrich itself by following the lead of the wicked Wall Street men—was keenly aroused over the growth of the giant corporations.

Spurred by the bitter pens and tongues of the muckrakers, the common man looked upon Morgan and his ilk as rough, red rogues who were plundering and stealing right and left. In many cases the estimate was not far wrong. Roosevelt was in touch with and responsive to the popular point of view. Morgan was not. He knew nothing and cared less about the ordinary run of human kind. Morgan sprang from whatever aristocracy this country may boast, and it was his chief pride that he was a *gentleman*. He and the young President were fated for conflict. "When I became President," says Roosevelt in his autobiography, "the question as to the *method* by which the United States Government was to control the corporations was not yet important. The absolutely vital question was whether the Government had power to control them at all."

Roosevelt found a way. He selected Morgan as his chief antagonist, giving the latter the shock of his life by suing to dissolve the Northern Securities Company, Morgan's gigantic merger of the Great Northern and the Northern Pacific railroads. Slur this action as so many have done, it seems to me that it was a dauntless act by a dauntless man.

The Northern Securities Company was an outgrowth of a tremendous contest for supremacy in the railroad world between Morgan and his ally, James J. Hill, and a coalition led by Edward H. Harriman and the Standard Oil. The struggle was like a great spectacle one watches in an arena. While the world looked on in breathless wonderment, men of illimitable power flung into the fray unheard-of masses of capital.

The result was a draw. Morgan, determined to place the Hill lines forever beyond Harriman's reach, hit upon the scheme of forming a huge holding company. Then Roosevelt took a hand.

In the Northern Securities suit Roosevelt forced the United States Supreme Court to reverse itself, in response to public opinion and a changing code of social thought. Roosevelt's victory was narrow, but the Supreme Court declared the merger an illegal combination in restraint of trade. The decision was a body blow to Morgan. It marked the end of an era in high finance.

The relations between Roosevelt and Morgan form a fascinating story. It will be given here so far as we have been able to gather it from those who were intimate with both men. These strong, forceful individuals, one feels sure, would have been comrades had not fate decreed that they should occupy opposing positions in great affairs.

Time and again friends of both sought to bring them together. There were many meetings, but no fusion of friendship. To Roosevelt, Morgan was a man whose talents were devoted entirely to entrenching the power of organized capital. To Morgan, Roosevelt was a gentleman gone wrong—a man who sacrificed all the privileges of his class for common applause. A politician. Morgan despised the tribe.

Morgan was no less colorful in his faults than in his virtues. He cared not a whit what the world thought of him. Each morning he held a levee, a rapid-fire affair, in his great red room at the western end of his lovely Italian Renaissance Library in East Thirty-sixth Street. Those who awaited him might include business associates, friends, art dealers, pensioners, what not.

Though his home was next door, he would often drive up to the Library entrance in an open barouche and come striding into the conference chamber. It mattered not the slightest to him that this fed gossip coupling his name with beautiful women. Let the world tell tales of a luxurious mansion on Forty-sixth Street, just off Fifth Avenue; of parties aboard his yacht; of Lucullan banquets in a private apartment at the Fifth Avenue Hotel where favors to the ladies were bracelets and necklaces of diamond and pearl.

Many women knew Morgan as a generous patron. In a way, his very defiance of convention was a protection. Who but Morgan would have dared to set forth for a church convention accompanied by a famous beauty? While the financier sat in solemn conclave with the men of the cloth, the lady enjoyed the luxury of the Morgan private car, drawn up upon a siding in a leafy suburb! Who but Morgan would have grandly bestowed "dots" of $100,000 each upon lovely young things, whose favors he had enjoyed, when they decided to anchor in the more placid harborage of matrimony? Who but Morgan would boldly have ventured an affair with the beautiful and intellectual wife of a famous and philandering architect?

Morgan's adventures in romance were many and varied. But they were never tainted by open scandal. His women were as loyal, as worshipful as the associates he chose in business. There was no touch of the tawdry in the lighter engagements of his life. Living today, on both sides of the water, are great ladies whose memories of Morgan the Magnificent are touched with a tenderness which time will never erase. They were privileged to see a side of this amazing man completely closed to others. Locked forever in the inner crypt of their natures are tales that will never be told. It is a pity.

Morgan was not a sensualist, but he found real stimulation in romantic as in religious emotion—a compound by no means rare. Fitting a certain need of his nature, women were attracted to him, irresistibly. With them he could be in turn Rabelaisian and delicate. He liked parties where the talk was free and joyed in the exuberant company of ballet belles. He was equally at home in the boudoirs of fastidious ladies. Few women could withstand his leonine love-making.

Like some of the fabled kings of the Old Testament he was eclectic in his choice of mistresses. He collected beautiful women as he collected objects of art. More than one young woman of humble station was distinguished by Morgan's attentions. While the affair lasted—sometimes long afterward—the financier was a lordly protector.

The path of a Morgan favorite was smoothed for life. He was ever solicitous of her welfare. He was genuinely pleased if she made a happy marriage. He deprecated the social cruelties inflicted upon women who defied the conventions.

In the heart of New York's lower East-side stands a great building—the Lying-In Hospital—devoted to the care of expectant mothers. Morgan founded this institution and lavished great sums upon it. From the tenuous filaments of a tempestuous romance this building grew. The lady of the liaison pointed out to Morgan the urgent need of a modern maternity hospital and led him into the project.

Many and varied were the ribald jests when it became known that Morgan had established a maternity hospital. It was a standing joke among the gay bloods of the bars and the clubs. But not even the boldest of his intimates ventured to twit the financier.

Lying-In soon became renowned, its medical staff including many noted specialists. Incidentally, several doctors married Morgan mistresses, though well aware of the nature of their former relationship. Does this not open a fascinating field for speculation? Why should physicians and surgeons be less squeamish than most men in such matters? Does their training tend to lessen respect for chastity and lead them to believe that modern Puritanism absurdly overvalues it?

Morgan's extra-marital ventures were no secret to his friends. Nor could they be concealed from his family.

But Morgan was Morgan and his life was his own.

He was not so tolerant of the indulgences of others, particularly those men whom he raised to positions of eminence and trust in his great consolidations. Charles M. Schwab will never forget an interview with Morgan shortly after the latter had made Schwab president of the Steel Corporation. Schwab had just returned from a sky-larking trip to Europe. The papers had been filled with tales of his exuberant exploits—gambling at Monte Carlo and the like. Morgan did not think these episodes consonant with the dignity of Schwab's position and bluntly told him so. Schwab pleaded that everything he had done had been done openly and not behind closed doors. "Humph," remarked Morgan witheringly, "that's what doors are for."

When Morgan was in a mood like that, the strongest quailed before him. His frown could cow the most ferocious of financial desperadoes. Morgan's eyes were awful in anger. Such eyes had seldom been set in human head. They blazed from beneath shaggy eyebrows. They seemed to change color with every emotion. They were really dark blue, but even those who knew Morgan well described them, varyingly, as of every shade from light gray to black.

At times they could soften and become as liquid as those of a woman, as when the financier indulged in a daily romp with his children and, later, with his numerous grandchildren. He permitted nothing to interfere with this phase of his family life. His children remember swarming over him, tugging at his sweeping moustaches and great double watch-chain, and exploring his pockets for hidden sweets and cookies. They rumpled his hair and pulled his clothing awry. But he didn't mind. He paid little attention to appearance or attire.

Morgan watched over his children as he did over his companies. In both cases, though, his authority was absolute, if benevolent. To this day the Morgan children look upon their father's memory with a degree of reverence approaching religious awe. In turn, Morgan's veneration for his father was almost Oriental in its intensity. Occasionally, generally late at night on some long journey or out alone upon the ocean, he would speak of his early life, the careful training his father had given him at home and in business, and the latter's pride when he first found his son standing upon his own feet.

Morgan's religion was a strange, depthful thing. It was the strongest impellent in his nature; and undoubtedly was linked with occasional waves of melancholy which swept over him. However, his religion, like everything else, was a private possession not to be shared with his fellow-man. Deep within Morgan burned the zealous doctrines of the old Puritan divines. From earliest childhood he had been taught that man comes into the world a sinner; and that only a favored few can escape the hell fire to which our sphere is doomed.

The only hope of salvation, Morgan believed, lay in

the doctrine of the Atonement. All his life he wavered not an inch from the beliefs of his boyhood. The first article of his will contains this remarkable declaration:

"I commit my soul into the hands of my Saviour, in full confidence that having redeemed it and washed it in His most precious blood, He will present it faultless before the throne of my Heavenly Father; and I entreat my children to maintain and defend, at all hazard, and at any cost of personal sacrifice, the blessed doctrine of the complete atonement for sin through the blood of Jesus Christ, once offered, and through that alone."

The grip religion had upon Morgan was extraordinary. Though no scholar and never a deeply read man, he was thoroughly conversant with the history of the American Protestant Episcopal Church. It was one of the curious anomalies of his nature that he could revel in gatherings of ecclesiastics where dull and dusty discussions of dogma and church law consumed the sessions. For decades he dominated the American Episcopal Church. He acquired the position, almost, of a lay Pope, and probably had more influence in church affairs than any member of the House of Bishops.

The Rev. Dr. W. S. Rainsford says of Morgan's religious nature:

"His beliefs were to him precious heirlooms. He bowed before them as the Russian bows to the 'Ikon' before he salutes the master of the house. The Evangelical 'Plan of Salvation' was to him what the Ark of the Covenant was to ancient Judaism. Of how that 'plan' grew, what other earlier plans were merged in it, he knew nothing. So Mr. Morgan had the peace and power of religious assurance, while the very nature of his assurance precluded in him the possibility of spiritual development. His religion was a talent to be wrapped in its own napkin and venerated in the secret place of his soul; laid aside in safe disuse, rather than passed from man to man in life's great barter."

For twenty-four years Dr. Rainsford, a picturesque Cambridge University Irishman, was rector of the Morgan church—St. George's on Stuyvesant Square in lower New York. Though total opposites in social outlook—Rainsford believed in "salvation by human touch"—these powerful individualists were irresistibly drawn to each other.

During the period of his pastorate, Rainsford breakfasted each Monday with his senior warden, Morgan; and perhaps drew closer to him than any other. The autocrat of the breakfast table confided in Rainsford as he did in few.

When Rainsford took over St. George's in 1883 the church was dying of dry rot. Rainsford made St. George's a free church and welcomed the teeming masses of the East Side. Preaching a religion of broad humanitarianism, almost of socialization, Rainsford restored St. George's ancient glory. Morgan grumbled at the revolutionary creed of the new voice in the pulpit, but recognized in Rainsford a man who got results, and so backed the vigorous young rector to the limit.

That was Morgan's way. Beneath the crust he showed the world, he was a creature of strong feeling and intense emotionalism. If he liked a man he gave him everything. If he didn't it was war to the hilt. Morgan was a man of fascinating prejudices and a good hater. He never sought to conceal his dislikes. He had a deep-seated anti-Semitic prejudice and on more than one occasion needlessly antagonized great Jewish banking firms. He judged men eye to eye and they went up or down in his estimation accordingly.

Some of his pet personal dislikes were E. H. Harriman, Andrew Carnegie, John W. Gates, and John D. Rockefeller. Colored by prejudice, Morgan always underestimated Harriman. It is interesting to speculate how far these men could have gone if they had joined their genius at the cross-roads in their careers. Morgan always winced when Carnegie addressed him as "Pierpont." Gates he considered an "unsafe" man. Rockefeller's cold money-lust chilled Morgan although he admired the Oil King's business genius and modeled his management of the Steel Corporation upon Standard Oil.

Morgan liked William Rockefeller and made John D.'s less pious younger brother a member of the Corsair Club, the highest honor that could come to a friend of Morgan. The Club was limited in membership to an even dozen and met at intervals aboard Morgan's yacht, the *Corsair*, or elsewhere. At Morgan's death in 1913 there were ten surviving members: Lewis Cass Ledyard, Joseph H. Choate, George S. Bowdoin, Charles Lanier, Francis R. Appleton, George L. Rives, Frank K. Sturgis, Charles Steele, Chauncey M. Depew, and William Rockefeller. Their names were not mentioned in the will, but to each was left a piece of silver plate.

Morgan was a kingly host aboard the *Corsair*. In successive decades, he built three great yachts called *Corsair*, each more imposing than its predecessor. The name satisfied his instinct for the dramatic. Did he visualize himself as a modern corsair as his splendid, black-hulled yacht bore him over the sea? Morgan was a great showman. He knew well the value of a setting just as he knew the force of a frown or the effect of a roar. For several years the *Corsair* was the flagship of the New York Yacht Club. Thereafter intimate friends called Morgan "Commodore." It was the only title in which the first financier of the world gloried.

At the height of his power Morgan grew to look upon himself as a modern counterpart of a gorgeous Renaissance prince. His pride expanded with his prestige. He growled angrily when he heard that a wit had dubbed him *Pierpontifex Maximus*; but beamed with pleasure when compared to Lorenzo the Magnificent. Morgan, too, could make gestures as magnificent as the greatest of the Medici, such as his coronation gift of a $500,000 tapestry to King Edward. Morgan, though, was no Lorenzo. He was the greatest collector of his time in many fields of art, but he did not support contemporary art.

Morgan's vast collections—paintings, porcelains, Bibles, miniatures, manuscripts, jewelry, and the like— were assembled with an apparent prodigality that no government could match. But Morgan was largely a checkbook collector; he was not a connoisseur in a finer sense. He loved beautiful things and liked to surround himself with them, but he bought under the guidance of expert salaried advisers, and seldom experienced the thrill of those personal discoveries that so delight the true connoisseur. He bought in batches; whatever plan and method there was may be credited to his advisers.

As an art purchaser, Morgan was difficult for dealers. He did not believe in giving the dealer a large profit. In the midst of a dicker he would turn his terrific eyes full upon his visitor and exclaim: "I have heard enough. I'll take this at the price you paid plus fifteen per cent. How much did you pay?"

It was a bold man who dared prevaricate as to price or seek to cozen Morgan into a more generous offer. Most items in the vast collections had appreciated enormously at Morgan's death, though admittedly underappraised.

Morgan had his disappointments as well as his triumphs as a collector. He was never able, for example, to persuade John Hay's widow to part with the original manuscript of Lincoln's Gettysburg Address, presented by Lincoln to his young secretary, Hay. Strange to say, Morgan was always eager to add to his imposing array of Lincoln letters and papers. His interest in Lincoln must have been the attraction of opposites!—another fascinating idiosyncrasy in the nature of Morgan the gentleman, the aristocrat, the Bourbon.

Although he believed in America and was an ardent patriot after his fashion, Morgan despised democracy. He was totally unable to deal with those whom he did not consider his equals. No duke of feudal France, no chieftain of a Scottish clan, was more contemptuous of the ordinary man than was Morgan. His boyhood was

passed in New England, a region of ingrown sectional-
ism; his later adolescence in a Europe where class lines
were rigidly drawn. From the cradle he had imbibed a
certain pride of blood and breeding. At twenty (1857)
he came into Wall Street, a lank, cocky youth thoroughly imbued with belief in his own destiny and with
the backing of a father who was rapidly becoming the
most forceful figure in a famous Anglo-American banking firm. Naturally young Morgan's thought was turned
eastward. It was so all his life. Not that he did not understand and take full advantage of the commercial
potentialities of the great crude country that was
America. But for his rules of conduct, his standards of
life, he drew rather upon England than upon the country of his birth.

Long after he had become a focal point, almost the
core, of the greatest movement of massed capital since
the world began, Morgan looked upon himself as the
agent, the trustee of clients largely European. He modeled his banking firm upon the great British and Continental establishments that came into being with the
development of power machinery. His career was in no
sense fortuitous. But events, of course, shaped him as
much as he shaped events.

It was this extraordinary man's most glaring weakness that he refused to place himself in touch with the
social currents that were influencing his time. He sold
his securities in every hamlet in the land but he never
troubled to meet the customers.

Hence it came to him as a shock when his acts were
questioned and the agencies of the law and of publicity

turned upon them. He hated most the parade of his personality and characteristics. In the late nineties it happened that a mystifying skin or blood disease manifested itself in an enormous enlargement of his already prominent nose. Specialists treated the member to no avail. Morgan's general health did not seem to be affected, but the nose remained bulbous and spotted with red and purple marks. The disfigurement was seized upon by the ribald cartoonists of the muckraking era, and the financier became painfully sensitive about it.

Until the very last year of his life (Morgan died a fortnight before his seventy-sixth anniversary) this was the only outward indication of physical deterioration in a man who had lived to the hilt, who was a heavy eater, a fancier of fine wines, an enormous smoker. From early manhood Morgan scorned physical exercise. In the mid-fifties he became alarmed over his increasing weight and toyed for a few days with dumb-bells and other gymnastic apparatus.

Feeling no better, he had himself thumped and tested by a famous physician. The latter told him: "You have worked all your life with your brain. Your body is secondary. Changing your habits might be fatal. Take no exercise in any form. Don't even walk a block when you can ride in a hansom. You have a magnificent constitution. Rely upon it."

Morgan had cut down to twenty a day the big, black, murderous cigars he smoked and had toned down correspondingly in his other habits. Thereafter, though, he ate and smoked and drank as he pleased—and lived to attend the funerals of most of his contemporaries.

Morgan was a large man, thick of chest, with a big head (he wore a seven and seven-eighths hat) set close down on burly shoulders, features large, a high, fine forehead, a square, bulldog chin. His dark hair gradually thinned and changed to iron-gray and to white, but his moustache until the final years remained a midnight hue.

Long past his seventieth year, he moved with almost nerveless alertness, surprising in a man of his age and bulk. His stride was elemental, jungle-like. To those who came before him, he seemed a citadel of silence and reserve force, cold, impressive, brusque, tramping forward, always making his visitor uncover his batteries first. He seemed as impregnable as a force of Nature. His mental power, as well as his physical resources, was the marvel of those who watched him. His mind seemed ever upon a distant purpose which he alone perceived. It was Bismarck's way. It was Napoleon's way.

"Morgan," remarked a noted lawyer who had many dealings with him, "had one chief mental asset—a tremendous five minutes' concentration of thought. A sort of clairvoyant instinct seemed to dictate his decisions. He always went to the main question intuitively and let the rest follow. He never puttered about among trifles."

The "trifles" were left to his partners. "I am not a good judge of men," he once told a friend. "My first guess is sometimes right. My second never is." Morgan was over-modest. He would never have been able to accomplish what he did unless he had possessed astounding selective ability in choosing men to work with and under him.

The house of Morgan was always known as a partner-killer. Morgan would not bother with details. His mind encompassed a greater picture. The detail work he left to the capable group surrounding him. These men adored their chief. "Senior," as they called him, had a certain love-compelling quality (when he chose to reveal it) which none could resist. Hence they accepted his lightest suggestions as orders from on high, gave themselves day and night to his mighty projects, and more than one died in his service.

Morgan, most likely, was totally unconscious of the terrific strain he placed upon these men. He judged others' powers of endurance by his own. Fierce in his friendships, he would have struck down in his tracks the critic who dared suggest that he was crowding cruel labor upon the frailer shoulders of his first partners—Egisto P. Fabbri, J. Hood Wright, Charles H. Coster, and Morgan's brother-in-law, Walter Burns. Yet these and others essayed to hold Morgan's soul-crushing pace and died under their burdens.

Morgan alone came through the mill. Business was never his bedfellow. If any particularly knotty matter was bothering him, he would retire to his den, riffle the cards at solitaire (as did Napoleon), and work out a solution quickly and decisively. Or he would corral two or three cronies in a private banquet room or in the cabin of the *Corsair* and sing the night away.

Morgan couldn't sing but thought he could. He had a deep voice and dearly loved to exercise it. He had at his command ditties by the dozen in French, German and English. What he lacked in voice quality he made up in quantity. Into these impromptu musicales the financier entered with as much gusto as he employed in singing hymns. He had a remarkable knowledge of hymns and loved congregational singing. This enthusiasm never deserted him. He would sing hymns alone if he could not find others to carry the verses with him. In the autumn of 1912 St George's Church completed a centennial chapel. Often Morgan drove from his home Saturday afternoons and entered the chapel alone.

"As soon as I learned of this habit," says Dr. Karl Reiland, the present rector, "I used to go over regularly to meet him there. Sometimes I found him kneeling in prayer, or reading or singing a hymn without organ, and alone. He seemed as happy as a child if I sent for one of our organists to play the hymns for us. He would stand in the chancel singing and beating the time, with book in hand, thoroughly enjoying every moment. The doors were always closed—none but the aged sexton and myself knew that the great master of men and things was worshipping in the Temple."

Often the financier would find relief in the companionship of birds or dogs. These and blooded cattle were the animals that chiefly interested him. He had cages of singing canaries in all his homes. They were tenderly cared for. Also, there was a standing order that breadcrumbs were to be distributed daily to sparrows. Woe betide the servant who neglected the duty!

Morgan always loved dogs. Once he possessed the finest kennel of collies in the country. For years Sefton Hero, a collie for which he paid thousands, slept under his bed. In later life he transferred his affection to Pekinese, and seldom traveled unaccompanied by a lively companion of this breed.

Morgan traveled much, but along a beaten path. London, Paris, Rome, the smart Continental watering-places saw him each year. Toward the end of his life, Egypt and Rome held greatest fascination. Although he spoke not a word of Italian, the Eternal City lured him for longer periods each spring. For hours he would sit in his rooms in the Grand Hotel, wrapped in thought, his revery broken only by the bells of the adjoining church, Santa Maria degli Angeli. Often he could be seen standing in the warm sunlight under the church's majestic arches, once a part of the Diocletian baths.

Rome, as did no other spot, appealed to the protean-mooded Morgan. The city and its atmosphere touched the rich emotional strata embedded deep in his nature. Here this extraordinary man found satisfaction for the conflicting elements that warred within him.

One must go back into his beginnings to gain an understanding of these curious and changeable characteristics.

CHAPTER TWO

THE HOUSE OF MORGAN TWO
GENERATIONS BACK

IN 1861 COLONEL HENRY WILSON'S TWENTY-SECOND Massachusetts Regiment was encamped on the northern bank of the Potomac. It was bitter fall weather. A man of seventy-six, in the uniform of a chaplain, doggedly tramped the muddy company streets, beating his thin body with his fists to keep from freezing.

He was a trim, high-headed old gentleman, with full beard, a mass of rebellious white hair, prominent, questing nose, and piercing eyes beneath shaggy brows. His lips were blue from the cold, but they uttered no word of complaint. He walked the night away, his arms flailing against chest and flanks.

Next morning friends found him in his windy tent shaking with a chill, and insisted upon his applying for leave. Reluctantly he signed the paper. A zealous young officer of the day wrote on the back of the application: "Why does he want three days? Give him two."

That afternoon, at the Treasury Department in Washington, the Rev. John Pierpont timidly presented a letter from Senator Sumner to Secretary Salmon P. Chase. The white-haired caller was a little bewildered when ushered at once into the presence of the Secretary. He flushed with pleasure when Mr. Chase asked him whether he was not John Pierpont the poet, author of "Warren's Address Before the Battle of Bunker's Hill"; and recalled the brave occasion in 1825 when Lafayette laid the cornerstone of Bunker Hill Monument. Daniel Webster delivered the oration, and John Pierpont read stirring verses beginning:

"Stand! The ground's your own, my braves!"

The old gentleman acknowledged his identity. Mr. Chase said he wished he could find something for the poet commensurate with his talents; but the only position he could offer was a minor clerkship, the chief duty of which would consist in copying records. Mr. Pierpont accepted this offer gladly.

John Pierpont died five years later holding this obscure post. It was the peaceful but pathetic end of a career that had been turbulent, brilliant, erratic, adventurous.

John Pierpont was the maternal grandfather of John Pierpont Morgan. From him the financier drew more than his given name. No approach to the complex mental and spiritual characteristics of J. P. Morgan is possible without careful examination of the traits and peculiarities of John Pierpont. Many of the qualities congenital in the stern and eloquent grandfather appeared in the grandson: terribly strong feeling, imagination, dash and initiative akin to recklessness, and—above all—insatiable love of the beautiful.

John Pierpont was at once a fanatic with a sense of humor and an intellectual rolling stone. His mind laid fierce hold upon whatever interested him. His life was a succession of triumphant failures, but he was always a gentleman and a fascinating personage. He failed as a merchant, scored no success as a lawyer, but won a measure of fame, if not fortune, as poet, preacher and reformer.

In these days he would have been called a crank or a faddist. He was constantly embroiled in controversy. He preached temperance to a congregation of rum-drinkers and rum-dealers and fiercely advocated freedom for the slaves long before Abolition became popular. He had strong leanings toward Socialism and was virulently opposed to the accumulation of great wealth. Twice he ran for political office in Massachusetts and, though certainly doomed to defeat, supported his cries for reform with such brilliant verse as:

A WORD FROM A PETITIONER

What! our petitions spurned! The prayer
Of thousands—tens of thousands—cast
Unheard beneath your speaker's chair!
But ye *will* hear us, first or last.
The thousands that, last year, ye scorned,
Are millions now. Be warned! Be warned!

He wrote these lines when campaigning for the abolition of imprisonment for debt in Massachusetts. In later years he lectured on spiritualism, insisting that everyone might be able to communicate with the dead if it were not for unbelief. Into all these causes he threw himself without regard for his personal fortunes. Alone, he waged what became known as the Seven Years' War against an influential element in his church, the Hollis

Street Meeting House in Boston; and resigned his pulpit only after he had gleefully demolished before an ecclesiastical court every charge brought against him. His defense was the delight and the joy of his literary associates—Whittier, Holmes, Dana, Mrs. Sigourney, and other figures of the New England renaissance.

In the church war, Mr. Pierpont's opponents charged that his attention had been diverted from his clerical duties "by the making of *books,* and the manufacture of *stoves* and *screws* and *razor strops*—and by entering into every exciting topic that the ingenuity of the fanatic at home, or the imported mountebank, could conjure up to disturb and distract the public mind, such as *Imprisonment for Debt,* the *Militia Law, Antimasonry, Phrenology, Temperance,* and last of all and above all, the *Abolition* of *Slavery,* a question which threatens above all else the destruction of our glorious Union."

In reply, Mr. Pierpont admitted his interest in books, stoves, screws, razor strops, phrenology, etc., and asserted his intention of continuing to preach upon "exciting topics" such as temperance and Abolition—"Sundays and weekdays, by daylight and candle-light, by lamp-light and moonlight; 'at sundry times and in divers manners'; in sermon and in song, in prose and in poetry, in rhyme and blank verse; in conventicles and conventions; in city and country, on both sides of the Alleghenies and both sides of the Atlantic; in pulpits heterodox and in pulpits orthodox; in stagecoach and steamer; in winter and summer; by petition and persuasion."

When the Seven Years' War broke out in 1838, John
Pierpont had already enjoyed a rich experience in life,
Born on April 6, 1785, in Litchfield, Connecticut (that
nursery of great men in and out of the pulpit), he was
a great-grandson of the Rev. James Pierpont who
was active with Elihu Yale in founding Yale College.
James Pierpont was father-in-law to Jonathan Edwards
and a close friend of Cotton Mather. The Pierponts had
been gentlemen and men of property for generations.
The first American Pierpont established a fulling mill
near Boston in 1658. The family traced its ancestry
back to a tenth-century Norman lord, Sir Hugh De
Pierrepont; and derived its name from a *stone bridge*
(*pierre-ponte*) built by Charlemagne in the eighth
century.

With such distinguished blood behind him, young
John Pierpont was graduated from Yale in 1804. One
of his classmates was John C. Calhoun. After assisting
for a short time in the Academy at Bethlehem, Connecticut, in the autumn of 1805 John Pierpont went to
Charleston, South Carolina, and passed nearly four
years as a private tutor in the family of Col. William
Allston, son-in-law of Aaron Burr.

The rich, ripe life of the Old South must have fed
the springs of poetry already bubbling in the young
man of New England. Returning to Connecticut in
1809, he studied law in the school at Litchfield, married
his fourth cousin, Mary Sheldon Lord, and spread his
shingle in Newburyport, Massachusetts. Here, in 1812,
he delivered before the Washington Benevolent Society
a poem that was to become famous, "The Patriot."

Here is one of the verses—with the swing, rhythm, lofty sentiment and patriotism of Kipling's "Recessional":

> What have we, Lord, to bind us
> To this, the Pilgrims' shore?
> Their hill of graves behind us,
> Their watery grave before;
> The wintry surge that dashes
> Against the rocks they trod;
> Their memory and their ashes —
> Be thou our guide, O God.

The law proving distasteful, the young poet afterward unsuccessfully tried mercantile pursuits in Boston and in Baltimore. He was utterly lacking in the business temperament. He and his young wife went through a period of poverty that was not lightened by the birth of successive children. Juliet, third of their six children, was born in Baltimore on July 30, 1816. The same year, the father, sadly miscast as a merchant, published a poem "Airs of Palestine."

Not long ago, the library of an ancient sectarian college in the South yielded this slender volume. It had gathered dust, apparently, for many decades. A note on the fly-leaf, stained almost to the color of parchment, furnished the intelligence that it had been "published for the author" by one B. Edes, printer, "on this thirteenth day of November, in the forty-first year of the Independence of the United States of America."

The poem is composed in heroic couplets. It shows a remarkable grasp of Biblical lore and contains passage after passage of rare beauty, filled with exquisite feeling and cadence. Frequent use of the liquids gives the poem a soft, stately, sonorous loveliness. Yet it was written by a man already turned thirty and struggling to find himself in life.

Already John Pierpont had begun the study of theology. Eking out a slender income as best he could, he completed a course in the Harvard divinity school.

In April, 1819, at thirty-four, John Pierpont was ordained pastor of the Hollis Street Unitarian Church in Boston. With the exception of a tour through Europe and Asia Minor in 1835, he preached continuously in this pulpit for twenty-six years. They were years of blossoming fame. In 1825, with other young ministers of Boston, Mr. Pierpont formed the American Unitarian Association. Before this, he had received M. A. degrees from both Yale and Harvard.

Soon the Hollis Street congregation, staid and conservative, realized that they had a firebrand for their minister. John Pierpont was a natural rebel. He conceived it the function of a preacher, in those troublous and changeful times, to denounce evil as and where he found it. Soon crowds began to throng his church to hear his denunciations of rum, of slavery, of various other issues that were slowly emerging to the fore. Naturally, he created a stir and began to attract attention beyond the bounds of Boston. Here is an impression of him by an anonymous writer in *The Christian Examiner* of the period:

"Mr. Pierpont united within himself the characteristics of two very distinct persons. One was graceful, cultivated, delicate, fastidious to the last degree, careful of etiquette, studious, dignified; with a certain loftiness of dignity, indeed, which strangers were apt to find somewhat frigid, but genial and expansive with his friends, and beautifully tender and loving with children. This was the clergyman and the poet.

"The other was the ardent knight, armed for battle, and seeking it far and near; . . . quick to discover injustice, he no sooner unearthed a new wrong than he attacked it with the fiery ardor of a nature whose enthusiasm was but the hotter for the restraints which the habits and tastes of the scholar ordinarily imposed upon it. He used all his weapons at once: logic, sarcasm, invective, poetry—and sharpened them all with a stern 'Thus saith the Lord!' This was John Pierpont, the Reformer; and . . . few names rang wider throughout the careless, prosperous land than his."

Another commentator of the period wrote:

"He was liable to open his Hollis Street pulpit any Sunday morning with either temperance or slavery, or both. He preached temperance to a congregation of men who drank rum, sold rum, made rum . . . of course he gave mortal offense . . . his fight lasted seven years, one man against many, poverty against wealth, right against wrong."

Before the ecclesiastical council, he was charged with failure to conduct himself "with Christian meekness" and with discussing, with too great freedom, "the meanness and crime which he saw about him in high places." Although he triumphantly sustained himself against the charges, the council passed a mild resolution of censure; and Pierpont, infuriated, resigned his pulpit.

He was now sixty and at the height of his powers as

an orator, scholar, poet, and preacher, but no formal pastorate could bound his restless nature. He gave up successive charges in Troy, New York, Medford, Massachusetts, and elsewhere. He ran for governor of Massachusetts as candidate of the Liberal Party; and in 1850 was candidate of the Free-Soil party for Congress.

From time to time, he wrote graceful and facile verse. At the Litchfield County centennial in 1851 he read a long poem, widely quoted, containing a description of the "Yankee Boy" and his ingenuity:

> Here dwells a people—by their leave I speak —
> Peculiar, homogeneous and unique,
> With eyes wide open and with ready ear
> Whate'er is going on to see and hear;
>
> Nay, they do say, the genuine Yankee keeps
> One eye half open when he soundest sleeps,
> And when his hand's on anything, you know,
> There is go in it and he'll make it go!

In the autumn of his life the good poet turned to spiritualism. He lectured and wrote with unabated enthusiasm, traveling the country over and solemnly assuring scoffers that he was in touch with the dead. In the winter of 1860 a friend sat down beside him in Musical Fund Hall, Philadelphia. The poet remarked: "I do not complain that our spirit interviews are doubted. Last evening, when I was speaking on this platform, I felt someone draw near me and, turning, I saw Dr. Channing there. 'Don't stop,' said the doctor to me, 'I was interested in your argument and came to hear you conclude. Pray go on, Mr. Pierpont!' "

Since Dr. William Ellery Channing, distinguished American Unitarian clergyman and author, had died eighteen years before, his just dropping in sounded spectral to the friend, but not to Mr. Pierpont.

During the five years of the Civil War, amid the din and thunder of great events, John Pierpont sat at a secluded desk in the Treasury Department, his fine copper-plate hand laboriously transcribing dull documents. He seemed to have been totally forgotten. But there were those who remembered his brave, fighting, creative days. On his eightieth birthday, in 1865, he was told in the evening that a few friends had called. On entering the parlor of his boarding-house to greet them, he was surprised almost into tears.

One presented him with a gold watch, another with a valuable cane, a third with a large photograph album containing the portraits of old Boston friends and parishioners, filled with autographed letters of congratulation in poetry and prose from Whittier, Holmes, Sumner, Wilson, Dana, Mrs. Sigourney, Wood, and Whipple, and other letters signed by Moses Williams, Gardner Brewer, and other solid men of Boston.

A year later, John Pierpont's tempestuous life was over.

Schoolboys still recite "Warren's Address."

While the brilliant John Pierpont was flaming across the intellectual skies of New England, a man of very different mould, and five years older, was slowly building a fortune in Hartford, Connecticut. This was Joseph Morgan, shrewd, keen, if undistinguished descendant of stolid farmers, capable artisans, and bony sea-faring Yankee traders. Joseph Morgan's earliest American ancestor was Miles Morgan, who landed in Massachusetts in 1636 and helped found the settlement of Springfield, now Holyoke.

With his thrifty wife, Sarah Spencer, Joseph Morgan moved to Connecticut in the second decade of the nineteenth century and bought a farm near the town of Hartford. He arrived in Hartford during boom times, when the town was rapidly expanding into a city. Hartford was rich with strategic trading possibilities. It was on the main line of stages that transported goods and travelers between New York and Boston— three days each way. Also, it was a key trading center for the Connecticut River Valley.

Joseph Morgan discerned a surer way to prosperity than farming. He decided to take a flyer in the transportation business, so he sold his farm and invested in stage lines. His judgment was good. Soon his stages were running east, west and north. Joseph Morgan also invested cannily in several of the innumerable roadside taverns that sprang up with the growth of the New York-Boston and the Connecticut Valley trade.

But the railroad was soon to make its slow way across the state and sweep aside the stage lines. Joseph Morgan foresaw its coming and its effect upon his fortunes. So, in 1835, four years before Hartford saw its first locomotive, Joseph Morgan had sold his stages, closed his roadside taverns, and was proprietor of a large hotel in Hartford which he grandly named the "City Hotel." Mine Host Morgan was a genial man who mingled freely with his guests and made them comfortable, but was always on hand when the bill was to be paid. He could toss off a noggin or two of rum or brandy with all comers, but it never affected the clearness of his head or the keenness of his wit. He was always ready to turn a trade or take a flyer in any enterprise that promised profit. Withal, he was a "solid" man and pious. He and Sarah, his wife, never missed a service in Christ Protestant Episcopal Church.

In 1835, by one shrewd stroke, Joseph Morgan amassed a fortune. Hartford was the home of several newly formed fire insurance companies. One of these was the Ætna Fire Insurance Company. Ætna, like other companies, had no cash capital, its resources consisting of notes for five or ten thousand dollars each pledged by the principal men of the town. The note-makers, Morgan among them, did not anticipate that they would ever be called upon for cash to meet unexpected fire losses. But the unexpected happened.

A disastrous fire swept New York, and gloom descended upon Hartford.

It seemed impossible to the more timid of the Ætna financial backers that their corporation could survive the shock. They gathered in the corridor of the City Hotel and talked over their troubles. Some of the note-makers got to feeling so blue that they began to offer their stock to whoever would buy, almost as a gift.

Proprietor Morgan heard all this talk and took counsel with friends. Then he conceived a brilliant scheme. Why not be an optimist amid this wave of pessimism? Why not pay the fire losses in New York promptly and set an example that would bring in a tremendous flow of new business, perhaps at higher rates? Would not the business community in New York be so impressed by Ætna's prompt acceptance of its obligations that it would hasten to take out renewed policies with the one company that had displayed courage and resourcefulness?

It was good psychology and it worked.

Joseph Morgan and his friends formed a $100,000 cash pool—the first Morgan pool. Within a few hours they secured a majority of the Ætna stock. Then they despatched agents to New York, grips loaded with greenbacks. While other companies were wavering and dickering for delayed payments, Ætna paid up promptly. The policy-holders were so grateful that they wanted to renew their policies at once. They were told that other agents of the company would call upon them in a day or two.

The second band of agents found it easy to write new business, though Joseph Morgan and his partners raised the rates from one-half and one per cent to three and five. Ætna was presently enjoying an unprecedented boom. Joseph Morgan and other holders of its notes received stock in proportion to the liability they had assumed. The net result to Joseph Morgan was a profit of $150,000, a splendid fortune in those days.

The nimble proprietor of the City Hotel could have lived in comfortable retirement for the remainder of his days. But he had other plans. He determined to invest part of his wealth to give his son, Junius Spencer Morgan, a flying start.

Junius was the pride of Joseph Morgan's heart. Born April 14, 1813, shortly before the family moved to Hartford, Junius had gone to work at sixteen as a clerk for Alfred Welles, Boston merchant. When he was twenty-one his father secured for him a clerkship in the banking house of Morris Ketcham in New York. Both employers had written glowingly of his aptitude for business. Junius was eager to become a merchant.

Joseph Morgan decided to further his son's ambition. He approached the prosperous dry-goods house of Howe, Mather & Company, of Hartford, and offered to purchase a junior partnership for Junius. The price paid was $50,000. In 1836, at twenty-three, Junius Spencer Morgan became a full-fledged merchant.

On May second, of the same year, Junius Morgan married Juliet Pierpont.

They had met in Boston during her father's stormy pastorate in Hollis Street. Young Junius Morgan, though bred an ardent Episcopalian, was drawn often to the Hollis Street Meeting House by the ardor of John Pierpont's orations.

One Sabbath evening, John Pierpont, then at the height of his fame, concluded a lofty sermon and sat down, exhausted. The congregation filed out into the night. A tall youth, with shining face, lingered. Timidly, he approached the famous pastor and uttered halting words of admiration. John Pierpont wrung his hand and took him home with him for further talk.

Thus Junius Morgan and Juliet Pierpont met. She was an unusual girl, sensitive to everything that was beautiful in art and Nature. There is still in existence a homely little collection of "art" objects—rude figurines, porcelain replicas of animals, etc.—assembled by Juliet Pierpont in her girlhood. These were treasured by her son.

Junius and Juliet Morgan went to live in a modest brick cottage on Asylum Street, Hartford. Here, on April 17, 1837, was born the first of their five children.

They named him John Pierpont Morgan.

CHAPTER THREE

PIP MORGAN

THE JUNIUS MORGANS DID NOT REMAIN LONG IN THE
cottage. Joseph Morgan had high hopes for his son and,
in the opinion of the new-risen capitalist, the small
snuggery on Asylum Street was not fit abode for a
rising young business man. Accordingly, he ordered the
construction of a substantial house on what was then
Farmington Road, now the famous Farmington Avenue of Hartford. The house was finished early in the
forties and there it was that John Pierpont Morgan
spent his boyhood days.

The house, a rambling, comfortable stone and wood
structure, sat well back from the road on a gently rising
slope. Today it is but one of hundreds of mansions that
line both sides of Farmington Avenue. Then it commanded a farm of one hundred acres, extending half a
mile west to the beautiful stream known as Little River.
As the years rolled by the farm gradually disappeared
and became residence property.

On its rolling fields have been built the homes of
such famous persons as Charles Dudley Warner, Isabella
Beecher Hooker, Samuel T. Clemens, and William Gil-
lette.

Morgan retained little recollection of the house in
which he was born. All of his early associations were

linked with the old Farmington Road homestead and his low ceilinged room on the second floor facing west. Pierpont, as he was always called at home, was a strong, healthy boy, large for his age and full of animal spirits. But there was in him a certain reserve that seemed forbidding to many and melted only in the presence of a chosen few.

At the age of six, when the time arrived for his initiation into the mysteries of the alphabet and the bothersome problems of geography and arithmetic, he was sent to a country school which then stood at the junction of Farmington Road and Asylum Street. This was the West Middle District School. The dingy old building has long since fallen before the march of progress.

Pierpont trudged to school alone and reported to Thomas K. Beecher, the teacher. At roll call, Mr. Beecher called upon the new pupils to rise in turn and give their full names. With forty pairs of eyes focused upon him, the latest arrival spoke up proudly: "John Pierpont Morgan, sir."

The usual titter which greeted uncommon names went around the room. At recess the boys practised on the name but could not master it. So they nicknamed young Morgan "Pip." All the years he lived in Hartford he was known as Pip Morgan.

The Morgan farm with its surroundings was an ideal place for a healthy, growing boy. There were tramps through the woods, frolics in the big, cool barn, and— best of all—swimming and fishing in Little River and in another famous but misnamed stream known as Hog River. This also skirted the Morgan farm.

As he grew older Pip Morgan was permitted to venture on boat and raft on the broad bosom of the Connecticut River. Many of his playmates were relatives, among them his cousins, Francis and Jim Goodwin. The former was to become the famous Rev. Francis Goodwin, the latter an early partner of Morgan as a banker in New York.

Young Morgan was a fair scholar in primary and grammar grades, but did not excel in any single branch of study. By nature he was taciturn and much given to having his own way. He was not morose, but most assuredly stubborn and independent. As a consequence he had his share of boyish battles. He won a fair quota of his fights, but at times went down to defeat grimly and defiantly.

Passionately fond of the water, he was a great hand at building boats and rafts. Once launched on the Little or the Hog River, these craft eventually found their way to the Connecticut, and their battered wrecks finally strewed the beaches of Long Island Sound. Hog River was his favorite playground. By name and nature this dirty creek was and is peculiarly attractive to boys. Rising in the Talcott Mountains, it picks up dirt, clay, and sewage on its way through the farm lands until it skirts the beautiful Capitol grounds in Hartford. Being muddy, it meets a boy's ideal as a place for swimming.

"Daniel's Dam" was a favorite swimming-hole. In these murky depths young Morgan and the Goodwin boys accumulated tanned skins, bloodsuckers, stone bruises, and all the ills and comforts that go to make up a well-rounded life for a normal boy.

Equipped at an early age with a shotgun and a rifle, Pip Morgan roamed the hills of the Boswell farm, the Porter farm, the Mather-Sill estate, and other places in quest of rabbit, quail, grouse, partridge, fox, and other furred and feathered denizens of the fields and woods adjacent to Hartford. The boy hunted with all his might and fished with skill and patience. As a rule, when he made his weary way homeward at dusk, his creel or his game bag was filled.

Pip Morgan and his chums were not above the usual small-boy pranks. Once, at an afternoon service in Christ Protestant Episcopal Church, Morgan and a friend, Clarence Sterry, were discovered in the balcony cutting up monkeyshines, seeking to tickle the risibilities of the girls from Miss Draper's decorous boarding-school. Lewis Downes, the organist, gave the ribald young gentlemen a sound cuffing and led them out of their hiding-place by the ears.

The episode, one may be sure, did not go unnoticed at home. For Junius Morgan was an old-fashioned parent and believed in the rule of rod. By this time, 1847, five children had come to bless the Morgan household. Four —John Pierpont, Sarah Spencer, Mary Lyman and Juliet Pierpont—grew to maturity. A second son, Junius Spencer, Jr., born in 1846, died at twelve.

The star of Junius Morgan was on the rise, decidedly. As a dry-goods merchant he had succeeded even beyond his father's expectations. Also, he was a pillar in the Episcopal Church and a civic leader. He was a liberal donor to charity, a founder of the public library, and one of the original subscribers to the Wadsworth

Athenæum, a famous forum of cultural discussion. The influence of his gentle, cultivated wife—true daughter to old John Pierpont, the poet—may be discerned in these pursuits.

In 1850 the dry-goods house of Howe, Mather & Co. became Mather, Morgan & Co. A year later Junius Morgan was invited by James M. Beebe, a prominent Boston merchant, to form a copartnership in Boston. Levi P. Morton, pioneer dry-goods trader, afterwards Vice-President of the United States, was associated with the Beebe house. The offer was too tempting to resist. Junius Morgan sold out his interest in Hartford, at a price reputed to be $600,000; and the summer of 1851 found the family in Boston. They lived first in Rowe Place, afterwards moving to 15 Pemberton Square. The new firm, soon to become one of the largest dry-goods establishments in the United States, began business at 37 Kilby Street under the style of J. M. Beebe, Morgan & Co.

Pip Morgan was fourteen when he arrived in Boston, not at all pleased with the change from the free, un-curbed life of Hartford to that of a metropolis. Indeed, for a time he considered running away to sea, but family discipline was too strong. He did not mind part-ing with his sisters (all girls were "silly" to him, then) but, in his undemonstrative way, he venerated his father and mother. So he bowed to the yoke and reluctantly entered the Boston English High School in Bedford Street. English High, established in 1821, the year before the old town of Boston became a city, was a noted public school.

Young Morgan was graduated from English High in 1854, twelfth in a class of twenty-six. His record card is still on file. The highest percentage obtained in the class was 410, the lowest 127. Morgan's rating was 368. His general conduct was marked "good." The subject of his graduating paper was Napoleon Bonaparte.

Classmates remembered him years later as "the richest boy in the school." Silent, reserved, he gave the impression at times of feeling himself above ordinary folk. Once he surprised his colleagues by giving a recitation entirely in French. Again, some verses he had written fell out of his algebra book. The boy who retrieved them read them surreptitiously and described them half a century later as "darned good poetry." Principal Thomas Sherwin sent Morgan one afternoon to a nearby stationer's to purchase rubber erasers. The youth returned with the erasers, also with a larger amount of change than Mr. Sherwin expected. "I bought 'em at the wholesale rate," explained Morgan gruffly.

During his last months in English High, the boy's health began to fail. From a chunky, stalwart youth he had grown taller and thinner. At times he seemed introspective and passed long hours walking alone on the waterfront. Doctors were called in, but their tonics and nostrums were of no avail. At precisely this period came an event that was profoundly to affect his future and the fortunes of his family.

A distinguished-looking gentleman, with shrewd kindly eyes and whitening side-whiskers, dined one night at Pemberton Square. This was George Peabody, founder of the noted mercantile-banking firm of George Peabody & Co., of London. The visitor was internationally famous, both as a business man and as a philanthropist.

A native of Massachusetts, George Peabody had begun life as a dry-goods clerk; opened stores in various American cities; and finally, at forty-two, in 1837 (the year of Pip Morgan's birth) established in London his great mercantile banking house. Peabody reached London at what John Moody, in his "Masters of Capital," describes as "the beginning of the greatest single revolution in human affairs—the change from man and animal power to steam power in the performance of the work of the world."

In London, financial capital of the earth, Peabody had taken the lead in financing America. His biographer, Fox-Bourne, thus describes the scope of this daring merchant prince:

"In London, and all parts of England, he bought British manufactures for shipment to the United States; and the ships came back freighted with every kind of American produce for sale in England. To that lucrative account, however, was added one far more lucrative. The merchants and manufacturers on both sides of the Atlantic, who transmitted their goods through him, sometimes procured from him advances on account of the goods in his possession long before they were sold. At other times they found it convenient to leave large sums in his hands long after the goods were disposed of, knowing that they could draw whenever they needed, and that in the meantime their money was being so profitably invested that they were certain of a proper interest on their loans. Thus he became a banker as well as a great merchant, and ultimately much more of a banker than a merchant."

[44]

At that time the United States had a disastrous reputation in England as a field of investment. Many of the states had repudiated or made lean compromises with creditors who had invested in canal bonds, unsuccessful state banks, or other unstable enterprises. In 1843 the English investor's bitter attitude was summed up in the "humble petition" to Congress of the Rev. Sydney Smith, Canon of St. Paul's in London, and famous wit, who held Pennsylvania bonds on which that state had defaulted. He wrote:

"Figure to yourself a Pennsylvanian, receiving foreigners in his own country, walking over the public works with them, and showing them Larcenous Lake, Swindling Swamp, Crafty Canal and Rogues' Railway, and other dishonest works. 'This swamp we gained,' says the patriotic borrower, 'by the repudiated loan of 1828. Our canal robbery was in 1830. We pocketed your good people's money for the railroad only last year.' All this may seem very smart to the Americans, but if I had the misfortune to be born among such a people, the land of my fathers would not restrain me a single moment after the act of repudiation. I would appeal from my fathers to my forefathers."

In seventeen short years, George Peabody had established a remarkable reputation for integrity and enterprise. He had largely overcome British prejudice against American investments. He had become the most trusted American banker in England. Annually he was host at a famous Fourth of July good-will banquet. The Duke of Wellington honored one of these occasions, and Queen Victoria sent her portrait and that of Prince Albert to hang in the dining-hall. Peabody gave millions for the housing of the poor in London and for the cause of education in the southern states of America.

He was rapidly becoming chief financial representative of America in England. But he was almost sixty and he needed an active young partner. Hence this visit to Boston in 1854. From his old friend, James Beebe, Peabody asked advice in the selection of a partner. "Junius Morgan is your man if he will go to London," said Beebe. "I should hate to lose him. He has been here only three years, but he is the best business man in Boston."

Peabody met the fine, tall, personable Morgan and offered him the partnership. Morgan accepted. One of the stipulations of the agreement, dated October 1, 1854, was that Morgan was to undertake the entertainment of the firm's friends. For this important function he was to be allowed $25,000 a year.

Soon 15 Pemberton Square bustled with activity. Trunks were packed, effects crated for the long voyage across the ocean. The children were full of excitement. Pierpont, the eldest, was seventeen. Sarah was fifteen, Mary ten. The babies of the family, Junius, Jr., and Juliet, were eight and seven.

The parents were worried about the health of their eldest son. Doctors advised for his puzzling malaise a climate milder than either Boston or London. Mr. Peabody suggested Fayal, an island in the Azores, where he had a correspondent, as an ideal spot for an invalid; and young Morgan set out alone for this garden spot. He looked up the place in an atlas and learned that oranges and wine were its chief industries.

Two months of boating and fishing and loafing at

Fayal worked wonders with the tall, silent youth. In the fall he reported to his father that he again felt fit. He was told to report at Feligh's School, at Vevey, on Lake Geneva, to prepare for college. He took ship to Portugal and made his way by stage and train to Vevey. Feligh's was a private school conducted by a Frenchman who made a specialty of preparing young men, chiefly English, for Continental universities.

Vevey was a picturesque spot, facing the perpetually snow-capped Dents du Midi of the Swiss Alps. Tiny farms clung to the hillsides. Life was quiet, though there were occasional excursions on beautiful Lake Geneva or visits to nearby kursaals where the music was good and the beer even better, and one could risk a franc or two at *petits chevaux.*

Young Morgan had no great yearning for the higher education, but did not demur the following year at his parents' selection of Göttingen University, in Germany, for a continuation of his studies. For several decades German universities had attracted a large number of English and American students. Emerson, Longfellow, Bancroft, Motley, and other famous Americans had studied at the Royal George Augustus University of Göttingen. Founded in 1737 by King George II of England, in his capacity as Elector of Hanover, Göttingen was famous for its thorough methods of instruction and its great libraries. Considerable emphasis was laid there upon mathematics and the natural sciences.

The old Prussian town had none of the beauty of Vienna or of Munich, its situation and environment possessed none of the historic charm of Heidelberg, but its teachers were of the greatest. And there were pleasant promenades along the banks of the River Leine or longer hikes (*spatzieren*) over the open country. It was a strange setting for a youth only a year or so out of old Boston town. But this youth was rapidly developing into a cosmopolite, and he was well able to take care of himself.

At Göttingen, for the first time, a branch of science absorbed young Morgan. He specialized in mathematics. Something in this exact science appealed to a side of his nature hitherto dormant. He passed long hours at problems. Many years later, in New York, a number of Göttingen men gave a dinner to their old professor of mathematics who happened to be visiting America. Morgan had become a famous banker, but this did not impress the guest of honor.

Looking quizzically at Morgan over his glasses, the old German remarked sadly: "I have always regretted that you did not remain at the University. Had you stayed with me you would have been my assistant so long as I lived and, unquestionably, at my death you would have been appointed professor of mathematics in my place."

At Göttingen, the young American's activities were not entirely confined to the curriculum. On occasion, he came out of his shell and reveled in the more gregarious phases of student life. He learned to smoke, for instance, when he joined a famous student corps which had been commanded twenty-five years before by the afterwards illustrious Otto von Bismarck. The corps smoked a very strong Virginia tobacco in big porcelain-bowled pipes with stems four feet long. A photograph exists showing Morgan in corps costume—round cap with a big feather, short jacket, tightly fitting leathern breeches, long cavalry sword dangling from a broad belt, big pipe in hand.

The Bismarck corps had another custom that had come down from the Iron Chancellor's time. One evening, so Göttingen tradition has it, the corps, after a long hike over the plains, turned into an inn for rest and refreshment. The year was 1832. While the landlord scurried for the beer, one of the students, John Lothrop Motley (afterwards American minister to Austria) slumped into one chair and *histed* his weary legs upon another. The landlord, returning, was outraged at this desecration of his furniture and rudely pulled chair No. 2 away from Motley. Whereupon Bismarck swore a mighty oath and decreed that each of *his* corpsmen must always be provided with two chairs, one for sitting, one for resting purposes. With the servility of their tribe, the inn-keepers and beer-hall proprietors yielded, and thereafter the twin-chair "regulation" obtained in the Bismarck corps. An American student was always solemnly selected as official "chair man" of the corps. Pierpont Morgan was honored with this distinguished duty in 1856.

On memorable evenings of conviviality, Morgan forgot his New England reserve. While glasses clinked, he sang many old German student songs and, to the end of his life, was fond of Körner's Sword Song, Heinrich Heine's "Lorelei," "Annie of Tharaw," and "Auf Wiedersehen." In return, he taught his fellow corpsmen to sing a number of Foster's and other popular American songs of the day—"The Old Folks at Home," "Oh, Susannah!," "Nellie Was a Lady," and "Old Dog Tray," and some of the rattling chanties of American sailors, as "The Shenandoah Is A-Rolling, Bully Boys" and "Boston Gals A-Pulling on the Bowline."

It was a cocky, self-assured, haughty youth of nineteen who entered his father's banking firm in the summer of 1856. Young Morgan was thorough master of himself. But his manner was abrupt and often so antagonistic as to puzzle his more genial father.

"I don't know what in the world I am going to do with Pierpont," remarked Junius Morgan. The father's anxiety was soon allayed. Pierpont applied himself to learning his trade and made astonishing progress. Soon he mastered the delicately balanced system of foreign exchange. He could tell in a moment what bills at sixty days on Paris or Amsterdam or Hamburg were worth in francs, guilders, the marc banco, etc.

Soon Junius Morgan—rapidly absorbing the executive responsibility of George Peabody & Co.,—began to rely upon his son's judgment. Young Pierpont had not been six months in the dingy old Peabody office when he took a flyer in a speculation of his own. Someone told him that coffee was selling low and might be a good investment. Pierpont bought a whole shipload. When he mentioned the transaction to one of the Peabody partners, the latter, an Englishman, remarked: "You are foolish, my boy. Where are you going to get the money to pay for it?"

Morgan tramped away angrily. Returning in a few moments, he slapped a draft on the table and said: "There! There is the money." The draft for the full amount was signed by Junius Morgan.

In 1857, Junius Morgan decided to broaden his son's experience by sending him to New York. The firm of Duncan, Sherman & Co. was the American representative of Peabody & Co. Junius Morgan wrote and asked for a billet for his son. Duncan, Sherman & Co. accommodated by offering a junior clerkship. When Pierpont Morgan took packet for America a new phase of his career had begun.

The world was different then. France was an empire. Germany was little more than a geographical expression. America was half-slave, half-free. Only the emigrant wagon had spanned the continent. Steamship and railway development were in infancy. Banking was provincial; enterprise individual, manufacture conducted in small units.

Pierpont Morgan came to a Wall Street trembling upon the verge of the terrible panic of 1857. "The Western Blizzard" this panic was ironically called. Of a sooth, it blew out of the West. Credit had been stimulated immeasurably by the vast tide of gold that had flowed for seven years from California. Unregulated by Federal supervision, state banks had issued gigantic amounts of notes secured principally by optimism and wind. The coming of the railroads had invalidated canal bonds. And the railroads were mostly wildcat projects in the hands of visionaries or crooks.

The eyes of Wall Street were magnetized on the West.

[51]

The gold rush, the defeat of Mexico, the annexation of Texas, the speeding settlement of the Middle West had fed the imagination of New York. Andrew Jackson's destruction of the national bank at Philadelphia, the opening of the Erie Canal, and other factors had intrenched Wall Street as the money capital of America.

New York, growing by leaps and bounds, was feeling its oats. Immigration was flooding the city, preparing to turn the East Side from the old Collect, where later stood the County Court buildings, into a slum reaching to the Harlem River.

Prosperity had gone to the city's head. Speculators were threatening the reign of the old Knickerbocker merchant princes with their professions of honor, their fine tables, and civic responsibilities. The town was pleasure-mad. Debts were fashionable among the upper crust. Blades in Delmonico's, the Astor House, the Irving House, boasted of the sums they owed their tailors and wine merchants. Daily, in *The New York Tribune*, Horace Greeley thundered a warning against approaching calamity:

"No man, no community, no nation can afford to buy and consume more than it produces for sale and sells. The farmer whose store bill is $500 a year, while he turns off but $300 worth of produce, may be a capital financier and have a choice farm and good backers and excellent credit—but all these things cannot save him from bankruptcy unless he stops to mend his hand.

"One of two things we must do, either stop wearing so many silks and drinking freely such capital wines, or we must produce them at home, or produce a great deal more withal to pay for them. And we do not believe that producing a great deal more of our present staples is a practicable alternative."

The Stock Exchange barometer was equally prophetic. The Exchange was housed in rented quarters in the Lord's Court building, with entrances on William, Beaver and Exchange Place. The brokers paid $1,000 each for their seats. Clothed in high choke-collars and stocks, brocaded vests, skin-tight pantaloons, and chimney-pot hats, they conducted their trades in dignity at tables. There were no tickers, no Wall Street extras to inform the public about prices. The brokers considered that their transactions were matters between themselves, as gentlemen, to be announced in due course when the calls had been completed for the day.

The crisis became acute in August with the failure for $5,000,000 of the apparently impregnable Ohio Life & Trust Co. Between then and the end of the year nine hundred failures were reported. Though perfectly solvent, even the firm of Peabody & Co. was caught in the backwash. It could not collect its American accounts. Peabody & Co. was saved, and a general panic in London averted by the suspension of the Banking Act. This enabled the Bank of England to advance Mr. Peabody one million pounds.

No such relief was possible in New York. In Wall Street there was a run upon the banks, and on October 13, a suspension of specie payment.

One can imagine young Morgan abroad on that hectic day when Wall Street surged with the army of the ruined, a wondering spectator amid the mob of swearing speculators, luckless depositors, feverishly hurrying brokers' clerks. Perhaps the cool, lanky young man from London saw honest old David Leavitt haranguing a mocking mob from the steps of his Merchants' Exchange Bank.

Perhaps he had pointed out to him the lean, slinking figure of Daniel Drew, that pious bear raider who profited by others' misfortunes. The time was not far distant when Morgan was to come into collision with this unconscionable scoundrel.

The panic of 1857 was Morgan's initiation into the tragic possibilities of a financial hurricane. Its lessons were not lost upon him.

CHAPTER FOUR

TRICKS OF A TRADE

YOUNG MORGAN TOOK TO FINANCE AS A CAT TO CREAM. In less than three years he went through the banking establishment of Duncan, Sherman & Co. from clerk to cashier. The firm's business manager was Charles H. Dabney, a shrewd New Englander and a clever accountant. Under Dabney's tutelage he became an excellent practical accountant and acquired that ability to analyze and dissect complicated bookkeeping statements that was forever after the wonder of all who came into contact with him. In manner he was still curt and gruff, and he wore a mask of grim asperity that did not tend to personal popularity.

These habits started him out with a misadventure that might have dismayed a less resolute youth. Through his father's influence a place had been made for him as director in one of the little railroad companies that in those days occupied the transportation field. After a year he was dropped on the ground of uselessness. With scrupulous fidelity he had attended every meeting and voted upon every question. But he had never made an observation upon any matter before the board, sitting for the most part fiercely staring straight before him as if he belonged somewhere else. The other directors could see no help in this kind of associate.

In 1860 Junius Morgan suggested that Duncan, Sherman & Co. take his son into partnership. The proposal was curtly declined. Angered, the elder Morgan directed Pierpont to take an office of his own; and made him American factor for George Peabody & Co. Soon the name of J. Pierpont Morgan appeared on a small suite on the second floor of the drab building at 50 Exchange Place, opposite the entrance to the old Stock Exchange.

For the next year or two young Morgan dealt in foreign exchange and purchased miscellaneous securities for the account of Peabody & Co. His eyes and ears were always open to opportunity, however, and he never overlooked a chance to speculate a bit on his own hook.

At the opening of the Civil War he took a private flyer that provoked the ugly charge that he had sold rotten muskets to the Government—a charge that was to pursue him all his life. In May, 1861, one Simon Stevens came to Morgan and told him that he and Arthur M. Eastman, of Manchester, N. H., had an opportunity to turn a pretty penny in the purchase and resale to the Government of 5,000 carbines in the Army arsenal in New York. Four years before, Army ordnance officers had condemned the guns as unserviceable and dangerous. Whether Morgan was told this never developed. However, he advanced part of the purchase money, taking a lien on half the carbines as collateral security.

Eastman and Stevens paid $3.50 each for the guns, which they promptly resold at $22 apiece to General Frémont, commanding the Federal forces at St. Louis. Tests showed that the carbines were obsolete. Frémont refused to authorize payment of the $109,912 agreed upon. A War Department commission investigated and awarded Eastman and Stevens $55,550. Stevens demanded the full amount and sued in the Federal Court of Claims for $58,000 additional. He won the case, the Court holding that Frémont had entered into a contract and "a contract is a contract." The Court stated that "by arrangement between Stevens and one J. Pierpont Morgan, the voucher for the first 2,500 carbines delivered was to be made out in the name of Morgan, which was done."

Gustave Myers, author of "History of Great American Fortunes," points out: "This decision opened the way for the owners of what were then cynically called 'Deadhorse' claims to get paid, and also for those contractors who had furnished other worthless arms and supplies of shoddy clothing, rotten tents and blankets, pasteboard shoes, adulterated food and other goods to the Government at exorbitant prices. A fine beginning for the great J. Pierpont Morgan, was it not?"

So far as the writer is aware, Morgan never answered oft-repeated allegations that he had knowingly profited through this legal but tricky transaction.

The dour young broker created his first real ripple in Wall Street when Charleston, South Carolina, was under bombardment and its fall expected momentarily. Gold was at a premium. Importers in New York were delaying remittances abroad, hoping to take advantage of a falling market. But Charleston did not surrender, and gold continued to rise both on the Exchange and in that curious institution at William Street and Exchange

Place known as "the Gold Room." This was a private enterprise of a man named Gallagher and was designed to facilitate trading on the Stock Exchange where gold was the last commodity "called out" at each session.

Already gold was flowing in small quantities to London. Any large shipment, it was evident, would advance the price sharply and force the dilatory importers to buy. Morgan and another keen young man, slightly his elder, sensed the situation and put their heads together. The other was E. B. Ketcham, of the firm of Ketcham, Son & Co. His father was Morris Ketcham, under whom Junius Morgan had served his novitiate in banking.

That afternoon the two young men boarded a puffy little train of the New Haven Railroad that ran from the Bronx River to New Haven, sixty-two miles away, and dropped off at Westport, Connecticut. Here was the summer home of old Morris Ketcham. They outlined their scheme to him. They would quietly purchase two million dollars in gold on joint account of Peabody & Co. and Ketcham & Co., and ship it abroad on Saturday's steamer. The result, they anticipated, would be an advance of several points in the price of gold; and they would have a clear exclusive exchange market to draw against on shipment.

"Why, we will get our money back and a big profit within a week," the crafty young gentlemen assured Morris Ketcham. They won his consent. The following Saturday saw $2,000,000 in double eagles on its way abroad, consigned to Peabody & Co.

On Monday morning Morgan and the **younger** Ketcham were anxious spectators in the Gold Room.

News of the large shipment had gotten about and the price shot up. The importers rushed to cover themselves. They had to buy sight drafts, and Morgan was the only foreign exchange dealer who could supply these in quantity. Within a few days the keen young financiers split a profit of $160,000.

Morgan employed part of his profits to buy his first painting. It was a portrait of a young and delicate woman by George Augustus Baker. He purchased it at auction for $1,500 at the Sanitary Commission Fair on Fourteenth Street; and hung it proudly over the mantel in his rooms at 42 West Twenty-first Street. It was the nucleus of his great collections.

The picture reminded him of Amelia Sturges, whom he was courting in his rough, impetuous fashion. She was the daughter of Jonathan Sturges and one of the beauties of New York. Morgan had many rivals, but was apparently outdistancing them all when, in the summer of 1861, Miss Sturges was stricken with tuberculosis. The disease made rapid progress. She was ordered abroad in a despairing effort to save her life.

Morgan dropped his business and followed. In Paris he found her—fragile, pale, declining. He knelt before her and begged her to marry him, swearing that he would devote his life to restoring her health. It was a side of the gruff, "uppity" young man she had not hitherto seen. She consented, and they were married quietly in the late summer of 1861. She died in February, 1862.

Her memory was the most poignant of Morgan's life. She touched in him an emotional chord no one else had been able to touch. Often he visited her grave in Fairfield, Connecticut. In his will he provided $100,000 to found a House of Rest for Consumptives, "The Amelia Sturges Morgan Memorial." To the end of his life he was ever responsive to appeals for aid in the ceaseless battle against the White Plague. His charities were always intensely personal. He maintained no bureaus, no scientific research committees (as do the Rockefellers) to distribute his millions. But there was scarcely an agency in existence for the relief of tuberculosis victims to which he did not contribute. And his private ledgers contained the names of dozens of sufferers whom he had aided. To his adoration of Amelia Sturges may be credited the welling to the surface of this wave of suppressed emotion.

Back in his office, Morgan plunged into work. The young widower devoted himself to foreign exchange (now more delicately balanced than ever) and kept his father thoroughly informed upon the shifting financial and military events of the period. Naturally, the Morgans and George Peabody were stalwart Union sympathizers. In England, where the opinion was generally held that the Union was doomed, Mr. Peabody and Junius Morgan did all they could to uphold the hand of Lincoln.

For their information they came to rely more and more upon their cool young correspondent in New York; and found Pierpont Morgan's interpretation of events invariably accurate. After the first battle of Bull Run, Secretary Chase came to New York and made a desperate appeal for gold to the bankers of the comparatively new Clearing House Association. Everyone was discouraged. But the bankers engaged to obtain gold from Europe—at twelve per cent interest. Peabody & Co. supplied a great deal of the gold.

Those were dark days, but young Morgan was firm in his belief in the ultimate triumph of the North. "The Union will win," he told a friend. "Then, if we work hard, we shall soon be the richest country in the world." Pierpont's letters to his father were invariably cheerful. They came at a time when the Rothschilds and other great European bankers were refusing to risk a dollar in American investments.

The youthful Morgan's optimism may have profoundly influenced one dramatic event in London. Confederate privateers were being built in many British yards. President Lincoln and Secretary of State Seward instructed the American minister, Charles Francis Adams, to inform the British Government that continuation of this practice would be regarded as sufficient cause for a rupture of diplomatic relations.

Unable to refute Lincoln's logic, the British authorities nevertheless demanded payment within five days of a "protection fund" of one million pounds in gold to meet possible damage claims from both the Confederate Government and British shipbuilders. The condition was apparently impossible. Adams appealed fruitlessly to British bankers. He was about to give up in despair when a representative of Peabody & Co. called upon him and said: "Peabody & Co. will advance the required sum within twenty-four hours and accept your receipt. But no one must know of the transaction except yourself, President Lincoln, and Mr. Seward." Adams, of course, leaped at the offer. Next day the gold was produced, and the British Government forced to declare an embargo upon suspected privateers. The effect throughout Europe and, indeed, the world at large, was enormous.

In New York, young Morgan kept in constant touch with the movements of the Army as well as of the financial forays of both North and South. He installed in his office a private telegraph wire (the first in Wall Street), and hired an expert operator, one Smith. The move was good for business also; for many distinguished men dropped in to get the news from the front. Jesse Bunnell, Lieutenant-General Grant's private telegrapher, and Smith were close friends. Often Bunnell would furnish live news direct from the line of battle.

Five minutes after Col. Washington Roebling, afterwards engineer of the Brooklyn Bridge, described from an Army balloon the movement of Lee's mighty army headed northward for the campaign that culminated at Gettysburg, the news ticked into the Morgan office.

After the war, during his tragic adventures in Wall Street, General Grant often dropped in to dictate letters and telegrams to his family and friends. The Morgan office had moved and expanded, but there was still a telegraph room, with Smith in charge. Grant had become so accustomed to the use of the telegraph in the war that thereafter he used it freely. He was a fair operator and could send and receive at the rate of fifteen words a minute. Incidentally, he was the only caller who could smoke the big, strong, black cigars liked by Morgan and Smith.

The troublous Civil War days required cool heads in Wall Street. Wartime suspension of specie payment led to periodic outbursts of speculation in gold. This was attacked as a national evil. The Stock Exchange crossed gold from its list, but the Gold Room vibrated with activity. Fatuously, Congress sought to solve the problem, in June, 1864, by passing the famous Gold Act, forbidding trading in gold under penalty of imprisonment. The New York bankers united in denouncing this drastic step:

"It is one of the most extraordinary and visionary acts of legislation ever passed in this country, or in any other country. So far from aiding the Government in its design to put down speculation among brokers and speculators, it has had, and will continue to have, an entirely different effect. The rate in Wall Street immediately advanced to 200, 205, 210, and, in fact, to 225. This Gold Act is only one more instance of utter lawlessness on the part of Congress to interfere with the ordinary business transactions of a commercial city. The cause of the rise in gold does not, did not, arise in Wall Street. The cause was the unwise issue of several hundred millions of paper currency at Washington and in the enormous importation following the uncalled-for inflation."

Congress repealed the farcical law a few weeks later. In 1864, having reached the age of sixty-nine and amassed $20,000,000, George Peabody retired. His firm had grown so steadily in British favor that he was offered a title of nobility by Queen Victoria. The sturdy old American would not accept. Mr. Peabody selected

Junius Morgan as his successor, but bitterly disappointed the latter by refusing to allow the firm name to be continued. Over the old-fashioned London dwelling house at 22 Old Broad Street went up the title: "J. S. Morgan & Company."

Junius Morgan, shrewd and daring, planned wide expansion. He knew that, with the close of the Civil War, a rich new continent of fertile farming and mineral lands would be opened and that capital, wisely invested, would multiply as at no other time in history.

If his plans developed as he hoped, his capable, energetic son would have to bear a greater load of responsibility. Pierpont would need help. Late in 1864 appeared this notice in *The Bankers' Magazine*: "Messrs. J. Pierpont Morgan and Mr. C. H. Dabney (for several years of the firm of Duncan, Sherman & Co.) have associated together as bankers, under the firm name of Dabney, Morgan & Co., Exchange Place."

In addition to Dabney the new firm took in Morgan's cousin and boyhood playmate, James J. Goodwin, of Hartford.

Morgan was now a ruddy, rather heavily built young man of twenty-seven. He had grown a moustache. He was staccato, emphatic in speech, unruffled, immutable in manner. Behind the jet glint of his eyes his inner thought was inaccessible. Only a few of those who came into daily contact with him sensed the power that was in him.

Since the death of his wife he had lived quietly, taking little part in the restricted social activities of a city numbed by war. In 1865 he married again and went to live at 227 Madison Avenue. His second wife was Frances Louise Tracy, daughter of Charles E. Tracy, one of the leaders of the New York bar and a vestryman in fashionable St. George's Episcopal Church. She was a striking beauty with wide eyes and classic oval cast of countenance. In 1866 the Morgans' first child was born—Louisa Pierpont, now Mrs. Herbert L. Satterlee. Their only son, the present J. P. Morgan, was born in 1867. A second daughter, Juliet Pierpont, now Mrs. William Pierson Hamilton, was born in 1870; and three years later came the last child, Anne Tracy Morgan.

Picturesque figures paraded the Wall Street stage in those days. Among them the gruff young banker, Morgan, passed unnoticed. There was Commodore Cornelius Vanderbilt, who had parleyed a Staten Island ferry line into a fleet of great ships, and was consolidating the Hudson River, Harlem and other small railroads into the New York Central trunk line—a vain, splendid-looking old man who toured Europe in his flashing steam yacht, the *North Star,* and drove a lovely young wife behind a pair of dappled grays in Central Park. Vanderbilt, the richest man in the country, with the stately appearance of a prince yet with the uncouth grammar and manners of a longshoreman, and so amazingly superstitious that he paid fortune-tellers and spiritualists to raise ghosts of dead men to consult in stock-jobbing ventures.

There was solid, conservative old Moses Taylor, president of the City Bank, who always had ample cash on hand and made his stockholders come to him to collect their dividends. There was A. A. Low, father of Seth

Low—a great merchant prince whose packet ships went to China and the Far East. And there were those precious rascals, Drew, Gould and Fisk. Uncle Daniel Drew, who could mouth pious phrases while he cut another's financial throat. Jason or Jay Gould, silent little ex-peddler, with ferret eyes, his face concealed as far as possible under a full black beard. Gould, boldest and most successful financial buccaneer of the day.

Grotesque Jim Fisk, chief lieutenant of Gould and Drew, was a world's wonder as a high-flying stock gambler. He had all the shrinking reticence of a drum major. Fisk lolled about town in gay clothes surrounded by gayer girls. He strutted the deck of his Fall River boats, his fat figure clothed in the uniform of an Admiral; or rolled ahead of his regiment in cockade and patent leather boots. He was finally shot to death in 1872 in a quarrel over a woman. His Grand Opera House at Twenty-third Street and Eighth Avenue ("Castle Erie" it was called) became a place of bizarre memories in which champagne, beauties of the ballet, and railway financing were very much mixed.

Gould, Fisk and Drew had selected as their pet field for gambling the Erie Railroad—"The Scarlet Woman of Wall Street." Gould had the most adroit brain of the trio. During the wild railroad expansion that followed the Civil War—the country's railway mileage was doubled between 1865 and 1873—Gould picked up railroads as one might collect old coins, manipulating their stock and unloading upon the public.

Quite by chance, in 1869, young Pierpont Morgan met and worsted Gould in a pitched battle. The victory made him widely known with a valuable reputation among the "solid" element in his world.

Planning, on behalf of the Erie, to fight Vanderbilt for New England traffic, Gould's greedy eyes had turned upon the little Albany & Susquehanna Railroad. The Albany & Susquehanna, 142 miles long, connected the Erie at Binghamton, N. Y., with the railroads centering in Albany. Gould set about acquiring a majority of its stock. The directors in power arranged to issue enough new stock to out-vote that purchased by Gould. The latter promptly obtained an order from Judge Barnard appointing Fisk receiver of the road, asserting that the A. & S. was bankrupt. The Tweed Ring was then in its glory and Judges Barnard and Cardoza were in the full tide of their infamous careers as its tools.

Such was the situation early in August, 1869, when President Ramsey, of the A. & S., and a frightened committee of directors called upon Samuel Sloan, who had been pioneer president of the Hudson River Railroad. "Why don't you fellows see Ed Morgan's young cousin Pierpont?" suggested Sloan. "He has brains and from what Ed tells me plenty of spunk."

"Ed Morgan" was Edwin Dennison Morgan, former Governor of New York and at that time the state's representative in the United States Senate.

Next day the A. & S. men called upon Morgan. Morgan's office was still "up one flight," but Dabney, Morgan & Co. now occupied four rooms at 53 Exchange Place. The interview was brief—and impressive. Morgan said: "Give me a statement of your exact condition. Let me know just what Gould and Fisk have done. Put it on paper. Come back day after tomorrow. I will give you my opinion."

That was all. But the visiting committee felt strangely reassured. There was something about this husky young man and the way he looked at one. At the next conference, Morgan said: "You gentlemen will have to fight those fellows in the courts. I think you can win. Do you want me to go ahead?"

The committee unanimously selected Morgan as their champion. He retained his father-in-law, Charles Tracy, and Samuel Hand, of Albany; and with them went to the Capitol where a stockholders' meeting was scheduled for the end of the week. Morgan had enough votes to control, but he knew the reputation of Gould and Fisk for rough-house tactics and acted accordingly.

The night before the meeting found Morgan and his attorneys working at the Delavan House. They were drawing up papers to present in the morning to Supreme Court Justice Rufus W. Peckham praying for an injunction restraining Gould and Fisk from interfering with the morrow's session. Lawyer Hand excused himself for a few moments, saying he had to drop down to the night boat pier to see a friend off. Hours passed and he did not return. Morgan and Tracy began to fear foul play. Finally, long after midnight, Hand rushed in, breathless.

"I was accidentally carried off on the boat," he gasped. "The captain was a stupid animal and would not put me ashore. Finally, I had to buy a life-boat and row ashore. I saw the lights of a station and stumbled over ties until I got there. I found myself in the village of Hudson. A train was just pulling out for Albany. I climbed aboard and was about to enter the only passenger coach when I saw Jim Fisk inside with a band of men who looked like Bowery toughs. They were drinking and carousing. I thought it best to stay where I was. I turned up my coat collar and rode on the platform all the way to Albany."

Morgan listened grimly to his colleague's tale. It was his first definite intimation that Gould and Fisk intended to ride rough-shod over the meeting. Next day, at noon, while Messrs. Tracy and Hand were arguing for the injunction before Judge Peckham, Morgan and Ramsey stood at the head of the stairs leading to the Albany & Susquehanna office. They were flanked by a couple of dozen husky trainmen.

Soon Fisk came along at the head of his Bowery crew. Attired in clothing of rainbow hue, Fisk marched alone up the stairs. No one ever doubted Jubilee Jim's personal courage. But, on this occasion, the battle was over before it began. Ramsey leaped at Fisk, seized him by the collar, and threw him bodily down the stairs. Here a policeman grabbed him and placed him under arrest. Noting the uniform of John Law, Fisk's followers scattered. His captor dragged him around the corner, thrust him through the doors of the police station—and disappeared. The bewildered Fisk found there was no charge against him. The "officer" was no officer at all—merely a Ramsey-Morgan man in a borrowed uniform.

But Gould and Fisk were not to be balked so simply. They began a struggle for physical possession of the Albany & Susquehanna. Soon the entire A. & S. territory was in a state of civil war. While Morgan and Gould were shooting injunctions at each other (twenty-two in all) Ramsey and Fisk were in command of rival forces in the field.

Fisk transferred his ragged Boweryites to Binghamton and sent them over the A. & S. in Erie flat-cars with instructions to capture every piece of rolling stock possible. The Ramsey-Morgan forces sent out gangs from Albany. Rails were ripped up recklessly. The Erie locomotive was thrown from the track, and Fisk's first band of skirmishers was captured and held prisoner. This was only a prelude to the major engagement, described by Carl Hovey, in *The Metropolitan Magazine:*

"The Erie had five thousand men at the tunnel a few miles from Binghamton, and held the station nearby. And the Albany party held the other end of the tunnel with about the same number. Just at dusk on an August afternoon the Erie captain determined to take the disputed tunnel. He put some two hundred products of the Bowery and neighboring streets on two cars, and, coupling on a locomotive, sent the train through the tunnel. The train passed through the darkness in safety, but as it turned a curve at the mouth a train with the Ramsey-Morgan men on board was seen approaching —on the same track. The Erie whistle shrieked for down brakes, but the other train never slackened its speed. The engines crashed together gloriously, and the collision was the signal for the fight. The men spilled out upon the track and fell upon one another with sticks and stones and revolvers and matchless profanity. After a time they got too much mixed in the darkness to fight any more and both sides drew back, taking with them the wounded and the drunken, and encamped beside the rails."

The State of New York looked on in wonderment. The newspapers sent correspondents into the field and devoted columns to "the Battle of the Susquehanna." Finally, Governor Hoffman threatened to call out the militia. Morgan trapped Gould and Fisk into signing a joint note to the Governor requesting the appointment of a state official to run the road. The Governor appointed A. Bleecker Banks, of Albany.

During the lull, Morgan stole a march upon Gould. At a few hours' notice he called a special meeting of the stockholders; produced the ledgers and stock transfer books which had been hidden first in an empty tomb in an Albany cemetery and later in a house in Pittsfield, Massachusetts; and elected a Morgan-Ramsey board of directors.

The new board empowered Morgan to lease the property. Morgan had already arranged with LeGrand B. Cannon, president of the Delaware and Hudson Canal Company, to take over the Albany & Susquehanna. The lease was signed and ratified at once—and Gould was licked. The A. & S. stockholders received a guaranteed rental of seven per cent, later increased to nine per cent. The stock jumped on the Exchange from eighteen to one hundred and twenty.

Morgan's firm received five thousand shares of A. & S. stock as its commission—rich reward for a few weeks' work. But richer yet was the prestige the affair brought him as "the man who had licked Gould."

Morgan was only thirty-two. But now Wall Street began to mark him as a Coming Man. Soon he was to enter a new and far more lucrative field of finance.

CHAPTER FIVE

FIRST MORGAN SYNDICATES

EVENTS MOVED FAST IN THE THROBBING POST-WAR days. And the Morgans moved with them.

In November, 1869, George Peabody died in London. During the five years of his retirement he had been a sort of emeritus adviser to Junius Morgan. Queen Victoria and many of the great people of England desired that the remains of the first great Anglo-American banker be interred in Westminster Abbey. But the patriotic old gentleman's death-bed request was that he be buried in his birthplace, the village of Danvers, Massachusetts.

Accordingly, the body was placed aboard H. M. S. *Monarch*, then the world's finest ironclad, and taken to Portland, Maine. The British man-of-war was accompanied over seas by the U. S. S. *Plymouth* and was met at Portland by a squadron commanded by Admiral Farragut. Young Pierpont Morgan was in charge of the arrangements. British and American sailors and marines marched together in the funeral procession, as did veterans of the Blue and the Gray. The suggestion came from Morgan.

In the business district of London—a stone's throw from the alley office where he had first set up in trade in 1837—a statue was erected to George Peabody.

Junius Morgan was left practically alone to chart the future of the house. The elder Morgan soon demonstrated that he possessed strength, daring and imagination no less remarkable than his predecessor's.

The following autumn Junius Morgan launched an enterprise that dazzled even lavish old Baron Lionel Nathan Rothschild. Baron Lionel was London chieftain of the family that dominated Europe for a century by the power of its wealth. He was a well-burgundied old gentleman, with beaked nose and white chin-whiskers. He was wont to overwhelm his friends by gorgeous, at times bizarre, hospitality. Junius Morgan had become his only rival in London as a lavish and princely host.

In the latter part of October, 1870, Junius Morgan was secretly summoned to Tours, where the French had set up a provisional government. On September 1 preceding, the German army had crushed the French at Sedan. Napoleon III had been captured, Paris besieged.

Junius Morgan, in Tours, was asked whether he could arrange to float a French loan of 250,000,000 francs ($50,000,000) in England and America, and upon what terms. Without hesitation, Junius Morgan offered to take a six per cent bond issue—at eighty. The terms were harsh, but the French were in no position to bargain. A few days later the bourses of the world were astonished by a brief announcement from 22 Old Broad Street that J. S. Morgan & Co. had closed the deal and that bonds, backed by the guarantee of the French government of national defense, were available to the public at eighty-five.

A portion of the French press denounced the terms,

finding it difficult to believe that "the credit of France can all at once have fallen to that of Italy, Peru, or Turkey." Nevertheless Morgan went ahead. The war ended quickly. The bonds were selling at par soon afterward. Junius Morgan and his associates pouched a profit of $5,000,000. "The former Boston dry-goods merchant," writes John Moody, in his "Masters of Capital," "took his place in the world, second only to the Rothschilds in the greatest financial operations of the time—the financing of great government loans—and held it throughout the '70's."

The French loan was a "syndicate" operation; in other words, the sharing of an underwriting among a group. The word originated in France. The staid London *Economist* deprecated its spread across the Channel, warning that the next financial crisis would be precipitated by a greedy syndicate's manipulation of the market. "A syndicate, if in relation to a new loan, is simply an association of persons who guarantee the subscription of the issue, either wholly or in part, each guarantor usually accepting the responsibility for so much to the actual contractor of the loan."

The same hostile attitude was soon to be taken in America where the syndicate seed, once planted, was to flower as in no other part of the globe.

Flushed with the success of the French loan, Junius Morgan turned toward a field that promised even greater profits: the refunding of the American Civil War debt. Naturally, he would operate through his son in New York. The latter had placed some of the French bonds in America. Slowly but surely the dour, undemonstrative Pierpont was justifying the hopes of his father. The brilliant success of the great Morgan loan to France had its repercussion in America. It brought to the younger Morgan an offer of alliance from Drexel & Co., a powerful banking house in Philadelphia.

Francis Martin Drexel, founder of the firm, came to America in 1817, at twenty-five. He was an artist of a sort, an Austrian Tyrolean who had fled from French conscription. After wandering about Europe and South America for some years, he settled in Philadelphia and sought to make a living painting portraits of respectable dons. But he found it more profitable to buy and sell state bank notes. In 1837, the year Pierpont Morgan was born, F. M. Drexel founded a small money change house in Third Street, that part of Philadelphia known colloquially as "the Coast of Algiers."

In 1863, when the elder Drexel was run down and killed by the cars of the Reading Railway, Drexel & Co. had grown powerful. Now, in 1871, the senior partner was Anthony Joseph Drexel, a popular, pushing man of forty-five. His office was a large marble block on the site where the Philadelphia Library stood during Washington's administration.

"Tony" Drexel and his partners—there were four— planned to have a share in refunding the huge Government bond issues. They needed a New York partner with powerful European connections. Pierpont Morgan was an ideal man.

In 1871, Dabney, Morgan & Co. was dissolved. The elderly Dabney retired with some $500,000 as his share of seven years' profit; and Drexel, Morgan & Co. came into being. Tony Drexel purchased the southeast corner of Broad and Wall Streets at $349 a square foot —a price for New York realty that was not to be approached again for thirty years—and erected an ornate seven-story "sky-scraper" at a cost of $1,000,-000. The Drexel Building, of white marble, was destined to become one of the famous landmarks of the world. It was one of the first elevator buildings in New York. The same solid structure, colored by time, and a mere pygmy among the gigantic buildings surrounding it, is still the home of the Morgan bank.

Drexel & Co. counted upon its new partner's ability and fighting spirit, together with the vast resources of J. S. Morgan & Co., to capture and control some of the enormous new Government bond issues. These plans came immediately into opposition with those of Jay Cooke, of Philadelphia. Cooke was known as "the financier of the Civil War." A fierce old man, with piercing eyes, long white beard and sparse hair flung back upon a high forehead, he was no mean antagonist.

Cooke had pretty much grown to consider as his own the bonding business of the United States Government. During the discouraging days of '61-'65 he had placed more than sixty per cent of the Union's $2,500,-000,000 war debt; and now did not hesitate to declare that he was entitled to the refunding profits.

Jay Cooke's services in the war had been, indeed, noteworthy and unique. He had come forward at a time when America's credit was so low that many economists predicted she would never be able to go to war. The Rev. Sydney Smith, he who had been cheated by the Pennsylvanians, observed: "The Americans cannot gratify their avarice and ambition at once. The war-like spirit of every country depends upon its three-per cents. If Caesar were to appear upon earth, Rothschild would open and shut the doors of the temple of Janus. Thomas Baring, or Bates, would probably command the Tenth Legion, and the soldiers would march to battle with loud cries of 'Scrip and omnium, reduced consols, and Caesar!' No, the Americans have cut themselves off from all resources of credit. Having been as dishonest as they can be, they are prevented from being as foolish as they wish to be."

However, when the war broke out, the Government did not risk refusal from the Rothschilds and other great foreign capitalists. Jay Cooke was appointed the Government's agent to sell its war bonds, and Cooke sold directly to the people. Only a man of his astonishing qualities could have done the job. "Cooke," writes John Moody, "was the typical American promoter of his time—a tremendous optimist, a great employer of friendship in high places, a sort of financial P. T. Barnum who exploited the Government's securities, and later his own, through a press-agent system—organized by him and never since equaled in this country—giving 'copy' to as many as eighteen hundred newspapers at a time; and who scratched every hamlet in the country through his canvassing to sell Government bonds."

With the success of the first issue of Civil War bonds, Cooke's task became somewhat easier. He was able to create a foreign market, particularly in Germany. The Germans were about the only people in Europe who supported the Union. German opinion, of course, was influenced by the fact that the great bulk of German immigrants, who had come to America after the uprising of 1848, had settled in the North. Thousands of them fought in the Union armies. With England, France, even Holland lukewarm toward the Union cause, the German-American support was of inestimable advantage to President Lincoln—and to Cooke.

When six per cent U. S. gold bonds began to sell at sixty, the Germans, especially the rich South Germans, began to invest heavily. America became the "land of ten per cent." In this movement, the German Jew was at the forefront. Even before the war a great many shrewd, enterprising young German Jews had come to America. These formed a class of traders as unerring in their money-instincts as our own Yankees.

By 1869 the great German money center of Frankfort controlled a large portion of the billion dollars of United States bonds that were held abroad. Historically, this was the beginning of the cleavage that has since distinguished the world of finance in America: the Yankee and the German Jew.

When refunding operations began in 1871, Jay Cooke naturally allied himself with his war-time clients, the Germans and the Jews. Against this coalition there now sprang into life a new combination—British and American capital represented by the Morgans, the Drexels, and others. One of the Morgan-Drexel allies was Levi P. Morton, Junius Morgan's old dry-goods partner in Boston, now head of the influential banking firm of Morton, Bliss & Co.

Levi Morton, who had begun life as a dollar-a-week clerk, had all the stalwart loyalty of his repressed New England school. He was bound to Junius Morgan by many ties. His former partner, Walter Haynes Burns, had married Pierpont Morgan's second sister, Mary Lyman, in 1867, and was now a member of the firm of J. S. Morgan & Co. Thus, it was a powerful group of Yankees and Britishers that sought the chance to refund the great war debts in 1871.

That year Cooke was the victor. He placed $130,-000,000 of the new issue. The transaction was so successful that the Rothschilds directed their American representative, August Belmont, to join Cooke in further operations. Belmont was a remarkable man. Entering the Frankfort house of the Rothschilds as a boy in 1829, he had come to America as the Rothschild agent in 1837 and married the niece of Commodore Perry, hero of the Battle of Lake Erie. In later years, the Belmonts, father and son, were to be associated often with Pierpont Morgan.

Undaunted by the first defeat in '71, the Morgan-Drexel-Morton alliance continued its efforts to break the Cooke monopoly. Tony Drexel and President Grant were intimate friends. Even closer to the President was George W. Childs, editor of Drexel's newspaper, *The Public Ledger* of Philadelphia. Drexel and Childs brought to bear all possible influence upon the administration. And the new Drexel partner, Pierpont Morgan, was not idle. In one of his letters, Jay Cooke acknowledges that "young Morgan and Morton were my most assiduous rivals."

In 1873, Secretary of the Treasury George S. Bout-well announced a $300,000,000 sale of bonds. Cooke and his cohorts and the Morgan alliance leaped into the bidding. Each side asserted that it would take the bonds at par. At once the skies clouded. The storm broke. The public, the press, the politicians were stirred at the possibility that large profits were to be poured into the pockets of small coteries of bankers. Debates burst forth in Congress.

The "Syndicate" was denounced as a ring to defraud the Government. Hon. Samuel Sullivan Cox of New York unleashed a speech of irony in the House. This gentleman, when editing the Columbus, Ohio, *Statesman,* had won the sobriquet "Sunset" Cox by an extremely rhetorical description of a sunset. His speech on the origin and purposes of the "Syndicate" exceeded even this florid effort. What sort of "animule" was the syndicate? Was it related to the Ku-Klux? The folks who sent him to Washington wanted to know. Well, here was his conclusion:

"While on the island of Corsica," related "Sunset," "I saw the devil-fish of Victor Hugo, a horrible monster with the most remarkable tentacula, which clasp the human form in their slimy claws. It has depopulated whole villages by the sea. It is called by the victims, in their mixed language, 'sundy-cato.' Revenue reformers write me that it is an animal peculiar to Pennsylvania, with a head of iron, eyes of nickel, legs of copper, and a heart of stone. It consumes every green thing outside of its own state."

The Ways and Means Committee held exciting public

sessions. These developed into a bitter fight between the Cooke and the Morgan factions. Newspaper doggerel asked:

> "Pray, what is a syndicate
> Intended to indicate?"
>   Is queried abroad and at home.
> "Say, is it a corner,
>   Where Jay Cooke as Horner
>   Can pull out a very big plum?"

During the spree of words, as some remembered later, young Pierpont Morgan sat alert but impassive, uttering not a word but taking in everything.

Cooke's friends told Secretary Boutwell it would be an "unpardonable outrage" to permit the refunding contract to be shared. Young Morgan listened—and said nothing. Very calmly, he had matched the Cooke offer and insisted upon participation, purposing to take either $100,000,000 or all of the remaining $300,000,000 of five per cent bonds. Cooke's friend, Senator Cattell, of New Jersey, wrote to Boutwell that the Morgan-Morton proposal was a thing that "can't be done and shall not be done."

The Ways and Means Committee took no action; and the Government divided the '73 issue evenly between the Cooke-Rothschild and the Morgan-Morton syndicates.

That was Jay Cooke's last great transaction, for in the autumn of 1873 he failed, carried down in a panic that left the country's business structure a ruin, temporarily. Cooke had over-extended himself seeking to push the Northern Pacific Railroad from Lake Superior to Puget

Sound. From that time until the end of the seventies his rivals had the field to themselves.

With the approach of the resumption of specie payment on January 1, 1879, European capitalists began to look more favorably upon our national obligations. The Morgan-Morton-Drexel alliance formed a syndicate with the Rothschilds and sold $260,000,000 four per cent bonds at an advance over the purchase price of from one to four points. The Morgan-Drexel share of the profits was computed at $5,000,000.

In sum the bond syndicates of the seventies disposed of $750,000,000 of Government securities. At the close of the operations the credit of the United States was on a four per cent instead of a six and one-half per cent basis. The Rothschilds, through August Belmont, disposed of the largest amount of bonds. The Morgan combination came next. The Rothschilds sold largely on the Continent, the Morgans in England.

In addition to splendid profits for themselves, the Morgans had succeeded in re-establishing American credit in England. With recurrent agitation in Congress over "fiat" money and silver "parity," it was often necessary for Junius Morgan to call upon his son to quiet the apprehensions of British investors. On several occasions, Junius Morgan summoned Pierpont to London by urgent cable over Cyrus Field's recently completed trans-Atlantic cable. Shouldering his way into staid tea-time conferences in Old Broad Street, young Morgan would assure timid English capitalists: "Every bond you buy from us is going to be paid in gold—backed by our pledge and the pledge of the United States Government. No responsible person in America pays any attention to the silver agitators in Congress."

The junior partner in Drexel, Morgan & Co. was an effective missionary. The British continued to invest in U. S. fives and fours; and soon American credit abroad was at its zenith. The effect of the changed spirit was felt in New York where the financial community hailed Junius Morgan as the leader in the new school of international finance. In 1877 the elder Morgan came to visit his son and he was tendered a public banquet in New York. Every financial magnate of prominence was present and cheered when Samuel J. Tilden, the toastmaster, lauded the guest of honor for "upholding, unsullied, the honor of America in the tabernacle of the Old World."

The demonstration marked the rise of a new financial oligarchy. Junius Morgan, now sixty-four, was preparing to retire from active business life. He was hale and hearty but the fleshpots had larded his great frame. "He presented," in the phrase of Moody, "the ponderous figure of an East India merchant prince in an old English play." His son was to come forward "as if chosen by circumstance and inheritance as the heir of North America."

Junius Morgan was confident that Pierpont could bear the scepter. Until then he had been merely the son of his father. But "he had learned the tools of his trade; he had watched and helped to operate great syndicates; and was perfectly well equipped to take first place in the security market of America. In one step he took his place as the greatest financial figure of his time or any other—greatest because the leader in the greatest and most momentous movement of capital in the history of the world."

In 1879, at forty-two, Pierpont Morgan stepped out upon his own and operated sensationally the first underwriting in American railway securities. Definitely, he emerged from the shadow of his father. He was as rugged as welded iron. His hair was thinning; his face unfurrowed and curiously soft compared with the mask it later wore. But there were the icy eyes, powerful nose, big brushy moustache and brusque, dictatorial manner.

Having piled up the first individual hundred-million-dollar fortune the world had ever seen, Commodore Cornelius Vanderbilt passed to his reward in 1877. His son, William H. Vanderbilt, came into control of the great New York Central system. Immediately, the politicians and rival railway promoters made Vanderbilt a target of attack. The New York Legislature, goaded by aroused public opinion, threatened to levy ruinous taxes upon the Central.

William H. Vanderbilt was of less firm stuff than his doughty sire. A stoutish man, with flowing side-whiskers, he divided his time between his stable of trotters and the Vanderbilt railroad system. He did not at all relish attacks upon him as a one-man power in a great railroad.

"The politicians are trying to ruin me," he told friends. "If I could see a way to do it, I would sell enough of my Central stock so it could no longer be said that I control a majority." One of the friends suggested that the frightened magnate consult Pierpont Morgan. That evening, in his Fifth Avenue mansion, under pledge of strictest secrecy, Vanderbilt laid the situation before the New York partner of Drexel, Morgan & Co.

"Mr. Morgan," exclaimed Vanderbilt, "I have word from Albany that the New York Central is going to be taxed to death! If I were not fearful of bringing on a panic, I would sell a great deal of my stock on the open market."

"How much stock do you own?" asked Morgan.

"Eighty-seven per cent."

"How much will you sell?"

Vanderbilt said he was willing to dispose of 250,000 shares, thus reducing his holdings to less than fifty per cent of the total capital stock. Morgan pondered a moment, then said: "I will sell 250,000 shares for you in England and no one will know anything about it until you make the announcement."

Morgan puffed a moment longer upon his cigar and added, quite casually: "There are two conditions, though, I would have to insist upon. First: a guarantee that the Central for five years will continue to pay its regular eight per cent dividend. Second: that a place on the board of directors be given to myself or some other representative of the purchasers. Those who invest their money through me must be assured that they are going to be protected."

Vanderbilt was startled. Never before had a banker or security broker formulated such a creed. "At what price can you dispose of the stock?" he asked.

"At the market price—130," replied Morgan, coolly.

Vastly impressed, Vanderbilt told Morgan to go ahead. Within a few days an agreement was signed. Not a hint leaked to the public. Several weeks later it was announced that Drexel, Morgan & Co. and J. S. Morgan & Co. had sold to English investors the great block of Central stock. The fact was purposely made public. Vanderbilt announced that he had invested the proceeds in Government bonds. Criticism of his one-man power in the Central system ceased, as did attempts to tax the railroad excessively.

It was not known who among the great investors in England were the purchasers. The British investors, however, showed striking confidence in Morgan, for they executed voting proxies in his favor. The House of Morgan holds these to this day.

The Central sale was the first outright disposal of American railroad securities by direct private negotiation. Morgan's profit was $3,000,000. Beyond this, he gained the good will of the richest man in America. Vanderbilt was so pleased that he presented Morgan with a costly and elaborate silver service and directed that the dies be destroyed so that the plate could never be duplicated.

The great and successful Vanderbilt stock deal established another precedent, incalculably valuable in future operations. Through it Morgan served notice, in a period of wild-cat speculation, that at least one international banking house would fight for its capital. Discounting the moral aspects of the matter, Morgan's attitude was good business. And it was time that such word should go forth.

The decade following the Civil War had been marked
by a moral breakdown, socially, financially, politically.
"Moral sense," writes Alexander Dana Noyes in "Forty
Years of American Finance," "seemed for a time to
have deteriorated in the whole community." The period
was marred by a succession of disgraceful episodes: the
Tweed Ring in New York; the vengeful impeachment of President Johnson; the tacitly admitted corruption of William Worth Belknap, Republican Secretary of War, 1869-1876; the Crédit Mobilier disclosures
of 1872 involving members of Congress; the infamous
gold-market conspiracy of 1869; the rise of crooked
railway promoters and their notorious corruption of
the courts; and, of course, the wreck of credit in the
great panic of 1873.

Rich, fertile America rode to recovery on the huge
grain and cotton crops of 1879. Specie payment was
triumphantly resumed. Immigration doubled and quad-
rupled between 1880 and 1882. Western lands were
opened to cultivation as never before.

The rapid development brought evils with it. The
choicest opportunities for plunder lay in the railroads.
Shrewd and unscrupulous promoters entered this field.
Their purpose was not to aid the growth of the West
but to enrich themselves. Their leader was Jay Gould.
"Few properties on which this man laid his hand escaped
ruin in the end," writes Mr. Noyes. "He mastered more
completely than any other promoter in our history the
art of buying worthless railways for a song, selling them
at fancy prices to a solvent corporation under his own
control, and then so straining the credit and manipu-

lating the books of the amalgamated company as to secure his own safe retreat through the stock market. He was not a builder, he was a destroyer, and the truth of this statement may be easily demonstrated by tracing out the subsequent history of the corporations which he got into his clutches."

In the Albany & Susquehanna foray, Pierpont Morgan had successfully opposed Gould and methods represented by Gould. Now an irresistible course of events was again to force Morgan into the arena—and permanently—as a foeman of Gouldism. During the next pregnant years he was to stand forth as champion of the real owners of the railroads—those whose money was invested in the stocks and bonds of the carriers.

No eleemosynary impulses motivated Morgan. He was a speculator, but always for a rise, an incorrigible bull on America. As such, he went forth to battle Gouldism and all that Gouldism represented. Capital— the capital that expected a safe, sure return upon its investments—had a protector. The issue was soon to be joined.

At forty-two, magnificent conceptions were stirring in Pierpont Morgan. He was at about the same age at which his father and his father's partner, George Peabody, had begun their notable careers in London. He was developing a vast pride in himself as capital's instrument in opening a huge continent. He began to play a part in the life of the community. As yet, however, there was little time for the lighter engagements to which he was to turn.

He joined the Union League and the New York

Yacht Club. He lent himself to the faithful little group which labored for a year to raise the paltry sum of $106,000 with which the Metropolitan Museum of Art was founded. His father was collecting canvases of Gainsborough, Reynolds and Romney. He himself was desultorily acquiring paintings and bits of sculpture, here and there.

He purchased a town house—a square, old-fashioned brownstone mansion at 219 Madison Avenue—and established a country home, "Cragston," at Highland Falls on the west bank of the Hudson. Cragston was a rambling, roomy house, built for comfort. Set upon an estate of 2,000 acres, its porches and windows commanded gorgeous views.

A black-hulled yacht, *Corsair I*, slid from the ways.

Pierpont Morgan came forward "as if chosen by circumstance and inheritance as the heir of North America."

CHAPTER SIX

RAILROAD LUNACY

ON AN AFTERNOON IN JULY, 1885, A GREAT YACHT with black hull and white superstructure sliced its swift way about New York Harbor. When the yacht crossed close under the counter of a ferryboat, passengers noticed four men on the quarter-deck. One, a man with square shoulders, thick neck, and heavy features, sat apart from the others. His face was set in a resolute scowl, lips clenched. His whole bearing spoke of warfare and relentless strength.

Indeed, it was grim war that impelled Pierpont Morgan, on this peaceful, sunlit day, to summon aboard his yacht, the *Corsair*, the directing heads of the country's two greatest trunk lines, the New York Central and the Pennsylvania.

As a climax to a crazy period of over-expansion, over-capitalization, and infamous speculation, the railroad world was in turmoil. Ruin threatened even the two systems—Central and Pennsylvania—that dominated the country east of the Mississippi. On the west bank of the Hudson river glistened the new-laid rails of a railroad called the West Shore, within sight of the Central which ran along the Hudson's eastern shore. The West Shore, partly completed, was designed to parallel and compete with the Central from New York to Buffalo.

William H. Vanderbilt, still master of the Central in effect, termed the new road "a miserable common thief caught with its hands in my pocket." Vanderbilt, partly in exasperation, had lent his backing to a line called the South Pennsylvania Railroad, projected to parallel the powerful Pennsylvania system.

The stability of all railroad securities was threatened, still shaky as a result of widespread and ruinous wars in '77, '78 and '79.

Morgan had returned from a European trip in June. He found the financial community in England with its face firm set against American investments, particularly railway issues. There was little Morgan could say to reassure his European clients. He was forced to admit that crooked or unduly sanguine promoters had built double the needed amount of trackage in the United States and issued three to four times as much security as interest could be paid upon.

British financiers had before them the gloomy story as set forth in yearly reports of Poor's Manual, recognized American railroad authority. Poor's Manual stated in 1884 that in 1883 almost $4,000,000,000— practically all the capital stock for the railroads of the United States—represented water. In the three years ending December 31, 1883, Poor's estimated, $2,000,-000,000 of capital and debt had been created, and "the whole increase of share capital, $999,387,208, and a portion of the bonded debt was in excess of construction."

Following the phenomenal grain and cotton crops of 1879 and 1880, there had been enormous increase in American railroad mileage. Get-rich-quick promoters were largely responsible. In two years almost 30,000 miles of railroad had been built, an addition of over one-third in the total mileage. Startling changes had come in less than a generation.

The first railroads had been built in sections, some less than twenty miles long. To travel from Albany to Buffalo, for instance, one used ten separate lines—all under different ownership. There were four distinct gauges or width of track in the country. Because of the work thus given to local labor in the transfer of goods from one terminal to another, these fragments of roads opposed any movement toward consolidation. But the movement was inevitable. Soon these tiny roads became links in the trunk lines.

The New York Central was originally a consolidation of eleven local roads. Similarly, the Pennsylvania system had grown from a combination of many local lines southwest of New York. These systems were vastly over-capitalized but, so long as they had the field to themselves, they could make the public "pay the freight." For a time their outlook was very comfortable indeed.

Then along came the unscrupulous promoter. He perceived the rich possibilities of building or threatening to build competing lines. In many cases he was a sand-bagger, a blackmailer pure and simple. The game was absurdly simple: the promoter bought a charter for a small sum. This gave him the right to issue first mort-

gage bonds. The proceeds provided a revolving fund
that could be employed as the promoter wished. The
stock alone held voting power and the promoter was
careful to retain control of the stock. Also, he often
controlled the construction company that was to build
the road, and contracted to pay himself anything he
wanted for this work.

Fired by the spirit of speculation, the public, both
here and abroad, bought railroad bonds by the tens of
millions. The victims believed they were aiding the
development of a great new country and that they
would enjoy a share of the limitless wealth the railroads
were creating. In every part of the British Isles, in cot-
tages and castles, folks had exchanged their savings and
surplus for crinkly bonds in American railroads. By
now, 1885, they had discovered that their money had
been tossed upon the tide. Accordingly, they were denouncing our railroad magnates as financial freebooters
and worse.

On his customary trip abroad, in the spring of 1885,
Morgan caught the backwash of this bitterness. The
British asked him very pointedly why New York Central dividends had dropped to four per cent and less
the moment the five-year period of guaranteed eight
per cent dividends expired. When he had placed a great
block of Central stock abroad in 1879, Morgan, it will
be remembered, had obtained W. H. Vanderbilt's pledge
to continue for five years eight per cent dividends.

As best he could, Morgan explained what had happened. There were now five independent through lines
to Chicago. Two more were building. Three roads

would have been ample. Ruinous competition had resulted. Passengers rode from New York to Chicago for a dollar a head. Freight was being carried at half cost.

The situation touched Morgan's pride to the quick. By now the house of Morgan was irretrievably linked with the fortunes of the trunk lines and the carriers of the middle Atlantic states. In addition to the Central sale, Drexel, Morgan & Co. and J. S. Morgan & Co. had placed with their clients in England great blocks of other railroad securities: Reading, Chesapeake & Ohio, Baltimore & Ohio, etc.

Despite their harrowing experiences British investors retained firm faith in the Morgans. In half a century George Peabody and Junius Morgan had built a mighty reputation. Was this invaluable prestige now to be destroyed through a situation which was not of the firm's making? During the spring there were many fateful conferences at 22 Old Broad Street. Junius Morgan was now seventy-two. After his brilliant successes he did not desire to end his career under a cloud. During hours of anxious talk with his son and his son-in-law, Walter Burns (now practically chief of the London house), Junius Morgan impressed upon the younger men that the honor of the house was at stake. Something must be done for the sake both of their own interests and of those of their clients, to breathe value into the securities sold through them.

Morgan was not especially touched by the plight of his British clients. But no hurt must come to his father. Him he worshipped as a deity, almost. So it was as though carrying a Grail that Morgan returned to New

York in June. He had formulated a plan which he thought would bring a measure of peace in the chaotic railroad world: he would persuade the Central to take over the West Shore, the Pennsylvania to purchase the South Pennsylvania. Study of the situation convinced him that these were the two sorest spots. His influence with Vanderbilt was powerful. He was not so intimate with the Pennsylvania, though Drexel, Morgan & Co. had jobbed several loans for that system.

Morgan's task was tremendously difficult. Vanderbilt shortly before had emerged from a costly contest with a road called the Nickel Plate, which Western promoters had partly built almost within sight of Vanderbilt's Lake Shore Railroad from Buffalo to Chicago. Vanderbilt purchased the Nickel Plate—and did not learn until afterwards that he could have saved millions by waiting a few weeks. Hence, when the West Shore loomed as a dangerous competitor of the Central, Vanderbilt got his dander up and vowed he'd spend his last cent before he'd compromise with the latest group of "blackmailers."

The West Shore was organized on lines familiar to that era of scandalous railroad financing. Its promoters were Charles T. Woerishoffer, a bear operator on the New York Stock Exchange; General Edward F. Winslow, a railroad engineer, and General Horace Porter. Through circulars so glittering that they gathered in even the guarded gold of the Astors and of D. O. Mills, $40,000,000 worth of bonds were sold. The promoters formed the North River Construction Co., controlled, of course, by themselves.

They assured the public that low-cost construction and rigid limitation of indebtedness would enable them to under-cut the Central with its watered millions. Within two years the investors learned that they had been rooked. The road was hopelessly insolvent. The contract with the construction company had eaten up more than $70,000,000 in the building of less than four hundred miles of railroad. The promoters, however, made good one boast: they hurt the Central vitally.

Under a flood of lawsuits, the West Shore went into the hands of a receiver in the spring of 1885. When Morgan returned from Europe the road was being operated through receiver's certificates at a cost of one hundred and forty-five per cent. The Central, too, was in dire straits. It was earning less than one per cent on its huge capitalization and was forced to cut into surplus to pay any dividend at all.

William H. Vanderbilt, then in the last months of his life, was suffering from some of the sins of his stock-jobbing father.

Morgan tackled Vanderbilt first. He found the Central chieftain fuming, vowing that he would never compromise with the thieving West Shore. Morgan, however, came armed with facts and figures to show that the West Shore, under proper management, could be made to pay. He argued that the Central's constantly increasing Mohawk and Hudson River traffic could employ the rival line. He told Vanderbilt: "Why, in five years the growth of trade on the Great Lakes will make it necessary for you to expand your Buffalo-New York facilities. Think what it is going to cost you to build additional roadbeds and new trackage. Why not buy the West Shore now when you can get it cheap?"

Morgan finally triumphed. Since their first meeting he had exerted almost hypnotic control over Vanderbilt. Now he turned the full voltage of his personality toward convincing Vanderbilt that he ought also to avert another disastrous railroad war by selling the South Pennsylvania to the Pennsylvania Railroad.

At every step Morgan found a friendly ally in Chauncey M. Depew, president of the Central. Morgan and Depew had been social intimates since the early seventies. Often in the evening, at the Union League Club, Morgan formed one of a group that gathered about Depew when the latter, a famous raconteur, was in a story-telling mood.

Grumpily, Vanderbilt finally yielded to Morgan's peace-making plan with the Pennsylvania. So far so good. But the hardest part of the business was yet to come. Morgan had to win over George H. Roberts, president of the Pennsylvania. Roberts was self-made and obstinate. He had begun life as a rodman with a construction gang. He was a Welshman, with all the stubbornness of his doughty race. Roberts was a gloomy person with prominent ears, deep-sunk eyes, and a moppy moustache, the weight of which seemed almost to sink his chin into his loose wing collar.

He had publicly denounced the South Pennsylvania and declared the Pennsylvania would crush it like a pebble. He was particularly incensed at the rival road's invasion of the Pennsylvania's Clearfield bituminous region. Roberts had practically chased Andrew Carnegie out of his office when the latter suggested gently that the new road could be better managed as part of the Pennsylvania system. The aggressive little ironmaster, eager as always to encourage railroad competition, had invested heavily in South Pennsylvania.

The outspoken Roberts asserted that all the king's horses and all the king's men could not make him change his mind. Vanderbilt, Carnegie, and other rich men who had put their money into South Pennsylvania were traitors to their class, raiders, pirates. Let them stew in their own juice. The Pennsylvania could take care of itself.

Morgan was well aware of Roberts' attitude. Undaunted, he went to Philadelphia and saw Frank Thomson, vice-president of the Pennsylvania. Morgan had decided upon a diplomatic attack. Thomson offered no hope but agreed to lure Roberts aboard the Morgan yacht for a conference with Morgan and Depew.

The president of the Pennsylvania boarded the *Corsair* under protest. He knew his own mind, he said. Everybody knew his position. Why waste time talking about it?

At first there was no discussion of business. Morgan was a genial host. He showed his visitors over his beautiful yacht and had an expansive luncheon served. Depew was in rare form. It was a new sort of business conference for the dour Roberts. A jovial group adjourned to the quarter-deck for coffee and liqueurs. Then, and then only, the matter of the moment came up.

While the *Corsair* steamed to the Highlands, Depew told of the Central's experiences with the West Shore. He said that Vanderbilt and his associates could hold out indefinitely in the South Pennsylvania fight. Did Roberts alone wish to be responsible for a war that might last for years and affect the credit of every railroad in the country?

Hours passed. The *Corsair* steamed back from the Highlands, turned up the Hudson as far as Storm King, and then retraced its way. Morgan sat smoking big, black cigars, one after the other. The sun dipped, casting gray shadows over the Palisades. Still Roberts was obdurate, determined that Vanderbilt and the other wealthy South Pennsylvania backers should be punished for seeking to "ruin" the Pennsylvania.

Depew displayed elaborate cost sheets and accounts showing that the Vanderbilt syndicate would lose millions under Morgan's proposal that the Pennsylvania reimburse the syndicate merely for its actual construction outlays. Roberts sat in silence.

Morgan came striding over and spoke, for the first time in hours.

"Yes," he said, "Mr. Vanderbilt and the others have had their lesson. They will not get out whole. Roberts, you must come into this thing now or"—his voice became ominous—"you will be forced to come into it soon if only to control your connections. Now you have a choice. Soon you won't have a chance to choose."

For a long time silence fell upon the group. Roberts puffed at his pipe. Morgan pulled at his cigar. The ship's bells chimed the hour—seven o'clock. The president of the Pennsylvania roused. "All right," he said sullenly, "I agree."

Morgan had won the most momentous victory of his career. An agreement was soon drawn up and ratified. Morgan lent the use of his name as purchaser of the South Pennsylvania. The Pennsylvania took over the contract, paying Vanderbilt and associates the actual cost of construction. The West Shore was bid in by Morgan and Depew at foreclosure sale for $22,000,000; and leased to the Central for 999 years.

The settlement of the costly squabble was hailed by the financial communities here and abroad as a masterstroke of negotiation. But one group was mournful. Shippers, who had profited by the competition of the independents with the Central and Pennsylvania, found themselves once more at the mercy of monopolies. Again the drawback and the rebate flourished. Favoritism and pull were once more in the saddle.

Small dealers who shipped from town to town were particularly downcast. They had seen hope in competition. For years their freight bills had mounted. They had largely paid the cost in the battle of the railroads to cut each other's throats on through traffic and to maintain illegitimate dividends upon hundreds of millions of fraudulent capitalization.

Morgan, of course, was not concerned in the least in the matter of rates. He was a representative only of capital, and capital demanded stamping out competition. Broader questions of social morality did not penetrate his consciousness to the slightest degree. He was looking out for himself and for his clients.

In the mighty cry that now went up for public regulation of railroad rates and for enforcement of unrestricted competition, a picture of Morgan was beginning to form in the public mind: a picture of a man cold and ruthless, devoted to one aim and one aim only, dollar profits for himself and those he represented.

Morgan's name began to creep into the newspapers. He was puzzled by the sudden notoriety. "I have done nothing except stop men fighting," he said. "I don't like to see men fighting. There is too much waste."

At the corner of Broad and Wall, Morgan still carried on his business personally. He was accessible to all comers. He had built up an enormous foreign exchange business for Drexel, Morgan & Co., and attended to its details himself. A veteran foreign exchange broker gave this recollection of the Morgan of those days to John Moody:

"I remember him in the early '80's. He used to do most of his exchange business personally then. I know I had to wait for him when he was out. He sat there in the front of his private office, his head down at his desk, and a big cigar cocked up in the corner of his mouth. When you offered him exchange, if he thought it was too high he'd say, 'No'; nothing more. Never an offer of what he'd give. You'd never know what he thought. Then you'd go out. If you could, you'd come back and offer it again, lower. If he thought the price right, he'd say, 'I'll take it'; nothing more. It was always 'Yes' or 'No'; no other talk at all."

Morgan, a quarter of a century of experience behind him, had schooled himself in a yes-and-no curtness. It paid. He managed most of his affairs yes-and-no style. But beneath the marble exterior was a nature of decidedly different texture.

During this period W. S. Rainsford, a radical young preacher, was summoned from a church in Toronto to the ancient and debilitated parish of St. George's in New York where Morgan was a vestryman and his father-in-law, Charles Tracy, senior warden. Rainsford had determined not to accept the call except upon his own terms—and these, he was convinced, were so revolutionary that no conservative vestry of the Protestant Episcopal Church would yield to them.

Accordingly it was with low heart that Rainsford arrived at the old Central Railroad depot in January, 1883. He was met at the station by J. Noble Stearns, one of the vestrymen, and driven to Morgan's home on Madison Avenue. Here were assembled the vestry, all men of wealth and standing.

Mr. Tracy outlined the serious state of affairs at St. George's. The church had fallen into a state of decadence. Old parishioners had drifted away and there were no new ones to take their places. The pew-holders were few. The church's floating debt had mounted to $35,000.

During the talk, Pierpont Morgan sat in an armchair and offered not a word. Rainsford, though, had instantly sensed that he was the most forceful man of the group. The preacher—thirty-three, bearded, six feet three—kept his eyes upon Morgan. Mr. Tracy concluded his remarks. There was silence. Morgan broke it. "Mr. Rainsford," he said, "if you will be our rector,

I will help you all I can. Will you accept a unanimous call to St. George's?"

"I will upon three conditions," responded Rainsford.

"Name them," from Morgan.

"First, every pew in the church must be absolutely free. Second, all committees with the exception of the vestry must be abolished and I must have the sole right to appoint new committees. Third, I want a fund of $10,000 a year for three years to employ as I see fit in church work."

Everyone in the room realized that Rainsford was asking autocratic powers. Mingled expressions were graved upon the countenances of Tracy, Stearns, David Dows, and the other men of power present. Only Morgan seemed to have made up his mind. One quick survey about the circle of tense faces, then Morgan looked full at Rainsford and uttered one word: "Done."

Thus began a lifelong friendship.

Rainsford soon saw that if he wished to democratize his church, he must first democratize his vestry, and Morgan first of all. For it was evident that Morgan was the commanding influence in the church and that he was accustomed to having his own way.

The young rector found that he could win Morgan not by flattery but by straightforward demonstration that his proposed radical changes would benefit St. George's. Next to those of his immediate family, Morgan seemed most concerned with the fortunes of his church. He and the other vestrymen were much disturbed by Rainsford's determination to bring into the fold the people of the tenements.

At one meeting Rainsford related a homely parable he had heard on the banks of a Canadian salmon stream.

"The salmon had deserted this stream," said Rainsford. "The fishermen were in a bad way. One man, however, was cannier than the rest. He sold his salmon nets and bought smelt nets. By merely changing the size of his mesh he was soon enjoying greater prosperity than ever."

By these diplomatic personal touches and the force of a great sincerity, Rainsford won point after point. Within a few months he had Morgan at the church door Sunday mornings greeting strangers and beaming upon the steadily increasing congregations.

Rainsford was enthusiastic for congregational singing and thought this should be led by a surpliced choir of women as well as of boys and men. With difficulty Morgan was won to this innovation. Elsewhere there was bitter opposition. One wealthy worshipper proffered Rainsford a check for $200,000 for the building of a much-needed parish and community house—provided the Rector would give up his cherished plan and permit the donor to hire organist and choir. Rainsford refused and the man left the church.

From the earliest days of his pastorate, Rainsford was in the habit of breakfasting weekly (usually on Mondays) with Morgan. Soon after the episode of the $200,000 offer, Rainsford told Morgan the whole story at the latter's breakfast table. Morgan listened but said nothing.

A year later, in early spring, a shabby hired coupé stopped at the door of St. George's rectory in East Sixteenth Street. In it was Pierpont Morgan. In those days he never drove in any other vehicle. "Just dropped in to say goodbye, Rector," explained Morgan. "I am on my way to Europe, sailing this morning." Extracting a letter from his pocket, he added: "I think this is what you want, Rector. If I have left anything out, you can tell me when I come back," and with a final handshake he was gone.

The paper was a deed of gift for a new church house. The cost was a quarter of a million.

That was Morgan's method—doing big things but in his own way. His way was autocratic and intensely personal, but result-producing. The principal drive in Morgan's nature may be expressed in one word: results. He set out to accomplish certain aims. Rainsford was to be his instrument in the rehabilitation of his church.

Other men were to be his instruments in the rehabilitation of the railroads. Now Pierpont Morgan was looked upon as the one man who could "save" the railroads. Capital regarded him as the only person who could lead the railways into the Promised Land—where strife was lessened and dividends were certain. For the next few years he was to be permitted to do little else than wrestle with the railroad problem.

He was willing to accept leadership. But there must be but one boss, one autocrat: John Pierpont Morgan.

CHAPTER SEVEN

"GENTLEMEN'S AGREEMENTS"—BUT THESE WERE NO GENTLEMEN

THE ERA OF WILDCAT SPECULATION, FRAUDULENT financing and dog-eat-dog competition in railroading swelled the country's clangorous cry for some sort of public regulation. American investors had been trimmed by the transportation confidence-men even more flagrantly than those in Europe. They had grown to regard the railroads—the good as well as the bad—as evil instruments designed by the devil to gobble up their savings.

They could think of but one way out: competition by force of law—an economic panacea as ancient as the republic. Hence, after a long fight, the Interstate Commerce Act was passed in 1887. The act prohibited pooling, a rate-fixing device to which some of the railroads had resorted since the mid-seventies. The pooling agreements, though generally broken as soon as signed, intensified the public's ugly mood.

Morgan was opposed to any and all form of Government interference. He was not in the slightest in sympathy with, nor did he deign to examine, the tangled social factors that had brought the new law into being. He believed in monopoly as the inevitable trend of capital, monopoly limited and supervised only by the demands and the requirements of capital. Law or no law, he was determined to protect the holdings of his clients and insure the prosperity and prestige of his firm.

Instinctively, the railroads turned to Morgan to show them the way out of the wilderness. Capital's new champion cast about for means to bring peace into the troubled railroad world. There was lustre now about the name of Pierpont Morgan. He represented achievement. Soon his old-fashioned brownstone residence became the gathering place of railroad executives.

In 1886, the year following Morgan's settlement of the Central-Pennsylvania quarrel, the presidents of the coal-carrying railroads had met at 219 Madison Avenue and agreed upon higher rates. This was the first of a series of memorable dinner-table conferences. At them were formulated so-called "gentlemen's agreements" and "community of interest" plans. The new dictator of railroad destinies wanted to bring peace by moral suasion, if possible. However, he soon showed that he was prepared to use force if necessary.

On March 23, 1887, Morgan had at his home at dinner presidents of some of the eastern lines which were principally engaged in the costly competition against the standard lines, among them John King of the Erie, Samuel Sloan of the Lackawanna, and Robert M. Olyphant of the Delaware & Hudson. An arrangement was perfected, to which the Pennsylvania and Central assented, by which each company bound itself by word of mouth to accept an agreed schedule of tariffs between competitive points.

Henry S. Ives upset that agreement before the year was out. Ives had attained a success as charming as that of Ferdinand Ward who had ruined General Grant and the Grant family only a few years before. Ives tried Ward's endless chain of railroad aggrandizement, a system which only the genius of E. H. Harriman ever carried out successfully. Ives had begun by getting control of the Cincinnati, Hamilton & Dayton and pledging its securities and his stocks and bonds. With the money thus borrowed he got another road, the securities of which he likewise pledged. He kept going in this way until he had acquired a system from Cincinnati to St. Louis which he called (aptly enough) the Vandalia and which had been used by the Pennsylvania as its outlet from Cincinnati west.

At this time the Baltimore & Ohio, under the management of Robert Garrett, became restless. It had built a line to Philadelphia but had been denied entrance into New York over the Pennsylvania tracks. Now Garrett sought reprisal by a union with the system built of flimsy fabric by the Young Napoleon, Ives. If B. & O. could be kept out of New York by the Pennsylvania, B. & O. would unite with Ives and keep Pennsylvania out of St. Louis.

No gentlemen's agreement could possibly hold the Pennsylvania against such a menace to its interests. The Ives-Garrett proposal was an entirely feasible and practical proposition except for one unknown quantity— the attitude of New York bankers.

Ives found that no money could be raised to finance his further projects. Appeals to Morgan and other New

York bankers, furthermore, brought only the pleasant tidings that Ives must pay up his other loans on maturity. Presently Ives failed. Garrett abandoned ambitious schemes, and a Morgan syndicate supplied the B. & O. with money urgently needed and brought it back into line. Morgan had repaid the Pennsylvania for furthering his peace plan of '85.

The Ives episode was the first instance of the exertion of concerted banking power on organized business. It was a force that neither Ives nor any of his contemporaries had been taught to reckon with. Previously the disturber, promoter, and corporation blackmailer had had no thought that his loans might be called because his plans ran counter to what capital considered "legitimate" investment. Morgan had made another departure both in finance and in American business.

In January, 1889, came the most momentous of the "gentlemen's agreement" meetings. Morgan assembled in his study eighteen railroad heads, together with representatives of the principal houses of issue of railway securities, and formed the "Interstate Railway Association."

Morgan's stature had grown. He was the acknowledged bellwether of the bankers. His name loomed large in the press. The railroad issue was the livest of the day. A Wall Street wag remarked admiringly: "Why, that man Morgan is a regular Jupiter!" and the nickname stuck. The newspapers heralded the 1889 conclave as the first step in a move to make Morgan chief of a great central company to regulate the entire railroad industry.

The country's chief organ of finance, *The Financial Chronicle,* said editorially:

"The consulting parties were practically all the heads of the competing lines on the one hand and the representatives of the world's capital on the other. When the party furnishing all the new money needed and the party that owns the old money invested and the party managing the corporations unite, the result means revolution. . . . The influence and authority of the board, when formed, can hardly be over-estimated. The standing of the members of the association would itself be a power not lightly to be resisted. But, in addition to that, every stockholder in Europe and America will be likely to gather around the board, giving it proxies when asked for or delegating to it any special authority which, in the board's opinion, it might need. Besides, it would substantially control the capital of the world. Against its advice or opinion we do not believe a dollar of money could be raised for any enterprise."

If not quite so ambitious, the meeting was sufficiently epochal. Present were partners of the three leading houses dealing in railway securities—Drexel, Morgan & Co.; Kidder, Peabody & Co.; and Brown Brothers. Morgan was their spokesman. He talked to the warring railroad executives as they had never been talked to before. He served blunt notice that existing evils must cease. He said that hereafter his house and the others represented would refuse to finance competing railroads.

The scene was dramatic. Morgan faced men jaundiced with jealousy—men who had been at swords' points for years. Some were visionaries; others so crooked they could rest comfortably on coils of rope. There were foxy little Jay Gould and his son George. Gould had long since been forced to give up his gutting grip on the Erie and had moved into western pastures. Now he controlled the Missouri Pacific.

There was George H. Roberts, grumpy president of the Pennsylvania. There was Charles Francis Adams the younger, who wrote in his autobiography this revealing summary of his six years' experience as president of the Union Pacific: "I made no friends . . . nor among those I met was there any man whose acquaintance I valued. They were a coarse, realistic, bargaining crowd." There were Marvin Hughitt, of the Chicago & Northwestern; R. R. Cable, of the Rock Island; Frank S. Bond, of the Chicago, Milwaukee & St. Paul; A. B. Stickney, of the Chicago, St. Paul & Kansas City; and many others.

At dinner Morgan had been jovial and hearty, full of badinage and pleasantry. He played the part of host to perfection, pressing choice viands and wines upon his guests. Now, in the study, his manner changed. He was like a pilot-fish turning upon a school of sharks.

"The purpose of this meeting," began Morgan, "is to cause those present to no longer take the law into their own hands when they suspect they have been wronged, as has been too much the practice heretofore.

"This is not elsewhere customary in civilized communities, and no good reason exists why such a practice should continue among railroads."

The railroad men gasped. The tart Roberts, of the Pennsylvania, was the first to find voice. "Speaking in

behalf of the railroad people of this country," he said,
"I object to this very strong language which indicates
that we, the railroad people, are a set of anarchists, and
this an attempt to substitute law and arbitration for
anarchy and might."

Stickney followed. "I am not in favor of secret meetings like this one. The public are sure to think we are
conspiring to do something we ought not to do."

Roberts returned to the attack. "The railroads would
be all right if it wasn't for the building of damnfool competing lines. The bankers can put a stop to this if they
want to. Mr. Morgan's language has been pretty harsh
for us to hold here. But I can stand it, I suppose, if the
others can."

Morgan took up at once Roberts' complaint against
competing lines. "I am authorized to say, I think, on
behalf of the houses represented here, that if an organization can be formed which shall accomplish the purposes of this meeting, and with an executive committee
able to enforce its provisions, upon which the bankers
shall be represented, they are prepared to say that they
will not negotiate and will do everything in their power
to prevent the negotiation of any securities for the construction of parallel lines, or the extension of lines not
unanimously approved by the executive committee. I
wish that distinctly understood."

Charles Francis Adams asked leave to put the railroad
question "into a nutshell." He said: "The difficulty in
railway management does not lie in an act of legislation,
state or national, but does lie in the covetousness, want
of good faith, and low moral tone of railway managers,

in the complete absence of any high standard of commercial honor. Now the question we are to decide here is whether any gentleman representing a railroad company is prepared to stand up and say before the public and before us that he is opposed to obeying the law, and, further, that in matters of controversy he prefers to take the law into his own hands rather than submit to arbitration."

An association was formed, high-sounding resolutions were passed. But Morgan's plan to bring about peace through "gentlemen's agreements" failed. Animosities were too deep-seated, morality at too low an ebb. There was too much capital buried in the railroads demanding impossible returns. Also, slippery men of the Gould type had played the game too long according to their own standards, to submit voluntarily to dictation by a confederacy of bankers. Morgan could awe such men into seeming acquiescence by the pressure of his personality. But once back in their own bailiwicks, they did as they pleased.

Morgan was not blind. He soon saw that he must control by force alone. He himself must have a decisive say, so far as possible, in the roads built by his clients. "Your roads?" he grunted once to a protesting railroad president. "They are not your roads. They belong to my clients."

For Morgan's clients there was a gloomy outlook in this year of 1889. Of American railway securities listed on the London Stock Exchange, with par value of more than half a billion dollars, but one company was paying dividends on its common stock. The London *Statist* pointed out that "the consequences of rate wars on American railways are proving so disastrous to the holders of securities, and the prospects are so gloomy, that some heroic remedy must be resorted to, else the whole investment will be lost."

In the continuing difficulties of the great Philadelphia & Reading Railway, Morgan determined to resort to a "heroic remedy." Reading had come to him for reorganization first in the spring of 1886. Through extravagant rental of leased lines and incompetent management, the road was drifting into bankruptcy.

There are two cardinal principles in railroad reorganizations: first, reduction of interest charges by exchanging high rates for low interest-bearing bonds; second, security holders must submit to a cash assessment, by their own consent, of course. After these primary requirements are met come naturally other elements of which better and more virile management is the most important.

Reading's 1885 deficit was $4,500,000. Drexel, Morgan & Co. arranged to underwrite a $15,000,000 syndicate. Security holders refused to pay an assessment and backed a reorganization plan of Franklin B. Gowen, president of the road. Gowen's plan failed. Austin Corbin was made president. In the fall of 1887, the Morgan plan was put through. The security holders "came through" this time; and were rewarded the following year when the road showed a profit of $3,000,000.

But Reading was not out of the woods by any means. A peppery gentleman named Archibald McLeod succeeded Austin Corbin as president. At once he launched an astonishing campaign to extend Reading into and across New England. He hoped to form a vast coal monopoly and planned to gain an independent entrance into Boston. He would control the Old Colony Railroad system, covering southeastern Massachusetts, and then Reading could carry coal direct from the mines into Boston and thence to Canada.

It was an ambitious scheme and it would have succeeded except for the opposition of Pierpont Morgan. The New Haven monopoly was forming, and Morgan was interested. Morgan undertook to dissuade McLeod from his dream of carrying Reading across the new railroad bridge at Poughkeepsie and into Boston. "You can't dictate to me," McLeod told Morgan. "I'd rather run a peanut stand than take orders from any banker."

McLeod began a historic battle to gain control of the Old Colony. From that moment, though he did not know it, his doom was sealed. Morgan and the Drexels exerted sufficient influence in both Philadelphia and New York to cut off McLeod's money supply. The Reading's New England plans collapsed. Soon Old Colony passed into the hands of the New York & New Haven. Another step had been taken in a scheme—in which Morgan then was but passively interested—to combine all the railways in New England into one dominating system.

McLeod, his race run, resigned the Reading presidency. He left behind him a new floating debt of $18,000,000. Once more Morgan was appealed to by a committee of bondholders to reorganize the road. This time Morgan took no chances of being over-ridden by a management whose plans might interfere with his own. He guaranteed to place sufficient Reading first mortgage bonds here and abroad to put the road on its feet, but stipulated that he was to control the road through voting proxies.

Morgan now committed himself to a course from which he never deviated: he determined to control every railroad into which his financial genius breathed life. He would control either through ownership of stock by himself and his friends or through a "voting trust." The possibilities of this scheme had just begun to occur to him. The voting trust was a spiral device by which one man or one small group could hold the proxies of millions of stock owners. Through it, Morgan was to make himself a "one-man power in American finance."

In these constantly expanding activities, Morgan could not have borne the strain without the aid of capable partners. For ten years Morgan's pace had been terrific. For the detailed working-out of his plans he required able men. He found them, offered them rich rewards—and broke them down with work. Egisto P. Fabbri, Charles H. Godfrey, and J. Hood Wright were his first partners in the New York office of Drexel, Morgan & Co. Fabbri was an international merchant, member of the old shipping firm of Fabbri & Chauncey. His health broke down in 1884. Godfrey retired the same year. Fabbri had endured eight years of the Morgan drive, Godfrey six. Wright lasted until the fall of

1894 when he dropped dead in an elevated railroad station at the end of his business day.

In 1884, George S. Bowdoin, of Morton, Bliss & Co., joined Morgan. The same year Morgan found his most valued coadjutor, Charles H. Coster, an accountant in Fabbri's former firm. Coster, for Morgan's purposes, was a man in a million. He had a mystic genius for figures. He possessed a mental solvent by which all the intricate and interwoven relations of railroad obligations, bonds and underlying bonds, collateral trust mortgages, every artificial form of securing a loan, resolved themselves into original and perfectly distinct elements.

A financial chemist was Coster, taking strange and unaccustomed quantities and by means of his mental processes reducing them to perfect simplicity. Having done his work, Coster could lay before his chief solutions clear and comprehensible. These enabled Morgan's spatial mind to create new structures. The two men reinforced and supplemented each other. The tremendous series of reorganizations perfected by Morgan, in the now traditional railroad reconstruction era between 1884 and 1895, would have been impossible without the aid of Coster. On the other hand, the latter's magic powers of mind found their opportunity in preparing material for his partner's creations. Morgan often paid tribute to the peerless genius of Coster, freely acknowledging his debt.

But Coster, too—to whom the most abstruse financial problem was as plain as a proposition of Euclid—broke under his burden. John Moody, who knew him, gives us this vivid description of Morgan's right bower:

"Men saw him by day—a white-faced, nervous figure, hurrying from directors' meeting to directors'
meeting; at evening carrying home his portfolio of corporation problems for the night. He went traveling
across thousands of miles of country, watching railroad
roadbeds from the back platforms of trains. The accountant from the old-time South Street shipping firm
with a genius for figures had reached a centre of business pressure where no man's strength could last. In the
first part of March, 1900, Coster took a slight cold;
within a week he was dead. The papers, as the chief
feature of his obituary, recalled that he was in the Di-
rectory of Directors as director in fifty-nine great corporations."

But we are ahead of our story.

Junius Spencer Morgan died in Monte Carlo on
April 8, 1890, of injuries suffered in a railroad accident. In his will, executed five months before his death,
he described himself as "a citizen of the United States
of America, of Old Broad Street, London, merchant."

"When I received a cable announcing my father's
death," Morgan told a friend many years later, "I felt
that something not to be replaced had gone out of my
life."

Early in May, Morgan bore the body of his father to
Cedar Hill Cemetery, in Hartford. The younger Morgan had established a family plot under the shadow of
an impressive monument of red Nova Scotia granite.
To this resting-place, in 1879, had been removed from
the Old North Cemetery the bodies of his paternal

grandparents, Joseph and Sarah Morgan. In 1891, the bodies of Morgan's mother and of his brother, Junius, Jr., who had died at twelve, were carried to Hartford from a cemetery in London.

Junius Morgan's estate totaled $9,211,740. He left $3,000,000 in trust to each of his two elder daughters: Sarah Spencer, who had married George Hale Morgan in 1866; and Mary Lyman, wife of Walter Burns. To his youngest daughter, Juliet Pierpont, wife of the Rev. John Brainard Morgan, he left $2,000,000 in trust. He dealt less generously with Juliet because of an apparent, though unexpressed, feeling against her husband. Dividing his "plate, pictures and watercolors" among his four children, he specified that Juliet's share should be only for life—"such use and enjoyment to be personal and independent of any present or any future husband." His paintings included examples of Gainsborough, Romney, Landseer, Reynolds and Millais.

Pierpont Morgan was his father's residuary legatee. Though he inherited little more than a million in money, Morgan's choicest bequest was a painting of his father that held a strange history. For years the painting hung over Morgan's desk in his office or home. Here is the story:

In the early eighties Junius Morgan dropped into the office of Sir William Agnew, of Agnew & Co., celebrated London art dealers. The Anglo-American banker was an old and favored customer. Sir William led him aside. "Mr. Morgan," he said, "I've found just the artist to paint your portrait. He came here last week and asked for a shilling. 'Why?' asked one of my salesmen. 'Because I am an artist,' said the fellow, 'and you people have made a great deal of money through us.' My salesman was toffy and asked him who he was. He said his name was Bragard and he was an American. 'Let me have a pencil,' said the fellow, 'and I'll show you what I can do.' My word, his hands were shaking; he seemed to need food and sleep. But he seized hold of the pencil and copied the nearest portrait with amazing fidelity! My man gave him five shillings and brought him to me. Mr. Morgan, this young man is a craftsman! You must sit to him."

A day or two later Junius Morgan met his young countryman, the artist who had given his name as Bragard; and ordered a portrait. There were ten sittings in a studio Agnew had rented for the stranger. At the tenth the work seemed to be finished. Junius Morgan was delighted. He counted out $2,500 in British pound-notes and handed them to the artist, "This is the last sitting, I suppose?" he asked.

"You might drop in tomorrow," advised the painter. "I am not quite satisfied with the hands."

Next day Junius Morgan appeared as usual. The studio was empty. The man known as Bragard had disappeared. The elder Morgan sought him fruitlessly and then became convinced that he was one of those geniuses who prefer to go through the world unsung. But he loved the painting and told the story in detail to his son. His son, he was sure, could understand such a nature as that of the artist.

Junius Morgan was right. For Pierpont Morgan's nature in some respects was not many removes from that of Bragard the artist. Pierpont, also, was a solitary. Even in his beloved family circle he fell into long periods of silence. His son, the present J. P. Morgan, remembers, while he was at Harvard, inviting a classmate up to spend the week-end at Cragston. "Just hop aboard the *Corsair*, tell my father who you are and come along," Jack Morgan told his chum. The latter followed directions. He boarded the *Corsair* at the New York Yacht Club landing, approached a stout, ruddy gentleman who sat reading in an arm-chair, and introduced himself. Then he too read his newspaper in silence until Highland Falls was reached.

Jack Morgan was waiting at the Morgan private pier. His father drew him aside. "Son," he exclaimed, "I am glad you asked that young fellow up! He is one of the nicest chaps I have ever met."

Morgan was a warm man, emotional at core. Now, fawning and flattery began to take inevitable effect. He lived constantly in a false environment. Often this led to periods of deep despondency. He withdrew into himself. Only occasionally were the depths of his nature stirred. Then he cried aloud for help and reached for the sympathy of the small number to whom he gave himself without reserve. One of these rare and revealing moments occurred, at this period, behind the locked door of a steamship cabin.

A few weeks before, at a meeting of the vestry of St. George's Church, Morgan had, surprisingly, introduced a resolution to reduce the membership of the vestry from eight members and two wardens to six members and two wardens. "This motion had best be passed without debate," said Morgan. The move stunned other members of the vestry and the Rev. W. S. Rainsford, the rector. The latter had planned expansion of the vestry to take in at least one representative of a flood of new parishioners. Rainsford demanded Morgan's reasons. Reluctantly, Morgan explained: "The Rector's responsibility is spiritual. The vestry's part is fiduciary. I do not want the vestry democratized. I want it to remain a body of gentlemen whom I can ask to meet me in my study."

The issue was joined. The battle was fought out until midnight. Morgan lost. Only his own vote sustained his position. Morgan rose and, speaking slowly, said: "Rector, I will never sit in this vestry again." He walked out. Next day Rainsford had his written resignation. This the rector acknowledged, but did not submit to the vestry. At breakfast the following Monday Morgan asked: "Have you submitted my resignation?"

"I have not and I will not," responded Rainsford.

"Why not?"

"Because I will not now or ever put you in the position of going back on your pledge to the rector and the vestry of St. George's Church."

"What do you mean?"

"You know what I mean. When I first came to you I came because you gave me your hand and your promise to stand by me in the hard work that lay ahead. I told you I was a radical. I told you I would do all I could to democratize the church. I am only keeping my word. I certainly shall not now, nor at any time, do anything to help you break yours."

Morgan was silent. Three times he and Rainsford breakfasted together with never an allusion to Morgan's resignation. Then Morgan sailed for Europe. His annual departure, by now, was almost a function. For the first time, Rainsford went to the dock. Morgan saw him and beckoned. The two men entered Morgan's cabin. The financier shut and bolted the door. What happened will never be known. Rainsford will only say: "We never had another falling-out."

To the world, Morgan was a man apart: an icy, heartless person with a Tarquin eye. There is a cutting before me from *The Sun* of February 29, 1892, headed "King of Financiers." It reads: "Mr. Morgan is a man of unassuming person and demeanor. He is not a popular man because he seldom indulges in public, political or social diversions. . . . He is a man of few words and uses them very sparingly. His manner is brusque and not always pleasant, though he is a trifle more cordial to his friends than Mr. Gould, Russell Sage or any other of the multi-millionaires. . . . His movements are watched more closely than those of any other man in the financial world."

Morgan was, indeed, a man apart. By choice, he represented a social and a financial class. He and his associates did not desire to penetrate the life of the common man. They were like water-beetles, carrying their own atmosphere with them. They could inspect the railroads they controlled or hoped to control through occasional junketing expeditions but, in the words of Rainsford: "Such expeditions were scarcely an adequate introduction to the millions whose well-being depended largely on those roads. . . . What did they know of the mighty people across the Mississippi?"

For years Morgan had been seeking to obtain a firm grip upon the American railroad. He had been thwarted by past conditions and by the eel-like elusiveness of promoters determined to continue their slippery manipulations without dictation. Now the panic of 1893 was approaching. This industrial upheaval swept into Morgan's hands what railroads he desired to control, and upon his own terms.

CHAPTER EIGHT

RE-MORGANIZING THE RAILROADS

THE PANIC OF 1893 TOOK TERRIBLE TOLL. COMMERCIAL failures were three times as numerous as those of 1873, with aggregate liabilities more than fifty per cent greater. No fewer than fifteen thousand houses went under. There were 158 national bank failures, 172 suspensions of state banks, 177 of private banks, 47 savings banks, 13 loan and trust companies, and 16 mortgage companies. The calamity prostrated trade, shook credit, depressed agriculture, and led to industrial and social unrest that at times approached anarchy.

In the Middle West a motley band of agitators, discouraged workmen, tramps and curious human freaks of all description started a march on Washington. "Coxey's Army," as these demonstrators were dubbed, terrorized towns, seized railway trains, and finally were dispersed by United States troops. Labor riots broke out in several sections of the country. The Chicago Railway Union strike of June and July, 1894, was the most serious. For more than a week the railroads centering in Chicago were actually in the possession of the unions. Again United States regulars were called in.

No other arm of industry was more paralyzed by the panic than the railroads. "So great had been the strain of the panic on these largely over-capitalized enterprises," writes Alexander Dana Noyes, financial historian of the period, "that within two years nearly one-fourth of the total railway capitalization of the United States had passed through the bankruptcy courts. Some of these failures had been of such a character as completely to shatter confidence in the methods of American corporations. Examination in one of the largest of these insolvencies proved that the company's officers, within two years, had sunk upwards of four million dollars in reckless speculation in the shares of other railroads. Deceptive balance sheets were repeatedly shown up in the subsequent investigation, as with the Atchison, Topeka & Santa Fé, whose $100,000,000 shares were distributed throughout Europe, and which, when its books were overhauled, was shown to have officially overstated income seven million dollars within three years. Disclosures of this sort, a large number of which came to public knowledge during 1894, were certainly enough to start a movement of foreign liquidation. Nor was there any improvement during the year 1894 in the finances of the companies; all of them went from bad to worse."

Upon one man, chiefly, fell the burden of leading in the rehabilitation of the railroads. The gigantic job was Pierpont Morgan's because he was the only man big enough and bold enough to tackle it. He took up the task not so much from choice as in sheer self-defense. His house was the leading vendor of railway securities and it had to "stick by its goods." John Moody tells us: "No single financial problem in the previous history of the world equaled in difficulty and magnitude this reorganization of the railroads of the United States. These crazy financial structures had been patched together by any possible method of cohesion. They were leased, interleased, subleased; bought in whole or in part; and securities of every degree of inflation represented questionable claims upon them."

Morgan undertook the great task without fear, but with renewed determination to apply that primal principle which was now his creed—force and force alone. He would waste no more time in kid-glove methods with men who had jockeyed and manipulated and bled into bankruptcy the most valuable properties in the world.

With thousands of miles of railroad going under the hammer, Morgan now had the eel-like promoter at his mercy. Away with moral suasion, "gentlemen's agreements," "community-of-interest" pacts! Now he would jump into the saddle, employing his new weapon—the voting trust. Since his clients, scattered all over the globe, could not vote their stock themselves he would vote for them, either in person or through "voting trustees" of his selection. Inevitably, this concentration of authority would make Morgan the greatest individual power the world of finance had ever known.

Morgan's first opportunity to clinch his position came when he was requested to reorganize a loose, confused combination of some thirty railroad companies in the South, all jealous, all involved in bankruptcy, all warring. This cluster of roads had been operated by a group of New York and Richmond speculators under the name of the Richmond & West Point Terminal.

Even in that crazy era, the Richmond & West Point Terminal was a thing to bring shudders to the economist. The so-called "system" was in a hopeless snarl. There were some nine thousand miles of trackage, most of it in miserable condition. There were leases, subleases, junior leases, and many subsidiary lines grafted upon four holding companies. More than one hundred stock and bond issues were involved.

Even before the panic a committee of bondholders had struggled with the problem. Finally they came to Morgan. The latter told them bluntly that if he took up the work he would insist that a majority of each class of Terminal securities be deposited with him at the very beginning; that all litigation should be under his control; and that he alone should have power to name new receivers. The committee received the Morgan ultimatum in amazement, then broke into outraged protest.

Morgan, they asserted, was seeking to lead them into a blind pool, to pledge them in advance to obey his will. It was unthinkable. They could not yield and retain their self-respect. While the tongues of his callers clanged, the new Colossus of Finance sat in serene silence. Then he showed them the door.

Along came the panic. Semaphores of distress were again signaled from the Richmond Terminal. The committee returned to Morgan in penitent mood and accepted his conditions, unequivocally. Morgan turned them over to his partner, Coster. "They were like the man," remarked Coster, "who came home at daybreak. His wife asked him why he had bothered to return at all. He replied: 'I would not have come, but every other place in town was closed.' " The Morgan office, in those days, was indeed the "last place open" for many snarled railroad companies. Chauncey M. Depew, after the panic of '93, dubbed Morgan "the doctor of Wall Street."

It is impossible to give more than a hint of the complications involved in such an achievement as the Richmond Terminal reorganizaton. There were no fewer than twenty-six foreclosures, for instance. But Coster's fancy played infallibly over the figures; and in three months he and Morgan had created the Southern Railway Company. It was Morgan's task to persuade, frighten or coerce crowds of creditors to bow to his will, besides providing the vast sums of money necessary to buy up claims and to support the railroad while the work of reorganization was going forward. And at the last, in this as in every reorganization, Morgan was confronted with the necessity of convincing the public that a bankrupt road could be made to pay a profit—else the stocks and bonds would not sell.

The Southern Railway was capitalized at $375,000,-000. New five per cent bonds were issued and allotted in certain proportions to the roads making up the system. The adjustment was bitterly fought by some of the old feudists; but Morgan, as we have seen, had placed himself in a position to quell rebellion. In its first year of operation under the new régime, the Southern Railway showed a profit of $3,000,000.

One after another, broken transportation corporations came to the Morgan repair shop—Northern Pacific, Erie, Lehigh Valley, and many others. The rebuilding process was generally the same: new companies were formed, share-holders assessed pro rata to raise required cash; and bond-holders, as a solace for accepting lower interest rates, received new stock. Then Morgan placed in command men of his own choosing.

When he reorganized Northern Pacific—of checkered history—Morgan levied a fifteen per cent cash assessment upon $49,000,000 of common stock and ten per cent upon the $35,000,000 of preferred. He guaranteed the new company an operating fund of $5,000,-000. Through scaling down interest or exchanging old bonds for new stock, annual fixed charges were reduced $4,853,000.

Statistics show the influence of the Morgan touch. In 1893, railways with $1,781,000,000 stock and bonds were placed in receivers' hands. As late as 1896, railways of $1,150,377,000 par value were sold under foreclosure. "For each process," says Noyes, "these were totals exceeding by nearly a billion dollars those of any other year on record. But as against the 169 insolvent railroads of 1895, with 37,856 miles of track and $2,439,000,000 capital liabilities, existing receiverships in the middle of 1898 covered only 94 roads, with a mileage of 12,745 and a capital of $66,500,000."

Within five years of the panic, more than a billion and a half dollars were in the securities of the corporations which Morgan had reorganized. The so-called "Morgan roads" comprised 33,000 miles—a sixth of the country's total. They earned yearly over $300,000,000. "The entire receipts of the United States Government," writes John Moody, "were only twice as large as those of the Morgan roads. They were not his personal property, of course, but the property of his clients, of the capital of England and the world at large. Other financial houses and interests were involved. In two of the great roads—the Baltimore & Ohio and the Vanderbilt lines—other strong interests were concerned. But even in these two Morgan dominated. The lead in the reorganizations of the Baltimore & Ohio had been taken by other firms, but not one of them was then strong enough to oppose Morgan, whose representative was in the 'voting trust.' The Vanderbilt lines held the family name, but the family itself had dwindled. The real vital force that remained was Morgan."

For many years Morgan had been interested in consolidating the railroads of New England into one system. After defeating Archibald McLeod's scheme to carry the Philadelphia & Reading into Boston, Morgan had financed the plan under which the New York & New Haven absorbed the Old Colony system. The New Haven proceeded to lease or purchase every railway line in Connecticut, with the exception of the Central Vermont; every line in Rhode Island; and all those in Massachusetts south of Boston. It secured steamboat lines connecting New York and Boston and bought up the great Boston & Maine system. Finally, at the solicitation of Morgan, the New York Central partly yielded to the New Haven the Boston & Albany and the Rutland Railway system.

The New Haven had its beginnings in the country of his boyhood, and Morgan superintended its growth pridefully. He rarely missed a New Haven board meeting. At these meetings he seldom broke silence but, when he did, his expressions were very much to the point. His longest "speech" contained exactly seventy-eight words. Called upon for suggestions at a meeting of directors in the old Grand Central Depot, Morgan rose and said: "There is just one thing I would like to say. I have been told that you are very slow about paying your just bills. I hear that some of your creditors have been held up, or staved off, sometimes as long as six months. Now I think this railroad ought to pay its just bills as soon as they are due; and, if you haven't the ready money in hand to pay them, I will advance the money." Having had his say, Morgan resumed his seat.

That was Morgan, a man of abrupt decision demanding sure results. In everything he touched he took command. Organizing one of his syndicates he parceled out the subscriptions just as a general places his units for a battle. He expected each dollar and its master to fall into line with military precision.

Morgan dominated his clients, his partners, and his friends. The late Bishop Henry C. Potter, of the New York Episcopal Diocese, was fond of an anecdote illustrating Morgan's habit of treating his friends as though they were still in swaddling clothes. One Sunday the Bishop was a guest at Cragston.

The afternoon had passed pleasantly and the Bishop was loth to leave. But he had promised to conduct an evening service in the city and prepared to take his departure on a five o'clock train. Highland Falls was on the West Shore Railroad, and trains, especially on Sunday, were few and far between.

"Don't bother about that train," insisted Morgan. "Stay and have supper with me. There is another train, an express, that passes through here a few minutes before seven. I'll have it stopped for you."

The Bishop yielded. Morgan said no more about stopping the train; but at fifteen minutes before seven ordered a carriage and drove the Bishop down a winding road to the tiny wooden shack that served Highland Falls as a station. The shack was closed and locked.

"Please, sir," ventured the coachman, "I think I hear a train coming, sir."

All three listened intently. Far away, beyond West Point, a whistle faintly pierced the silence.

"Damn it!" ejaculated Morgan, "that's the express. We've got to flag it. Let's find a lantern. What, there isn't any around? All right, Tom, break in the door."

A huge rock in the hands of the coachman splintered the frail lock of the station. The track was vibrating with the thunder of an approaching train. "Hurry, hurry, find a lantern!" ordered Morgan, impatiently. Tom rushed out with the station-master's lantern. The train's headlight was in sight up around the bend. Morgan grabbed the lantern, lighted it quickly and waved frantically.

With a crash of breaks the train came to a halt. It was a freight!

The brakeman and the conductor came rushing up. Both were blue with anger.

"What the hell do you mean stopping us here?" demanded the conductor. "There's an express train right behind. There's liable to be a collision that'll knock out your blankety-blank eye-teeth. Who the hell are you, anyway, and what do you want?"

Morgan identified himself. This made not the slightest impression upon the doughty conductor. "You ought to know better!" he shouted and unleashed a new flood of profanity. All the while Morgan had been edging the Bishop down the tracks towards the caboose. "Now, now, Bishop," he said soothingly, "get in here and ride down to Weehawken. This is a fast freight and it has the right of way. You'll be on time for that service."

In a daze, the Bishop obeyed. His last impression, as the train gathered speed, was of Morgan and the conductor shaking their fists at each other. Bishop Potter was a whimsical man and it tickled him immensely that the trappings of majesty with which Morgan was clothed in the public eye did not at all impress at least one free and untrammeled railway employe.

Indeed, by now, there was an aura almost sacerdotal about Morgan.

Morgan was the apotheosis of an abstruse science— finance—which then, as now, attracted the imagination while it repelled comprehension. As the first outstanding Captain of Industry of the new school, he was becoming an object of curiosity and admiration.

To the popular imagination, there was something captivating in a man who could toss millions about as the juggler does his spangled spheres—something mysterious in the way Morgan took moribund properties and worked upon them his financial legerdemain. Hi! It is nothing. Presto! It has life and is moving. Change! It is a great property and the country (or someone) is so much the richer.

There were minds, singularly constituted, that comprehended Morgan's magic. But the common man stood aghast. He worked by the sweat of his brow and accomplished commonplace results. But here were great fortunes apparently materialized out of thin air by the wave of a wand. No wonder the ordinary citizen regarded with awe and admiration the magician who had wrought so momentous a change.

Morgan was operating in those days in a metropolis of susceptibility. New York was the ruddy, uncouth harlot of the continent's cities, drunk on Pittsburgh steel, Ohio oil, California gold—the capital of the Gilded Age, of Canfield's, of Anna Held, of Anthony Comstock, and Koster & Bial's; of Olga Nethersole's "Sapho" and Eleanora Duse's "Camille"; of Bradley Martin's monkey ball and Ward McAllister's Four Hundred.

It was the epoch of the dollar rampant. Materialism piled up vast, incongruous palaces on the soil of the Red Man; made the American tourist despised abroad; and erected a papier mâché effigy of pure American womanhood. Mamma and the girls found little old New York and the shopping bazaars of Fifth Avenue and Twenty-third Street stuffy. They were abroad, with their heedless millions, buying titles and culture. It was Edith Wharton's Age of Innocence and Thomas Beer's Mauve Decade.

[135]

Pierpont Morgan was part of the period's panorama. Unlike other great figures of the counting houses, Morgan never permitted his work to become his jailer. He left his office at three, rode uptown on the "L," and went about in an open barouche drawn by a single horse. Though almost defensive in his dignity, he cared nothing for the ordinary trappings of greatness.

Pleasant afternoons he drove in the Park or on Fifth Avenue. He was seen often in art auction rooms or at the Metropolitan Museum. Occasionally he dropped in upon a select and limited circle to chat, smoke a cigar, or view objects of art. The ladies found that he could be as friendly and adaptable in social intercourse as he was frigid and forbidding in his office. He was an indifferent attendant at opera and theatre, preferring to pass most evenings alone in his study before a grate fire. Sometimes he loitered in smart shops buying trinkets for his women folk. He was always presenting unusual or quaint gifts to those he liked.

Though by nature a "man's man," Morgan reveled, at times, in the companionship of women. He was most drawn to women who possessed both beauty and brains. One of his feminine friends was Lillian Russell. Morgan and the beautiful actress, at the heyday of her fame, enjoyed many cosy tête-à-têtes during which he would view the latest additions to her distinctive collection of Chinese porcelains.

Another close woman friend was Maxine Elliott. The rare brunette beauty of this young actress had taken New York by storm. Though born in Maine, her languorous charms were tropical. People followed her on the street and in stores. Her skin was as clearly pale as porcelain. In every feature and glance, in every movement of a tall, perfect, lissome figure, Maxine Elliott was pure Grecian. She reminded one of Gautier's description, in "Arria Marcella," of the fair Pompeiian: "Dark and pale. In her pallid face beamed soft, melancholy eyes heavy with an indefinable expression of voluptuous sadness and passionate ennui; her mouth, with its disdainful curves, protested, by the living warmth of its burning crimson, against the tranquil pallor of her cheeks, and the curves of her neck presented those pure and beautiful outlines now to be found only in statues."

Morgan was interested in statues. But he was more interested in Maxine Elliott. In the latter '90's, she repeated in London her New York triumphs, both artistic and social. Her train of admirers was numerous. She was often seen with Morgan and more than once met the financier's friend the Prince of Wales, afterward Edward VII. Sometimes she graced the small, intimate parties which the Prince (and Morgan) most enjoyed. Later, she became the wife of the inimitable (and oftmarried) American comedian, Nat Goodwin.

Maxine Elliott had a peculiar influence over Morgan. She never hesitated to break lances with him. "Why, you men in Wall Street are like a lot of cannibals," she told him once. "You devour anything that comes along—if it is edible!" Time and again, Morgan permitted her to "tame" him—as he permitted all those whom he really loved.

Morgan despised the very shadow of a newspaper

man. Yet, on one occasion, returning to America by chance on the same ship with Maxine Elliott, Morgan suffered her to lead him before an assembled press delegation. And he actually uttered a few pleasant words!

Not alone industry, but the United States Government itself suffered disastrously from the panic of 1893. A nest of tangled and unmanageable circumstances brought on a series of crises in 1894 and the early part of 1895. Drained of its gold reserves the Government was several times on the verge of bankruptcy. Only bold and secret action by Treasury officials and New York bankers, led by Morgan, averted disaster.

Since the resumption of specie payment in 1879, the Government had maintained a minimum gold reserve fund of $100,000,000 to redeem outstanding notes. The reserve had proved ample during the prosperous and money-careless '80's. The panic of 1893, however, brought a startling and disheartening change. European security holders dumped one hundred million dollars' worth of stocks and bonds upon our markets. Foreign exchange rose rapidly. It was necessary to export gold by the tens of millions. The Treasury at once felt the effect.

Twice in 1894 the Treasury was forced to issue emergency bonds. Investors, in the troubled state of affairs, showed no enthusiasm. John G. Carlisle, Secretary of the Treasury, came to New York and begged the banks for aid. "It might have been imagined, from the extraordinary nature of the episode," historian Noyes informs us, "that it was Turkey or China which was

standing hat in hand in the money market. The out-
come of this humiliating incident was, however, that
the fifty millions in bonds were taken, eighty per cent of
them going to the New York banks at the upset price.
If the 'syndicate bid' from the New York banks were
to be eliminated from the reckoning, the actual bids received for the bond issue of February 1, 1894, would
cover less than ten millions out of the fifty millions offered."

Almost half the payments for these bonds were made
by withdrawals in gold from the Treasury, in exchange
for legal tender notes. Under the Resumption Act of
1878, the Secretary of the Treasury was directed to pay
out and re-issue these notes. The result, in hard times,
was a drain upon the Treasury—and there seemed no
way of stopping it. "We have," asserted President Cleveland in his annual message of December 3, 1894, "an
endless chain in operation, constantly depleting the
Treasury gold, and never near a final rest."

There was another element in the situation even more
disheartening. Technically, the legal tender notes were
payable in "coin"—that is, either gold or silver. Silver
had depreciated. Money sharps were exchanging it for
gold and exporting the more valuable metal. "Free coinage" agitation was rampant in Congress.

In the hard times then upon it, the silver-producing
West believed that Wall Street was plotting its ruin.
In the West everyone cursed the Gold Bugs, and de-
voured woodcut cartoons showing Wall Street, the busy
milkman, pinching the last drop from the poor farmer-
cow. Folks in the West and South formed their eco-

nomic theories from such widely read books as "Coin's
School of Finance," by Harvey.

In schoolmaster fashion, this book taught the iniquity
of the gold dollar. The nation's currency policy, in
sooth, had degenerated into a clash of camp-meeting
dogmas. In New York's exclusive Union League Club,
Gold Bugs cut Bimetalists. In Washington, Silverites
identified their cause with the Vicarious Atonement.
Of a pending gold resolution in Congress, a young member from Nebraska named Bryan (we quote *The New
York Herald*) "amused the House by offering himself
as a martyr to the cause of free coinage and cheap dollars, declaring that he would willingly give up his life
to secure the defeat of the pending resolution."

In the white marble building at Broad and Wall
Streets, James Stillman one day found Morgan with his
head in his hands. For three years Stillman had been
president of the National City Bank. He was a subtle,
myopic little man—a financial genius with a manner so
cold and repellent that frequently stenographers, from
very fright, were unable to take his dictation. On this
occasion Stillman found Morgan in a state of emotion.

"The Treasury had asked him for fifty millions,"
narrated Stillman, many years later. "Then they came
to me and I went around to see what I could do. Morgan
was upset and overcharged. He nearly wept, crying:
'They expect the impossible.' So I calmed him down and
told him to give me an hour; and by that time I cabled
for ten millions from Europe for the Standard Oil and
ten more from other resources and came back. I told
him, 'I have twenty millions.' I told him the sources.

He became perfectly bombastic and triumphant, as the Savior of his Country. He took all the credit. But then, you see, Morgan was a poet. Morgan was a poet!"

Morgan, though, as Stillman was to discover later, and frequently, was more than "a poet."

The Government's emergency bonds were to be paid for specifically in gold. They were taken, grudgingly, by Morgan, Stillman, and other bankers. But they were mere makeshifts and did not save the Treasury.

At the close of 1894 it seemed impossible to preserve the gold standard and the public credit. In panic, foreign and domestic capital rushed to escape before the anticipated crash. In January, 1895, the enormous sum of $45,000,000 was withdrawn from the Treasury; and gold to the amount of $25,900,000 went abroad. On the last day of January, the gold reserve had fallen to $41,340,181. Withdrawals were continuing at the rate of almost $2,000,000 daily.

It seemed that nothing could prevent suspension of gold payments. Business circles were gripped with excitement. The markets fell. Merchants and bankers arranged their affairs as though anticipating invasion by a foreign army. Nothing, they believed, could avert the surrender of the Treasury.

But something did.

Pierpont Morgan, boldest man the world of cash had ever known, came forward with a proposal involving a unique experiment in finance.

CHAPTER NINE

"SAVING THE COUNTRY"—FIRST, 1895

PIERPONT MORGAN SAT IN A ROOM IN THE ARLINGTON Hotel, Washington, playing solitaire. It was four o'clock on the morning of Friday, February 8, 1895. Snow slashed against the windows. The storm was not more foreboding than the situation which confronted the country. There was but one day's supply of gold left in the United States Treasury.

The Government and the financial world were facing a catastrophe such as had never before been known.

Uninvited, indeed risking open rebuff, Morgan had come to the Capital to consult President Cleveland. The previous day a bill authorizing issuance of emergency gold bonds had been defeated in the House by Silverites. To Morgan this had but one meaning: the Government must depend upon private sources to save the Treasury. President Cleveland was bitterly opposed to such an expedient. The stalwart old Democrat in the White House clung stubbornly to his belief that relief should and must come through the representatives of the people.

Though much alike in mental mold, Cleveland and Morgan divided sharply in social philosophy. The President, son of an indigent traveling parson, held a naïve belief in popular government. Morgan believed that democracies were devices where the most ruled the best. Both were men accustomed to command. In a situation such as this their wills were bound to clash.

At the station, the night before, Secretary of War Daniel Lamont had delivered a blunt message from the White House. "The President has made up his mind to rely upon Congress. He will not see you," he told Morgan. Morgan's response was equally blunt. "I am going to the Arlington Hotel," he said. "I shall wait there until the President is ready to see me."

To Morgan this was no time to stand upon ceremony. Cleveland, he realized, was no financier. Morgan nevertheless respected him for his sturdy championship of the gold standard at a time when his political future was at stake. The silver issue had split both parties wide open. Morgan had decided that relief of the Treasury could be brought about only by his firm and one other —August Belmont & Co., American representatives of the powerful foreign house of Rothschild.

He had in his pocket a contract for restoring and maintaining the Treasury gold reserve. Whether the President and the Secretary of the Treasury could legally consummate the covenant without the consent of Congress was the problem which now concerned him as he sat and smoked and riffled the cards. His presence in Washington capped a fortnight of exciting and dramatic events.

For two weeks Morgan and August Belmont had been engaged in guarded parleys with various Treasury officials, negotiations conducted in the greatest secrecy. The Government did not dare permit the press and

public to learn in actual measure how close the Treasury
was to repudiation. On January 24 Belmont and John
G. Carlisle, Secretary of the Treasury, had been closeted
in conference. Carlisle asked Belmont to ascertain
quietly whether it would be possible for the Government to float an emergency loan in Europe. On January
28 the President sent a special message to Congress.
Without revealing in detail the terrible straits of the
Treasury, Mr. Cleveland thus pictured conditions:

"The real trouble which confronts us is the lack of confidence, widespread and constantly increasing, in the continuing ability of the Government to pay its obligations in
gold.

"The only way left open to the Government for procuring
gold is by the issue and sale of its bonds. The only bonds
that can be so issued were authorized nearly twenty-five years
ago. . . . They are made payable in coin instead of specifically in gold. . . . It is by no means certain that bonds of
this description can much longer be disposed of at a price
creditable to the financial character of our Government.

"The most dangerous and irritating feature of the situation
. . . is found in the means by which the Treasury is despoiled
of the gold thus obtained without cancelling a single Government obligation, and solely for the benefit of those who find
profit in shipping it abroad or whose fears induce them to
hoard it at home. . . . The same notes may do duty many
times in drawing gold from the Treasury; nor can the process
be arrested as long as private parties . . . see an advantage in
repeating the operation.

"Whatever ideas may be insisted upon as to silver or bimet-
alism, a proper solution of the question now pressing upon
us only requires a recognition of gold as well as silver, and a

concession of its importance, rightfully or wrongfully acquired, as a basis of national credit, a necessity in the honorable discharge of our obligations payable in gold, and a badge of solvency."

On January 29, Secretary Carlisle's chief assistant, William E. Curtis, saw Belmont at the latter's home in New York. Curtis was the Treasury liaison man with the New York bankers. Many times, in that trying period, he had gone to New York on confidential missions. On this occasion Belmont silently handed Curtis a sheaf of private cables. They were gloomy. The Rothschilds would not touch American Government bonds—unless payable in gold and gold alone. "Why don't you see Morgan?" asked Belmont. "Perhaps he can suggest something."

Morgan had been strangely inert. With the Treasury drifting daily nearer the rocks, he had made no move. It was unlike him. His attitude puzzled the panicky and timid men of his world who had grown to look to him, in every emergency, for decisive action.

On this morning—January 30—Morgan received two communications. One was a request from Curtis for a conference at the Sub-Treasury. Another was a cable from his London house. The latter, signed by Walter Burns, informed him that the London house of Rothschild had approached J. S. Morgan & Co. and suggested joint action to avert a calamity. The growing gravity of the situation apparently had caused the Rothschilds to modify their earlier insistence upon "gold only" bonds.

In a few minutes the immaculately groomed Belmont walked into Morgan's office. He also had received a cable from London. To his astonishment he found that Morgan had already drawn up a rough outline for a syndicate proposal. The two worked over the plan for a little while, incorporated certain changes into a memorandum and, arm in arm, crossed the street to see Curtis. They told him they had decided to come to the aid of the government—at a price.

"I don't know whether we can get hold of enough gold, either here or abroad," said Morgan. "But we are willing to try. In our opinion, no popular loan is possible. Here is a memorandum of our terms. You can take it to Washington and let us know what the President and Mr. Carlisle think of it."

The Morgan memo measured with little mercy the Treasury emergency. Morgan and Belmont offered to take a thirty-year four per cent bond at a price equivalent to 104½. Existing U. S. four per cents were bringing 111 on the market. No such concession had been asked of the Government since the resumption of specie payment.

The Treasury, however, was in no position to bargain. On Saturday Morgan and Belmont received word from Washington that the President and Carlisle favored their proposal. Saturday morning rumors circulated in Wall Street that Morgan had agreed to come to the relief of the Treasury. On the mere strength of these reports, some $4,000,000 in gold, boxed for export shipment, was returned to the Sub-Treasury. It was a surprising illustration of the potency of one man's name.

As the day advanced, the newspapers got wind of the negotiations. Though they could only guess at the extraordinary nature of the situation, the papers were healthily suspicious. One or two editorials appeared on Sunday in which such phrases as "dark-lantern financiering" were freely used. The New York *World,* under the quick spur of its almost prophetic proprietor, Joseph Pulitzer, at once launched a campaign that was to last for months—and prove insufferably irritating to Morgan. *The World* warned Cleveland and Carlisle that they were delivering themselves to the money interests and permitting private individuals to pouch large profits at the expense of the nation. In bold, black type the President was advised to stand out for a three per cent loan—"If the banks won't take it, the people will."

On Monday, when he thought the matter practically settled, Morgan received a letter from Secretary Carlisle. The Secretary wrote that the administration had decided to depend upon a popular loan. Morgan spluttered with anger. The newfangled telephone was one of the financier's pet dislikes. When he had to use it, he swore, tore his hair and worried his vest as a terrier does a mouse. But, on this occasion, he got through a call to Carlisle and urged the latter to do nothing until he and Belmont got to Washington. Carlisle agreed to delay for a day before inviting subscriptions to a popular loan. August Belmont started for Washington at once. Morgan followed.

With Morgan went Robert Bacon and Francis Lynde Stetson. Bacon was a junior partner in the new firm of

J. P. Morgan & Co., formed January 1, 1895. Lovable, handsome as a god, Bob Bacon, '80, had been "Harvard's Model Man" by selection of his classmates. Morgan took him from a brokerage house in Boston and was now breaking him in. Bacon adored "Senior" and survived Morgan's remorseless pace for several years with but one breakdown. Then, upon orders of his physician, he went to England and restored his shattered nerves by riding to hounds fifty miles a day, five days a week.

Anthony J. Drexel had died in Karlsbad in June, 1893. Though changing the firm name in New York, Morgan continued alliance with Drexel's successors in Philadelphia.

Stetson was a former law partner of President Cleveland. The wags of the Street called him Morgan's "Attorney General."

In Washington, Morgan found Congress aflame. Party lines had disappeared. Gold men and Silver men were battling like bandits. Gold was denounced as a badge of oppression. "The President has declared war on silver," shouted Senator George T. Vest. "He would make us accessories to this effort to fix the gold standard upon us. This supposed emergency can be met by Treasury payments in silver." The Senator raised a vibrating hand to heaven. "So far as I am concerned, I will never vote to issue bonds to secure gold to place us on a single gold standard!"

Morgan paid no more attention to these forensic outbursts than to attacks in the press. He regarded politicians and editors as a semi-literate crew, anyway.

President Cleveland received Morgan and Belmont on Tuesday morning, February 5. Morgan and Cleveland were old acquaintances, having met frequently, during the period between his first and second terms, when Cleveland practised law in New York. Both men were wedded to tobacco. It had been Morgan's habit, when in Washington, to drop into the White House for a chat and a smoke.

This morning, though, there was tension. For once Morgan's personal force failed to magnetize. "Thank you for calling, Mr. Morgan," said Cleveland, shaking his shaggy head, "but I have decided to rely upon Congress. The Government does not desire a private loan." The meeting was soon over.

For two more vital days Congress beat the tomtoms but did nothing to put a dollar in the Treasury. On Thursday afternoon the Springer bill was buried in the House by a vote of 167 to 120. This bill authorized bonds specifically payable in gold. Even the New York _World_ then abandoned hope for a popular loan—"The only thing left for the Administration to do is to make a loan on the best terms obtainable. That these terms will be harsh and discrediting is due as much to the wilfulness and imbecility of Congress as to the incapacity of the Administration—that party leadership which is a part of its obligation to the voters who placed it in power."

To expert observers the situation now seemed hopeless. Only a miracle, it appeared, could prevent suspension of the Treasury within twenty-four hours.

In New York Morgan received word at three o'clock

of the failure of the Springer bill. He jammed on his hat and picked up a satchel. "Come on, Bacon," he said, "we'll take the Congressional." Fiercely staring straight before him, he brushed aside a knot of waiting newspaper men, jumped into a cab and drove to the Cortlandt Street ferry. On the way to Washington, Bacon recalled, he uttered scarcely a word. News of his departure had been telegraphed ahead. He shook his head grimly when asked for a statement; received Secretary Lamont's message from the President without change of expression; and went to the Arlington.

Throughout the evening there was a constant stream of visitors. Curtis and other Treasury officials came in, also many congressional leaders. All seemed in a panic. They asked Morgan what he purposed to do. He was silent. The last of the callers left at midnight. Bacon went to bed. A light burned in Morgan's room until almost daylight.

While he played solitaire, he thought out the problem. He had no doubt that Cleveland and Carlisle would capitulate on the morrow. But, even if they accepted the Morgan-Belmont proposal, how could they overcome the legal difficulties?

As he sat alone in the small hours of the morning, his mind floating in the backwaters of introspection, a solution came to him.

He and Bacon breakfasted at nine. "Bacon," said Morgan, slowly, "there is a law on the books, unless it has been repealed, which gives the Secretary of the Treasury power to purchase gold whenever the Government needs it, at the best price he can make, and to pay for it in any authorized obligations of the United States. I think the section is number four thousand and something of the Revised Statutes. It was passed, I think, in 1862 during a Civil War emergency. I remember Mr. Lincoln's sending Secretary Chase to New York where he worked out the legislation with some of the bankers. I know the Government got gold because my house furnished some of it."

Before the meal was over the telephone rang. It was a message from the White House. The President would see Mr. Morgan.

Not even pausing to light a cigar, Morgan, with Bacon, started across Lafayette Square for the White House. It was still snowing and a nasty wind was blowing.

In the President's study were gathered Secretary Carlisle, Attorney General Olney, and other officials of the administration. Mr. Cleveland was curt in his greeting. He seemed worried. He was not smoking, so Morgan's cigar remained unlighted. Morgan and Bacon sat in an inconspicuous angle of the room. They looked about for Belmont. He had been delayed by the storm and did not appear.

Business had begun in New York. The run on the Treasury continued. From time to time bulletins were brought into the room. All were disquieting. Several times the President reiterated his determination to resist a private bond issue. Hours passed. Finally a yellow slip was handed to Mr. Carlisle. "Mr. President," announced the Treasury chieftain, "only nine million dollars in gold is left in the New York Sub-Treasury."

Now Morgan, for the first time, broke silence. "Mr. President," he said, "the Secretary of the Treasury knows of one check outstanding for $12,000,000. If this is presented today it is all over."

Carlisle nodded confirmation. Then, and then only, did the harassed head of the United States Government turn to Morgan. "Have you anything to suggest, Mr. Morgan?"

During the long conference no one had marked the slightest change in Morgan's demeanor. The Sphinx of his face had been impossible to read. Now, though, he talked rapidly and decisively. He told the President of "Section number four thousand and something" of the Revised Statutes; and recalled the circumstances under which it had been passed.

"That may help us," remarked Cleveland quietly. "Let's have a look at the law." The book of Revised Statutes was sent for. Attorney General Olney quickly identified the section Morgan had in mind. It was number 3700. Olney read the Act aloud. Passed March 17, 1862, it provided:

"The Secretary of the Treasury may purchase coin with any of the bonds or notes of the United States authorized by law, at such rates and upon such terms as he may deem most advantageous to the public interest."

The President took the book and read the Act to himself, intently, amid silence that had become painful. Then Cleveland closed the thick volume and a smile crossed his countenance. "Gentlemen," he said, "I think our problem is solved. This Act seems to empower us to negotiate a bond sale at our own discretion. Congress, though, of course, must and shall be informed of our intentions."

The Government had surrendered to that inevitable power known as Morgan.

At once the President and his advisers took up the Morgan-Belmont syndicate proposal. The terms as originally set forth by Morgan were agreed upon. But sudden doubt assailed Mr. Cleveland. "How about this drain of gold abroad?" he asked. "Suppose the Government does purchase gold from the bankers and it is immediately withdrawn from the Treasury and sent abroad. Mr. Morgan, can you guarantee that such a thing will not happen?"

This was a consideration that had occurred to no one in the room—except, possibly, Morgan. Could any syndicate prove powerful enough to prevent foreign exchange dealers from taking profits by shipping gold abroad? Morgan did not hesitate. "Mr. President," he said, "I will so guarantee."

"All right," said the President. "It is now two o'clock, and you gentlemen had better go out and get some lunch, while I formulate the terms of the plan for transmission in a message to Congress so as to send it up to the Capitol without delay."

As the company rose, someone noticed that brown powder was strewed over Morgan's coat and trousers. It was the remains of the financier's after-breakfast cigar which he had ground to pieces during the long conference. Amid general laughter, Morgan shook the powder from his clothing. The President reached into his desk, drew out a box of cigars, and said with a smile: "It is time we all had a smoke. Mr. Morgan, will you remain while I dictate a message to Congress?"

Under its contract with the Morgan-Belmont syndicate, the Government was to receive, over a six months' period, gold worth $65,116,244, and to issue in payment $62,315,400 in bonds. The contract provided: "At least one-half of all coin deliverable hereunder shall be obtained in and shipped from Europe," and "the parties of the second part and their associates hereunder . . . as far as lies in their power, will exert all financial influence and will make all legitimate efforts to protect the Treasury of the United States against the withdrawal of gold pending the complete performance of this contract."

These provisions had never before appeared in any bond agreement between the Government and private purchasers.

The contract provided, also, that the Government was to be permitted within ten days to substitute at par a straight three per cent bond, provided payment should be expressly stipulated in gold. On its face this was a generous offer. It would have saved the Government $16,000,000 in interest charges. But there was not the slightest possibility of such provision's passing.

Indeed, with the receipt of the President's message, wilder clamor broke out in Congress. The administration party was almost stunned. The outcries of the Silverites were echoed in the opposition press. Many of Cleveland's most ardent supporters were bewildered. The

President's purpose was not comprehensible to the general public. He was accused of having sold himself to Wall Street.

In the storm of denunciation, two men remained quite unmoved: Cleveland and Morgan. Morgan returned to New York to perfect his syndicate and stop the outflow of gold. Psychologically, the Cleveland-Morgan agreement proved instantly effective. That very Friday night, $18,000,000 in gold was taken from the strong boxes of ships in New York harbor and re-deposited in the Sub-Treasury.

Morgan's pledge to the Government, despite the possibility of handsome profits, encompassed extraordinary difficulties. He planned to dam a natural economic movement. He would stop the flow of gold by permitting gold shippers to participate in the bond issue. It was a new idea.

"The syndicate proposed," says Noyes, "to sell in New York whatever drafts on London should be needed by the banking and mercantile community, and to meet the drafts in London through the use of their own credit on the London money market. The magnitude of this undertaking will readily be perceived. . . . Both they and the Government, however, took the chance. With the double purpose of insuring themselves against competitive sales of exchange and of insuring the Treasury against export-gold withdrawals by competing bankers, the syndicate next took the unprecedented step of binding together in the undertaking every banking house and every bank in New York City with important European connections. All of these firms and institutions were admitted to the syndicate, part of the new four per cent loan being distributed among them at profitable rates. In return for this allotment, they bound themselves, as the Belmont-Morgan syndicate had already bound itself, to draw no gold from the Treasury pending the execution of the contract."

The remarkable experiment went smoothly forward. On July 8, 1895, the Treasury gold reserve reached $107,571,230. The success of the operation was aided by an unexpected and favorable turn in trade conditions. Stimulated by the Rhodeses, Barnatos and other picturesque figures of the new South African gold and diamond domain, an old-fashioned fever of speculation broke out in London. Nothing in the penny shockers could rival the career of Barnett Isaacs Barnato, son of poor Jewish parents, peddler, and billiard marker, who found fortune in the Kimberley diamond mines and the gold mines of Johannesburg. As a partner of Cecil Rhodes and a member of the Cape Legislative Assembly, Barnato returned to London in 1895. He became the centre of the speculation in South African mining stocks known as the "Kaffir Circus," and he was popularly known as the "Kaffir King." Two years later, his reason undone by reverses, he was to commit suicide by jumping into the sea near Funchal.

But he and Rhodes now stirred into life a spirit of speculation in England. And Morgan reaped the reward. The British again began to buy securities and they took Americans with the rest. The Morgan-Belmont bonds appreciated rapidly, touching 124 in the early summer of 1895. There were some anxious moments when the tempting price induced speculative sale of the bonds; but by autumn, when the syndicate operation was concluded, the Treasury reserve was well over $100,-000,000.

All this time violent criticism of President Cleveland and of Morgan continued. Morgan was accused of having made millions out of the Government. He became a symbol of the hated Captain of Industry—a target alike of Populists, Silverites, and other elements already forming to carry their discontent to the polls in 1896 under the banner of the fiery and humorless young Congressman, William J. Bryan of Nebraska.

Morgan regarded personal attacks as so much twitter-twatter. "Almost any other man," comments Carl Hovey, "would have spoken in his own defense . . . The subject simply irritated him. He never thought of meeting the public half-way with an explanation."

Even when testifying before a congressional committee of investigation, Morgan treated his critics with cavalier contempt. However, in a colloquy with Senator Vest and Senator Platt of Connecticut, he did deign to make what may be termed a defense of the bond syndicate.

Senator Platt: Why did you not want to have an issue of bonds after you had commenced your negotiations? You asked the President not to issue a bond call. What was your reason for doing that?

Morgan: Because I knew that if the call was made, the public would understand that the foreign negotiations had been abandoned.

Platt: When it was understood that you were negotiating, shipments ceased?

Morgan: Absolutely; and they did not commence until a month afterward.

Platt: And so your real purpose, as I understand you, in this transaction was not the idea that you could take this bond issue and make money out of it, but that you could prevent a panic and distress in the country?

Morgan: I will answer that question, though I do not think it necessary in view of all that I have done. I will say that I had no object except to save the disaster that would result in case that foreign gold was not obtained.

Senator Vest: If that was your sole object, why did you specify in your telegraphic communication to Mr. Carlisle that your house, or you and Mr. Belmont, were to have exclusive control of the matter?

Morgan: Because it was absolutely impossible for more than one party to negotiate—to make the same negotiation for the same lot of gold. It would only have made competition.

Vest: If the gold was abroad I take it for granted that anybody could get hold of it who had the means to do so. If you were actuated by the desire to prevent a panic, why were you not willing that other people should do it, if they wanted to?

Morgan: THEY COULD NOT DO IT.

Just a plain, bald statement of fact, as Morgan saw the situation.

A year or two later, when the storm had blown over, a friend one day twitted Morgan about his profits in the gold deal. "Take a look at that dog," directed the financier, pointing to a fox terrier playing on the lawn. The dog seemed smart. The friend paid it a casual compliment. "Look closer," insisted Morgan, calling the dog to him. The other bent over and read this inscription upon a bronze tag attached to the dog's neck:

"EMERGENCY. Presented by August Belmont to J. P. Morgan as a souvenir of February, 1895."

Many years after this episode, in one of his rare communicative moments, Morgan told the complete story of his negotiations with President Cleveland. The occasion was a small dinner party at his home. A chance question brought up the subject. The ladies of the party were leaving for the opera. Their wraps had been brought when Morgan began to talk. He held his listeners spellbound. One by one the ladies resumed their seats. That evening the Morgan box at the opera was unoccupied.

The syndicate manoeuvres were absorbing. But they were merely an interlude in the financial flowering of Pierpont Morgan. He was still chiefly concerned in his huge railroad reorganizations. These had been confined principally to New England, the South, and the region east of the Mississippi. Now, new powers were appearing both in the Northwest and in the Southwest.

If Morgan was to become caliph of a continent's capital, he must concern himself with these—either as ally or as enemy.

CHAPTER TEN

HILL AND HARRIMAN

AMERICAN RAILROADING TEEMS WITH CLASSIC TALES of individual achievement. No stories, though, are more romantic, more enthralling, more extraordinary than those of James Jerome Hill and Edward Henry Harriman. In a few short years these men re-arranged the railroad map of the country; divided organized capital into two great hostile groups; and rocked the financial world. They vitally affected the fortunes of Pierpont Morgan.

Let's have a look at them:

In 1876 Jim Hill, a waggish, whimsical sort of fellow, sat outside his coal and wood yard on the levee at St. Paul, Minnesota, and boosted the Northwest to everyone who would listen. A fatherless boy of eighteen, Hill had drifted into St. Paul twenty years before from Ontario. The Scotch-Irish lad had grown up with the town. He was a jack-of-all-trades and had a great gift of gab. He was a short, stocky man with one eye. He wore his hair long, plainsman fashion, and grumbled when his wife forced him to have a few inches sheared off now and then.

Folks liked Hill though they rather smiled at his ambitious "schemes." Just now he was glowing over the possibilities of what could be done by "live fellows" with the St. Paul & Pacific Railroad. This road, built mostly by Dutch capital, had wobbled into receivership during the panic of 1873. Its main stem ran from St. Paul on the Mississippi, two hundred miles west to Breckenridge on the Red River. Hill was agent for the old side-wheel boats that brought freight up the Mississippi to St. Paul. He also represented Norman W. Kittson who operated a couple of tiny stern-wheelers on the Red River from Breckenridge to Winnipeg— then Fort Garry.

Kittson's chief customer was the Hudson's Bay Company. Donald A. Smith—later Lord Strathcona—was company commissioner at Winnipeg. Smith, a soft-spoken, red-bearded Scotchman of fifty-six, had led a life packed with melodrama. He had spent thirteen years in Labrador alone among the Indians. Louis Riel had captured and sentenced him to death during the first Half-Breed Rebellion of 1869-70. In a contest of wills, Smith outgamed Riel and saved his life.

Both Kittson and Smith were disgusted with the service they were getting from the receiver-operated St. Paul & Pacific. For three years Jim Hill had been dinning into their ears the advantages of buying and building up the road. But the deal would require a sum that none of them possessed. The Dutch bondholders had put $20,000,000 of their good money into building the road and had returned very decided negatives when asked by the receiver to take further risks.

Nevertheless, Hill, Kittson, and Smith believed in the project. Every time Smith went east he talked the matter over with George Stephen—later Lord Mountstephen. Stephen was president of the Bank of Montreal, with which the Hudson's Bay Company banked. Stephen and his vice-president, Richard B. Angus, both Scotchmen, promised to run out some time and look over the property. Now chance intervened.

In 1875 a lawsuit carried Stephen and Angus to Chicago. The litigation dragged and they had a few days to kill. They flipped a coin to decide whether to visit St. Paul or St. Louis. St. Paul won. On a certain Sunday morning Jim Hill, wildly excited, escorted the big bankers from Montreal over the St. Paul & Pacific to Breckenridge. Ordinarily the line shut down on Sunday, but that didn't stop Hill. He provided a special train—a puffy engine and a dingy passenger coach.

When enthusiastic, Hill used to wave his little finger in a curious, rotary motion all his own. One can imagine him on this trip, waving that little finger and attempting to impress the silent, reserved bankers with the possibilities of the streak of rust that was the St. Paul & Pacific.

The country through which Hill's "special" passed was dismal. For two successive years the prairies had been ravaged by a plague of grasshoppers. The farmers fought the pests by dragging sheets of iron smeared with coal tar about their fields, but to no avail. Hundreds of farmers had given up in despair and abandoned their properties. But the great stretches of country were soothing to eastern eyes; and before Stephen and Angus left for Chicago Hill had interested them in the grandest of his schemes.

The next year Stephen went to Amsterdam and ob-

tained an eight months' option on the Dutch bonds.
The Dutch were so eager to rid themselves of a bad
bargain that they exacted for the option just one gilder
—forty cents—and offered to sell their holdings at
thirty cents on the dollar without regard to interest
defaults.

Stephen sailed for New York and interested John S.
Kennedy, a cautious, old-school private banker who
wore his whiskers sidewise. Kennedy, also a Scotchman,
was trustee for the principal St. Paul & Pacific mort-
gage holders. Kennedy knew Stephen as a careful, able
business man, and came into the combination at once.
Hill was set at work to secure a franchise from the
Minnesota Legislature. He succeeded after a hot fight.
In the spring of 1877, six men—Hill, Stephen, Smith,
Angus, Kittson, and Kennedy—took over the St. Paul
& Pacific.

Now enters that element of luck to be noted in so
many romances of industry: the grasshoppers left the
country! Stranger still, no one ever knew where they
went. That season, as though conscience-stricken over
the plague, Nature balanced the books by pouring forth
the greatest wheat crop the region had ever known.
An avalanche of business flooded the road—grain going
out by tens of thousands of bushels, farmers and immigrants pouring in. Hill, under tentative appointment as
general manager of the road, worked twenty hours a day.
He partly satisfied a desperate need for new cars by
buying in New York a lot of discarded old coaches
with board seats and box stoves.

The stream of prosperity swelled. During later

revolts of the granger states against the railroads, folks used to say: "The grasshoppers went out and Jim Hill's Scotchmen came in. We got rid of one plague only to catch another."

This was hardly fair, though it was true that the departure of the grasshoppers made Hill and his associates multi-millionaires almost over night. The combination had put only $283,000 in actual cash into the purchase. Now, their dizzy fortune still on the upcurve, they had no trouble finding money for expansion and improvement. Stephen, in Montreal, and Kennedy, in New York, managed the finances. Hill ran the road. In 1879 they paid for everything and issued $16,000,-000 in new bonds. Also, the lucky six divided $15,000,-000 in stock—a fifth each going to Stephen, Smith, Kennedy, and Hill, a tenth each to Angus and Kittson. At the same time they incorporated the St. Paul, Minneapolis & Manitoba Railroad; and began to push out into new territory.

A curious metamorphosis had come over Jim Hill.

The man still preserved a certain engaging and faunal simplicity. He talked over his plans as of yore with the bootblack, the barber and the banker. His appearance and manner had not changed. But he had developed a surprising genius for practical railroading.

Year by year the St. Paul, Minneapolis & Manitoba grew. By 1893—as the Great Northern system—the road had pushed to the Pacific and had a mileage of 4,300 and a capitalization of $143,000,000. By 1898, when the system had expanded to 5,000 miles, stockholders had received $56,000,000 in profits and bonuses.

The original group was still intact, though two able, vigorous men had been admitted into the family. These were D. Willis James, head of the great metal firm of Phelps, Dodge & Co., of New York, and George F. Baker, president of the First National Bank of New York. Both were friends of John S. Kennedy—friends and allies also of Pierpont Morgan.

Baker, indeed, was perhaps Morgan's most trusted adviser. He was a conservative banker of the Kennedy type. The Street called Baker Morgan's "Secretary of the Treasury" just as it termed Francis Lynde Stetson, the lawyer, Morgan's "Attorney General." Morgan relied upon Baker's judgment as upon that of no other man. Time and again a word from Baker curbed Morgan's impetuous instincts. Baker's bank had become a sort of training school from which Morgan selected likely young men to take into his firm.

When Hill began to push through to the Pacific in 1887 he came into natural competition with the Northern Pacific. The Northern Pacific was a loose aggregation of fifty-four separate companies. Poorly built, costing half again as much to operate as the Great Northern, the Northern Pacific was hopelessly handicapped in the race for traffic. The panic of 1893 swept it into receivership. Northern Pacific security holders in this country turned to Morgan. Foreign investors were represented by the Deutsche Bank of Berlin.

Through Baker and Kennedy, Morgan had closely followed Hill's phenomenal successes. Several times in New York he had met Hill and he liked him. Hill exercised over Morgan some of that curious chemical charm the rough-and-tumble fighter always has for the man surrounded by the conventional and the artificial. Now Morgan decided that a merger between the Northern Pacific and the Great Northern was the only sure method of insuring railroad harmony in seven states of the Northwest from the Great Lakes to the Pacific. Hill had the same idea. Willingly, he became Morgan's agent on the ground.

Negotiations went on for two years. Finally, in the spring of 1895, Hill crossed the ocean and met Morgan and representatives of the Deutsche Bank in London. Morgan had purchased a square, ivy-covered mansion at Prince's Gate, overlooking Hyde Park, large enough to house the random objects of art which he was gathering with increasing enthusiasm. Here it was that he, Hill, and the German financiers talked over the proposed merger.

On May 10, 1895, a plan was placed upon paper. The so-called London Agreement tied the Northern Pacific and the Great Northern by a Siamese-twin ligature. The Northern Pacific was to be reorganized through new issues of $200,000,000 in bonds and $100,000,000 in stock. The Great Northern would guarantee payment of principal and interest on the bonds; and in return was to receive one-half of the new company's capital stock.

The plan was announced at once. Instantly there was a wave of public criticism. Morgan and Hill were accused of seeking to fasten a monopoly upon the Northwest. A Great Northern stockholder brought suit in the Federal courts, alleging that the proposed merger violated an act of the Minnesota Legislature forbidding consolidation of competing and parallel lines. On March 30, 1896, the Supreme Court of the United States upheld this contention and forbade the merger.

But Morgan and Hill were not yet beaten. While the matter was in litigation, in the autumn of 1895, Morgan attended the triennial convention of the Episcopal Church in Minneapolis; and, between sessions, he and Hill were much in each other's company. Morgan was determined to bring the two systems together, both to avoid ruinous competition and to take care of his discouraged bondholders, scattered through Germany, Switzerland, France, Belgium, Holland, England, Austria, and Scotland. He and Hill worked out a substitute plan. Says Hill's biographer, Joseph Gilpin Pyle:

"The new plan . . . simply substituted the principle of joint ownership by individuals for that of corporations. What the companies could not do legally was entirely lawful for their stockholders in a private capacity. . . . A new company was organized with $80,000,000 common and $75,000,000 preferred stock, and the issue of not to exceed $130,000,000 prior lien four per cent bonds and not to exceed $60,000,000 three per cents . . . Hill and his friends were to have the right to ask such portions of the stock as were not subscribed for by the old stockholders.. . . . This amount turned out to be about $16,000,000. . . . The right to retire the preferred stock at par on any first of January during the next twenty years was reserved, a provision whose importance, soon to be tested, was not then foreseen. Both classes of stock were vested in five voting trustees for the first five years, the voting power of the trust expiring November 1, 1901. Mr. Morgan was placed at the head of it."

[167]

The new alliance worked out brilliantly. At last Morgan had found a man with whom he could work in a perfect "community of interest." Under Hill's able management, the Northern Pacific soon showed profits almost comparable to those of the Great Northern. The Morgan-Hill group now controlled in the Northwest a system of some 11,000 miles. Northern Pacific stock gradually advanced 100 points.

The combined system, nevertheless, was in the hands of a small group of men who considered it as much their personal property as their homes. It was theirs to do with as they liked. Morgan explained the principle—pure Bourbonism—as a witness in the stockholders' suit (Peter Power *vs.* Great Northern).

Morgan: The community of interests is the principle that a certain number of men who own property can do what they like with it.

Q: But they sha'n't fight one another?

Morgan: There is no fighting about it. If they choose to fight their own property—but people don't generally do that.

Q: Is not this community of interest one of working harmony?

Morgan: Working in harmony, yes.

Q: Even though they own competing and parallel lines?

Morgan: No; they own them all.

Now, Morgan and Hill decided that it was necessary for the system to extend east into Chicago. In the same suit quoted above, Morgan told of the genesis of the idea.

Morgan: I think it was 1899—it may have been 1898—I made up my mind it was essential that the Northern Pacific Railroad Company—Railway, or whatever you call it—what is it?"

F. L. Stetson (Morgan's counsel) : "Railway."

Morgan: Railway should have its eastern terminus practically in Chicago. And in the same manner, the New York Central, of which I am a director, at that time or soon after decided the same thing with regard to their line; that the western terminus of their line should be in Chicago. . . . In other words, that the transcontinental line should come to Chicago, and the eastern line should go to Chicago. So that was to be the central point. And I talked it over with a great many people interested in the Northern Pacific, and I found they all agreed with me. The question came up as to how it could best be done. Of course, we were confronted with the question which is always arising and repeats itself, as to whether a line that you want is an independent line, or whether it is a competing and—what is the other term?"

Stetson: Parallel.

Morgan: Parallel and competing line; and from a study of the case I came to the conclusion that there were but three lines available. . . . I said, take St. Paul, because the financial responsibility was less.

Hill, however, did not want the St. Paul. He was convinced that the Chicago, Burlington & Quincy was a better feeder for the Great Northern and the Northern Pacific; and Morgan let him have his way. The Burlington, with a mileage of 7,911, stretched fanwise through the richest traffic country in the West. It tapped the river valleys of the Mississippi and its tributaries, the mining industries of Colorado and the Black Hills; the fertile lands of Illinois, Iowa and Nebraska; the coal mines of Illinois and Iowa. It could supply Hill with westbound traffic in abundance and help him fill empty freight cars on their way back from unloading eastbound lumber and grain.

Hill, on behalf of Morgan, began to dicker for the Burlington early in 1901. The negotiations brought them into sudden collision with another group casting longing eyes upon the same property.

This group was led by E. H. Harriman, a nervous, rapid-fire little man with a genius as a practical railroad operator equal to that of Hill, ability as a financier comparable to that of Morgan—and in audacity surpassing both Hill and Morgan.

Harriman was a pouncing sort of person with an ambition hitched to the stars. He had a bomb-proof conscience and a world of self-confidence. "Let me be but one of fifteen men around a table," he said once to Otto Kahn, a young financier who danced admiring attendance upon him, "and I will have my way."

Son of an impecunious Episcopal curate, Harriman began his business career at fourteen as office boy, salary five dollars a week, in a stock exchange house. This was in 1862. He was short, stocky, bow-legged. In a year the sharp-eyed boy had been promoted to "pad shover." The pad shover was a messenger clerk whose duty it was, in those days before the ticker or quotation boards, to display pads of paper containing latest stock prices. A mate in this humble but opportunity-making occu-

pation was the late Thomas Fortune Ryan, then plain
Tommy Ryan.

Before he passed out of his teens Harriman was thoroughly familiar with the brokerage business. Soon
Dewitt C. Hays, his first boss, made him cashier at
$2,000 a year. The youthful cashier always had an eye
out for the main chance. He was animated and ingratiating in manner when he wanted to be. Though poor,
his family was of old and respected lineage.

As soon as his finances permitted, Harriman began
to train with wealthy and sporting men about town,
popularly identified as the Younger Society Set. He
joined the Seventh Regiment and the Travelers' Club
on Fifth Avenue. He made many useful friends.

Ned Harriman was a good marksman, a fine billiard-
player and an exceptional boxer. He gained considerable
fame through exhibition matches with Billy Edwards,
former lightweight champion, whose talents were later
employed to quell disturbances that might arise at the
Hoffman House bar.

At twenty-two Harriman borrowed $3,000 from
his uncle, Oliver Harriman, a well-known merchant,
and purchased a seat on the New York Stock Exchange.
His first office was a modest room, up two flights by
leg-power, at the corner of Broad Street and Exchange
Place. A few doors away was the office of Pierpont
Morgan, whose name even then meant something in
the Street. Harriman and Morgan must have passed
each other often, but it is doubtful whether the latter
then knew of the former's existence.

Harriman's rise was rapid. He attracted an unusual

clientele. He took his brother William into partnership. In the panic of 1873 he plunged into several stocks which had been hammered down to rock bottom, speculated with every cent he could beg or borrow, and emerged with a profit of several hundred thousand dollars. Some of the surplus he invested in securities of the Illinois Central Railroad.

Illinois Central was known far and wide as a "solid" proposition. Old New York families—the Astors, Goelets, Cuttings—owned large blocks of stock. One of Harriman's social friends, Stuyvesant Fish, was secretary to and heir-presumptive of William Henry Osborne, merchant-president of the Illinois Central. For some time Harriman's alert eyes had been focused upon railroading. In 1879 he married Mary Averell, of Ogdensburg, N. Y. Her father, a leading up-state banker, was president of the Ogdensburg & Lake Champlain Railroad Company. Mr. Averell made his son-in-law a director of the Ogdensburg & Lake Champlain.

In 1881 Harriman's keen eyes lighted upon a tiny railroad in the northern part of New York state. It was called the Sodus Bay & Southern. Its length was thirty-four miles. It ran from Stanley, N. Y., to Lake Ontario. Its equipment consisted of two rusty locomotives, two passenger cars, and seven freight cars. Harriman bought it for a song.

"It has the best harbor on the Lake," he told his brother. "The Pennsylvania will have to buy it." The youthful owner improved the track and began to erect a large grain elevator. In a few months he sold out to the Pennsylvania for $200,000.

Now the restless little man turned his attention to the Illinois Central. The road was striking south toward the Gulf of Mexico. Harriman placed some of its bond issues for Osborne and Fish. Also, he invested heavily on his own hook. In 1883 he was elected a director. The aging Osborne turned over the operation of the road to Fish and Harriman. These young men were a study in contrast—Fish a great, easy-going blond chap affectionately nicknamed the "White Elephant"; Harriman, small, dark, secretive.

Harriman resigned his brokerage business and devoted all attention to the Illinois Central. Soon it was apparent that a new and bold force was at work. Harriman and Fish began to buy up scraps of roads here and there and add them to the Illinois Central. Some conservative men in New York shook their heads. "I don't like that Harriman," remarked old Sam Sloan, railroad pioneer, a summer neighbor of Mr. Osborne at Garrison, N. Y. "He and 'Stuyv' Fish are going to get Osborne in trouble with the Illinois Central if he don't look out."

Nevertheless, the young men, and the road, went forward. Harriman and Fish negotiated loans at more advantageous rates than had ever been known. They actually sold one Illinois Central three and one-half per cent bond issue at a fraction above par—a far cry from the old eight and ten per cent days. From then on "cheap money" was one of Harriman's slogans. Also, he determined never to let any part of the road run down.

Harriman's domineering, combative methods left a trail of hostility. The little man, indeed, was always an adept in "the gentle art of making enemies." Soon this propensity brought him across the path of Pierpont Morgan—and he made his most implacable enemy.

The initial clash came in 1887—and it was doubtless also Morgan's first intimation that there was such a person as Harriman—over the control of a railroad in Central Iowa known as the Dubuque & Sioux City. Illinois Central had this road under lease and wanted to purchase. Majority stockholders objected and placed their securities in the hands of Morgan. At the annual meeting of the railroad in Dubuque, Harriman showed up with a lawyer and defeated Morgan on a technicality. Harriman prevented voting of the majority stock on the flimsy ground that proxies were signed by Drexel, Morgan & Co., personally and not as trustees.

The contest was carried into the courts. It dragged along. Finally, Harriman addressed a brief note to Drexel, Morgan & Co., offering eighty dollars a share for the majority stock and stating bluntly that the offer would not be renewed. Dubuque & Sioux City stockholders accepted, much to Morgan's disgust. It went against the grain to be defeated by what he termed a "snide trick." From that time on Morgan conceived a dislike for Harriman amounting almost to hatred. Contemptuously, he spoke of Harriman as a "two-dollar broker." Morgan vendettas were always personal.

The next clash came in 1894 when Morgan announced his plan of reorganization for the Erie Railroad. Harriman owned a comparatively small amount of second mortgage six per cent Erie bonds. He objected to the Morgan plan. "Whom do you represent?" he was asked.

"Myself," was his reply. Harriman went into court and raised so much rumpus that the reorganization plan was changed. He was not forgiven, however, by either Morgan or the Erie management.

One day Harriman telephoned the executive offices of the Erie and asked that the Chicago express be stopped at Goshen so that he could attend the trotting races. Harriman was then vice-president of the Illinois Central. Such simple favors were generally granted readily, but this request was curtly refused. Harriman, however, knew that the express could be flagged at Goshen if there were any passengers for points west of Buffalo.

So he telephoned a friend in Goshen to buy a ticket to Chicago; and blithely took his seat in the express at Jersey City. The train stopped at Goshen. Trainmen peered about for the Goshen-Chicago passenger. This mysterious person did not appear. But Harriman hopped out gaily and went off to the races.

Until now Harriman had simply been a "nuisance" to Morgan. Soon, though, the former was to prove himself in a great battle. "At first Morgan brushed Harriman aside," Otto Kahn tells us. "Before many years he was to raise his hand in salute."

In 1895 Morgan gave up as impossible the reorganization of the Union Pacific Railroad. No road in the country was in a more hopeless condition. The Union Pacific system had slowly disintegrated until its mileage had been reduced from 8,167 to 4,469. Its subsidiary companies were desperately tangled. In addition, the Government was insisting upon payment of the huge debt with interest that had accumulated for thirty years.

The Union Pacific region, west of the Mississippi and southwest of the Missouri, was in fact outside of Morgan's sphere of influence. The road served a country with which he was totally unfamiliar. He was rather relieved when Jacob H. Schiff, senior partner of the growing house of Kuhn, Loeb & Co., came before him, deferentially, and asked whether he would object to Kuhn, Loeb & Co.'s having a try at the reorganization. "Go ahead," said Morgan genially. "I am through with the Union Pacific. I won't even take a financial participation."

As it turned out, this was the chief tactical mistake of Morgan's life.

Schiff was a patient, skillful man, a suave diplomat with a complex Oriental nature. He formed a strong committee and for a year wrestled with the Union Pacific problem. Then he became aware of a curious undercurrent of opposition—an undercurrent that pulled at his plans like the tide. There were strange delays in Congress; a portion of the press became hostile; bondholders abroad, on various pretexts, held off from definite agreements.

In Schiff's mind, there was but one force strong enough to stir up this antagonism. Accordingly, once more, he called upon Morgan. No love had ever been lost between the two. But it was impossible for Schiff to doubt Morgan when the latter turned his Tarquin eyes full upon him and said: "I am not responsible, but I will find out who is. No, I have not changed my mind. I want nothing to do with the Union Pacific."

A short time later Morgan sent for Schiff. "It is that little fellow Harriman who is interfering," he said. "Look out for him. He is a sharper." Followed a remarkable conference between Schiff and Harriman.

"Mr. Harriman," said Schiff, looking at the other through lazy, half-closed lids, "we are everywhere meeting opposition to our plans to reorganize the Union Pacific. Is this opposition being directed by you?"

"Yes," replied Harriman, "I am the man."

"Why?" asked Schiff.

"Because," answered Harriman, without batting an eye, "I intend to reorganize the Union Pacific myself."

"How can you do it?"

"Well," said Harriman, "I can get money cheaper than you. The Illinois Central ought to have the Union Pacific."

Something about the man impressed Schiff immeasurably.

"Can we work together?" he asked.

"Sure," replied Harriman, "if you will make me chairman of the executive committee."

Schiff refused and Harriman left. The opposition grew stronger. Again Schiff bargained with the cocksure little Illinois Central executive. "We'll make you a member of the executive committee," said Schiff. "Then, if you prove to be the strongest man, you'll be chairman in the end."

"All right," said Harriman, "I am with you."

Now the reorganization of Union Pacific proceeded smoothly. The executive committee held the names of

Winslow S. Pierce, Marvin Hughitt, Otto Kahn, E. H. Harriman, and James Stillman. Stillman was taken in because, as president of the National City Bank, he represented "the greatest reservoir of cash in America." The Union Pacific reorganization involved payment to the Government of an immense sum, $45,000,000. The National City had become known as the Standard Oil Bank. With incomes rolling in at the rate of a couple of million a week, the Standard Oil magnates required outlets.

Stillman was their agent. Through this cold little man, the curtains of whose countenance were never drawn, Harriman now touched undreamed-of sources of capital. In the Union Pacific board, Otto Kahn tells us, "Harriman was a newcomer, looked at askance, somewhat in the light of an intruder. His ways jarred upon several of his new colleagues. By some of them he was considered as not quite belonging in their class from the point of view of business position or financial standing—a free lance, neither a railroad man nor a banker nor a merchant. Within one short year he had placed himself at the head of the Board, and become the ruling spirit, the dominating force of the enterprise. If you ask me how this amazing transformation was accomplished, I can only refer you to other examples which history records of the phenomenal rise of those exceptional beings whom Providence has endowed with such qualities as to compel the acceptance of their leadership by their contemporaries."

Harriman impressed James Stillman similarly:

"A very prominent man had told me to 'look out' for Ed Harriman. 'He is not so smart as some people think, and he is not a safe man to do business with.' For that reason I steered clear of him until the matter of the Union Pacific re-organization came up. In my association with him after that time he impressed me as a remarkable man—a man of unalloyed frankness and honesty and in all respects loyal and trustworthy. He soon showed, moreover, great money-making possibilities. . . . I have been acquainted with all of the prominent men of this country during the last forty years, and I can truly say that Harriman, in his conception of vast achievements, and his skill, energy and daring in bringing them to realization, far surpassed any other man I have ever known. His brain was a thing to marvel at; and yet if you could take it apart as you would a clock, you would find its mechanism extremely simple. Nevertheless, it could make the most complex problem understandable and solvable."

That was the way Harriman impressed people who came into contact with him. On his first trip over the Union Pacific, the general manager remarked to his superintendent of machinery: "Joe, did you notice that dark-complected man with glasses who seemed to know so much about scrap, and a great deal about things in general? Well, that's the man who is going to have a great deal to say about this railroad. Ned Harriman. He's a comer!"

After he became chairman of the executive committee Harriman's first move was to go personally over the whole line from the Missouri River to the Pacific Coast. He had a train made up with an observation car in front, a locomotive in the rear. With his daughters,

Mary and Cornelia, he sat out forward, noting rails, curves, grades, ballast, etc.

Operating officials were amazed at the dynamic little official's knowledge of practical railroading. "He saw every poor tie, blistered rail, and loose bolt on my division," remarked one superintendent, admiringly. Harriman asked immediate permission to spend $25,000,000 for improvements. On his own authority he closed several contracts. The directors grumbled at first, but Harriman's tremendous enthusiasm lured the most cautious into voting unheard-of sums. Harriman spent $45,000,000 within five years in improving the Union Pacific's physical condition.

From the start, fortune favored him, just as it had favored Jim Hill in the sudden flight of the grasshoppers. Unusual rainfalls in the arid belt brought heavy crops and prosperity at a crucial time. Annexation of the Philippines stimulated transcontinental and Oriental business. Earnings increased rapidly. Once again the U. P. paid dividends. In three years the system expanded to 15,000 miles. Dismembered branches were taken back.

After the death of C. P. Huntington in August, 1900, the Union Pacific bought forty-five per cent of the Southern Pacific stock. Branch lines were absorbed by exchange of securities; the main line of the Southern Pacific by sale of $40,000,000 four per cent bonds. Within three years, in the phrase of John W. Gates, Harriman had transformed the Union Pacific into "the most magnificent railroad property in the world."

And now the new monopoly of the Southwest came

into collision with that of the Northwest. Harriman heard that Morgan and Hill were negotiating for the Chicago, Burlington & Quincy. Harriman's mind had been upon more immediate projects. But he, too, wanted the Burlington, "partly because," in the words of his biographer, "it was a competitor for business in Union Pacific territory, and partly because it might at any time extend its main line from Denver to the Pacific Coast and thus become a rival of the Union Pacific in transcontinental as well as local traffic."

Morgan and Hill stole a march on Harriman. They bought the Burlington on behalf of the Great Northern and the Northern Pacific. Harriman asked an interest in the purchase. If Morgan had consented the whole western country would have been parceled out as Morgan had split the East between the Pennsylvania and the New York Central. But Morgan refused.

Without hesitation, Harriman set out to purchase the Northern Pacific, which owned half the Burlington. He proposed to buy control of $155,000,000 of stock in the open market. "The boldness of the plan," comments Hill's biographer, "allied it to a work of genius. From those grim old lions (Morgan and Hill) who guarded the way, the quarry was to be snatched before they sensed the presence of an enemy. The implications of the project were tremendous. Suppose the Union Pacific gained control of the Northern Pacific. At once the Great Northern would have to make terms with its new owners, or bear the brunt of incessant attacks along two thousand miles of battle front. It would be shut into its narrow strip between its line and the Canadian border. As the Union Pacific would succeed also to a half-interest in the Burlington, the situation there would be a permanent deadlock. . . . There could be but one issue from a position so intolerable. He [Hill] would have to make the best terms he could. And the terms dictated by an interest that would then reach from New Orleans and Galveston to Winnipeg, and from San Francisco, Portland, and Tacoma to Chicago, St. Paul, and Duluth, were not likely to be tolerable. The victor could then make them almost what he pleased."

It was a situation that stunned the imagination.

The schemes of Hill and Harriman brought on the most stupendous financial conflict Wall Street had ever known.

CHAPTER ELEVEN

NORTHERN PACIFIC PANIC—THE BATTLE OF THE GIANTS

JAMES J. HILL ARRIVED IN NEW YORK FROM WASHING-
ton one night in mid-April, 1901. At the ferry he was
met by Mortimer Schiff, son of Jacob H. Schiff, senior
partner of Kuhn, Loeb & Company. "Father is waiting
for you at Mr. Baker's house," explained young Schiff.
"Did you get his message?"

"Yes," replied Hill. "Is Harriman there also?"

"I believe so."

The railroad chieftain of the Northwest knew full
well the significance of the conference. On behalf of
the Great Northern and the Northern Pacific he had
concluded negotiations for the purchase of the Chicago,
Burlington & Quincy. The contract was to be signed
on the morrow. Harriman and Schiff were making a
last effort to have Union Pacific declared in on the deal.
They had persuaded George F. Baker, Hill's long-time
associate, to arrange this parley. But Hill's mind was
clamped tight: he would not yield. He had the backing
of Pierpont Morgan, whose will was law in Wall Street.
He knew that Morgan detested Harriman and snorted
contemptuously when he heard the latter hailed as the
railway genius of the age, a veritable Colossus of Roads.

In Baker's library the atmosphere was strained.

Schiff, by no means so suave, so conciliatory as usual, began the discussion by asking Hill why he had positively denied to him a month previous that he had any intention of buying the Burlington. The bearded little banker reminded Hill of their friendship of many years and former close business alliance.

"Schiff, I am sorry I had to mislead you," said Hill, not in the least abashed, "but it was necessary. I knew your relations with the Union Pacific."

Schiff did not press the point, but he and Harriman urged Hill to permit Union Pacific at least a minor participation in the Burlington purchase. Genially but positively, Hill declined. As Hill rose to leave, Harriman, who had been pacing the floor in suppressed excitement, turned his piercing, dark eyes full upon his rival and said: "Very well, this is a hostile act and you must take the consequences." Hill merely waved his hand and excused himself.

On April 20 Hill announced that the Great Northern and the Northern Pacific had concluded a joint purchase of more than ninety-six per cent of the Burlington stock. Morgan and Hill paid $200 a share—far above the market valuation. Morgan sailed off to Europe, and Hill exultantly returned to the territory where he was king. They would have stuck closer to Wall Street, perhaps, if they had realized the full import of Harriman's warning. Swayed by personal prejudice, Morgan again under-estimated Harriman.

The bold little "two-dollar broker" was not long in showing the temper of his metal. He launched a sudden flank attack. He had determined to buy up the huge

Northern Pacific and thus assure the Union Pacific a half-say in the management of the Burlington. The audacity of the scheme quickened even the controlled pulses of James Stillman, the cold, inscrutable president of the National City Bank, and of Harriman's Standard Oil allies. These were Ten Per Cent Boys and they were now almost affectionate in their friendliness for Harriman, their tireless little dividend-developing machine. Harriman was no longer an "intruder" in Union Pacific councils. He had been given full control of the system's finances. He was empowered to issue $60,000,-000 worth of bonds.

Harriman would need this amount and more to carry to success his astounding scheme. Mind you, this was no simple proposal to pick up a bankrupt road at twenty or thirty cents on the dollar. It meant going into the stock market and into the highways and byways—as quickly, as secretly as possible—and wresting from the strongest Wall Street-railroad combination in the country control of a $155,000,000 corporation.

The "two-dollar broker's" joust with Jupiter meant even more. It crystallized a rivalry that was to remove Morgan from his lone pedestal as sole monarch of money. Never again would the will of a single man be supreme.

Harriman's strategy was subtle. He and Schiff had accomplished much before the Morgan-Hill alliance suspected the purpose of their manoeuvres. Of course, Northern Pacific stock appreciated sharply the moment Harriman's brokers went into the market. But the rise was generally ascribed to the acquisition of the Burlington. Ironically, the Morgan-Hill group accepted this explanation and sold blocks of "Nipper" stock to the enemy.

On April 1, the house of Morgan held almost $40,-000,000 in Northern Pacific. Noting the rise to par and better of securities for which they had paid only 16, the firm got rid of some of its holdings. On May 1, Morgan & Co. held but $26,000,000 in N. P., par value.

"Jim" Hill was a baby in Wall Street. But he was a player of "hunches." He was in Seattle the last day of April when a premonition came over him that all was not well. He ordered a special train and broke the record getting to New York. On the forenoon of Friday, May 3, he walked into Schiff's office and asked the meaning of the rapid rise in Northern Pacific. One may imagine Schiff smiling slyly into his beard as he informed Hill that Kuhn, Loeb & Co. were buying N. P. upon orders from the Union Pacific.

"All right," said Hill, "do your best, but you can't get control. It is impossible for you to buy enough stock to control. Why, Mr. Morgan and my friends alone hold $35,000,000 or $40,000,000 worth of Northern Pacific. So far as I know, none of them have sold a share."

"Perhaps," replied Schiff enigmatically, "but we've got a lot of it. You secretly bought the Burlington and refused to give us a fair share. Now we're going to see if we can't get a share by purchasing a controlling interest in the Northern Pacific."

Schiff always insisted that he had again offered to make peace if Hill would permit the Union Pacific to share control of the Burlington. In a letter to Morgan written a fortnight later (May 16, 1901) Schiff asserted: "In the evening of the same day, Mr. Hill came to my house, stayed there until after midnight, and repeatedly assured me that there would be no difficulty in accomplishing what I had proposed. Evidently, however, Mr. Hill must have put no credence in the statement I had made to him of the ownership by Union Pacific, for on the following Monday the frantic buying began, both here and in London."

In addition to the written records of the principals in the dramatic events that followed, we have, fortunately, much first-hand information.

Schiff informed Hill on Friday night (May 3) that Union Pacific already controlled about 370,000 of Northern Pacific common and about 420,000 of the preferred—a total of approximately $79,000,000 on a basis of par valuation. Taken together, this was a clear majority of the two classes of stock. Taken separately, though, the Harriman alliance lacked some 30,000 to 40,000 shares of a majority of the common stock.

Harriman knew this and it worried him. He knew that the preferred stock could be retired at the will of the Northern Pacific directors, leaving control to the common stock. The directors, naturally, were enemies. The situation is best explained in Harriman's own words, as he gave it after the tumult and the shouting were over:

"On the morning of Saturday, May 4th, I was at home, ill. We had somewhat over $42,000,000 of the preferred shares of the Northern Pacific, or a clear majority of that issue, and somewhat over $37,000,000 of the common shares, which lacked being a majority of the common shares by about 40,000 shares. But we had a majority of the entire capital stock, as represented by both the common and preferred shares, and I had been competently advised, and was convinced, that this holding was sufficient to enable us to control the Company. Nevertheless, the fact that the Northern Pacific could, on the 1st of January following, retire the preferred shares, of which we had a majority, bothered me somewhat, and I felt that we ought not to leave open to them any chance of retiring our preferred stock and leaving us with a minority interest in the common stock, or involving us in litigation about it.

"Some of our friends, however, felt that our position was secure enough, and that it would be foolish to go in and buy more Northern Pacific stock at the prices which then prevailed. Nevertheless, I made up my mind that we should have a majority of the common shares, and on that morning I called up Heinsheimer [one of the partners in the firm of Kuhn, Loeb & Co.] and gave him an order to buy, at the market, 40,000 shares of Northern Pacific common for my account. He said: 'All right'; and as dealings that day in Northern Pacific common shares continued to be very heavy, I felt that, come what might, I had control of Northern Pacific, common stock and all.

"On Monday, the 6th of May, Northern Pacific came strong from London and opened with a burst of activity in the Street; and having had no confirmation from Kuhn, Loeb & Co. of the purchase of the 40,000 shares of Northern Pacific which I had ordered on Saturday morning, I called Heinsheimer up and asked him why I had gotten no report of the execution of my order. He told me that before giving out the order he had to reach Schiff, who was at the synagogue. Schiff instructed him not to execute the order and said that he (Schiff) would be responsible. I then knew that matters were in a serious way and that the whole object of our work might be lost. Meanwhile, the day (Monday) had become so advanced, and prices of Northern Pacific shares had gone so high that I realized the impossibility of buying, in such a market, 40,000 shares of stock. So I determined to go down and see Schiff, find out what it was all about, and fight the question out with what material I had in hand."

Meanwhile, Hill, his old guard of Scotchmen (John S. Kennedy, Strathcona, Mountstephen and the rest), and his new cohorts (Morgan & Co.) rallied. Hill passed Saturday with Robert Bacon. Bacon was a charming fellow, but Hill cursed his luck that Morgan was enjoying the baths and basking under the bland, blond skies of Aix-les-Bains. Bob Bacon was no Pierpont Morgan in a pinch like this.

Hill and Bacon collaborated in a frantic cable to Morgan. They summarized the situation and asked Morgan's authorization to buy enough shares of Northern Pacific common to give them control. Morgan was about as pleasant as a teething crocodile when he received news of the Harriman raid. On Sunday, May 5th, Bacon got a cable peremptorily instructing him to buy the needed shares "at the market."

At the moment Morgan's immediate thoughts were far from Wall Street. In a villa at Aix lived a Frenchwoman of title and quality. She was tall and dark and of that oval Grecian cast of countenance that most appealed to the financier. Soon messengers were streaming between quiet

Aix and the jewelers and couturiers of Paris. The colony observed the affair with delighted approval. Morgan's attentions invested the lady with an aura of added distinction. No one was surprised when she exchanged her modest villa for an imposing chateau in the nearby Savoie countryside.

Morgan's view of the Northern Pacific contest was given a year later on the witness stand in a stockholders' suit (Peter Power *vs.* Northern Pacific):

"When I heard of it, I felt in this position: we had organized the Northern Pacific; he had placed all the securities of the Northern Pacific, and I knew, as I had always supposed, that there were people, friends of ours and other people, who practically held enough Northern Pacific—we had always supposed we had with us people upon whom we could depend to protect our moral control of the property.

"And consequently, when that news came to me, I hadn't any doubt about the fact of the matter. And at the same time this news came so strong—whoever had acquired it— I felt something must have happened. Somebody must have sold.

"I knew where certain stocks were, and I figured it up. I feel bound in honor when I reorganize a property and am morally responsible for its management to protect it, and I generally do protect it.

"So I made up my mind that it would be desirable to buy 150,000 shares of stock ($15,000,000 worth) and with that I knew we had a majority of the common stock; and I knew that actually gave us control, and they couldn't take the minority and have it sacrificed to Union Pacific interests. The stock was bought absolutely for my house. . . .

"Mr. J. S. Kennedy has been a friend of mine for forty

years. He and I were in Aix together. He came down to see what in the mischief all this meant. I said I didn't know and he said, 'Whatever you want done, I want done with my Northern Pacific.' Whatever I was willing to do, they wanted, and they wanted to put the stock just where I said it would be safe. That was what they wanted. Well, I appreciated that; I cannot help being touched by a thing of that kind."

On Monday, May 6th, the Morgan-Hill forces sent "Jim" Keene, famous stock manipulator, into the market. By Tuesday night, Keene's swarm of brokers had the 150,000 shares Morgan had ordered—and brought on the swiftest and most paralyzing financial paroxysm the country had ever known. The conflict was wanton, fostered by the ambitions and vanities of two men— Morgan and Harriman. Both, though never publicly admitting it, were afterward thoroughly ashamed. These men trampled ruthlessly upon the rights of the public, bankrupted thousands, depressed values by the hundreds of millions; and almost brought the world in which they lived crashing about their ears.

Beyond that, they rolled the drums for an even greater conflict. They fed the hatred that millions of Americans already entertained for Captains of Industry and all they stood for. Henceforth, Morgan and Monopoly were synonymous terms. And the issue was soon to be joined: Who shall rule: People or Plutocrats? Wall Street or Washington?

However: Northern Pacific common jumped forty points in two days. By Tuesday night, Morgan had 30,000 shares more than a majority of the common. But Harriman and the Union Pacific controlled a majority of the preferred; and, of the total stock, they had in their possession 781,080 shares—or about 6,000 more than one-half.

Now came the most disgraceful episodes in the whole tawdry affair. On Tuesday and Wednesday speculators and the "outside public" sold in expectation of a break. These late-comers believed, of course, that they could buy in later at lower prices and close out their contracts. They were totally unaware that Morgan and Harriman did not intend to take profits but purposed to lock up the actual N. P. shares. On Monday European bankers became alarmed and reversed previous liberal policies on American loans. The Bank of England warned the London joint-stock banks against New York.

On Thursday morning, the 9th day of May, Wall Street suddenly awakened to the fact that Northern Pacific was cornered. The stock soared to $1,000 a share. The only profit-takers were a few dozen individuals who held tiny lots. Their offerings were but a drop in the bucket. Wall Street realized that it had sold millions of dollars worth of N. P. which it did not possess. It could not get the millions needed to settle. The result was "finance run mad." Cornered brokers either fell into a mental palsy or scrambled madly in a futile effort to protect themselves. "While this was happening to Northern Pacific stock," writes the financial historian, Alexander Noyes, "all other stocks broke violently, declines of fifty per cent or more occurring in many of the soundest shares. It was admitted, afterward, that on the books of the lending banks, and on the basis of the day's low prices for collateral pledged against stock exchange loans, a good part of Wall Street was for a couple of hours technically insolvent."

To avoid general ruin the leading banks hastily formed a temporary pool and loaned $20,000,000 to the money market. At the same time, the Morgan and Harriman interests, frightened by the havoc they had wrought, permitted shorts to settle at $150 a share.

It was a sort of foundling panic, this. No one would father it. Both sides were full of specious excuses. Hill blamed the public, saying:

"All I can do is to liken it to a ghost dance. The Indians begin their dance and don't know why they are doing it. They whirl about until they are almost crazy. It is so when these Wall Street people get the speculative fever. Perhaps they imagine they have a motive in that they see two sets of powerful interests which may be said to be clashing. Then these outsiders, without rhyme or reason, rush in on one side or the other. They could not tell you why they made their choice, but in they go, and the result is such as has been seen here for the past few days."

Harriman later excused himself as follows:

"Our holdings [of Northern Pacific stock] were all acquired prior to the supposed contest between Morgan & Co. and ourselves. During the days of the panic we did not buy any Northern Pacific stock, nor give orders for any. Many of our shares had been bought in Germany, Holland, or England, for delivery in New York, and the certificates were on their way to their destination. Meanwhile the agents of the foreign sellers were making their deliveries by using stock borrowed from other people. Then, when the supposed contest took place and other parties bought Northern Pacific at very high prices and demanded immediate delivery, the agents of these European sellers had great difficulty in getting stock to fill their contracts. But, in every case, we gave them all the time they needed. We were not in the supposed contest and had no hand in it."

A week to the day after the panic, Schiff addressed a long letter to "Dear Mr. Morgan." Though perhaps unintentional, it reads like a masterpiece of delicate irony. Setting forth, as tenderly as possible, to demonstrate that Hill was a double-tongued liar, Schiff proceeded blandly to absolve Morgan of any responsibility for the situation and ended upon this curious, almost fawning, note:

"I trust you will accept my assurance that nothing was further on the part of Union Pacific interests than to do aught meant to be antagonistic to you or your firm, and that, as far as my partners and I are concerned, we have at all times wished, as we continue to do, to be permitted to aid in maintaining your personal prestige, so well deserved. You will find Union Pacific interests, and certainly my firm and myself, entirely ready to do anything in reason that you may ask or suggest, so that permanent conditions shall be created which shall be just to all interests and not bear within them the seed of future strife, discord, and possible disaster.

"Trusting, then, dear Mr. Morgan, that you will understand the spirit in which this letter is written, and hoping that the rest of your stay abroad may be pleasant and not interrupted by any unsatisfactory events, I am, with assurances of esteem,

"Yours most faithfully,

"JACOB H. SCHIFF."

[194]

Friendships, however, are somewhat flexible, particularly between men who may prove useful to each other. So it need not surprise us to find Schiff, a short month later, addressing Hill also as "Dear Mr. Hill."

Truly, this catastrophe had a purifying effect. A few days after that dreadful May 9th, Hill sauntered into the office of Kuhn, Loeb & Co. and asked for Schiff. The senior partner was out. "How is he?" Hill asked Felix Warburg, another partner. "Not very happy," replied Warburg. "Oh," commented Hill, airily, "Schiff takes these things too seriously."

Nor did Harriman seem heartbroken. During the height of the excitement Harriman was operated on for appendicitis. He was a difficult patient and the doctor could keep him quiet only by promising permission for him to use the telephone the moment he came out of the ether. Much to the surprise of those at his bedside, he asked to talk to Hill. "Hello, is that you, Hill?" he said weakly. "This is Harriman. I just wanted to let you know the operation is over and I am all right." With a sigh of satisfaction, Harriman sank into his pillows and went to sleep! He and Hill had never been hostile personally. After their first few meetings, they called each other "Ed" and "Jim."

After all the fanfaronnade, the Battle of the Giants resulted in a pyrrhic victory. Neither party was quite sure of its ability to defeat the other, legally. As Hill's biographer puts it:

"Nothing was to be gained for either side by fighting. Both might have continued to tear up Wall Street and injure large property interests including their own. They could have engaged in endless litigation, which would have cost a lot of money without materially altering anything. They might have maintained their divided ownership and kept up a tug-of-war until the rope broke. The end of that would be two pieces of rope and two parties covered with bruises from severe falls. . . .

"On both sides there were big men. . . . Recent events had broadened and instructed their view. Things being as they were, they were ready for agreement."

Late in May, Kuhn, Loeb & Co. gave this statement to the press:

"It is officially announced that an understanding has been reached between Northern Pacific and Union Pacific interests under which the composition of the Northern Pacific board will be left in the hands of J. P. Morgan personally. Certain names have already been suggested, not now to be made public, which will especially be recognized as representatives of the common interests. It is asserted that complete and permanent harmony will result under the plan adopted between all interests involved."

Upon his return from Europe in July, Morgan appointed both Hill and Harriman members of the new Northern Pacific board. The war was over, temporarily. Harriman was balked of his main purpose. But, at last, he had won his way into Morgan councils. It was not long before he was on the Northern Pacific executive committee; not long, either, before he was buying up other roads on the credit of the Union Pacific and defiantly announcing that, if the law would only let him alone, he "would spread not only over the Pacific coast but over the Atlantic. I would go on as long as I live."

Had Harriman captured the Northern Pacific in 1901, the Interstate Commerce Commission declared he would have "subjected to a common will and policy nearly one-half of the territory of the United States—a comparatively undeveloped, rapidly growing, and extremely rich territory, into which must necessarily extend the population and business of the Eastern States."

Meanwhile the marts of the world buzzed with the name of Pierpont Morgan and the fame of a great industrial combination he had welded. This was the United States Steel Corporation, the world's first "Billion Dollar" merger. In every town and hamlet, people were talking of "Steel" just as in previous eras they had talked of gold and oil. *Life*, leading comic weekly, published a cartoon:

Q. Who made the world, Charles?
A. God made the world in 4004 B.C. but it was reorganized in 1901 by James J. Hill, J. Pierpont Morgan, and John D. Rockefeller.

A soubrette of the period popularized a song fashioned about "Morgan, Morgan, the Great Financial Gorgon." Everywhere a weary pilgrim seeking a place to rest was turned away—"It's Morgan's; it's Morgan's." Finally—

> "I went to the only place left for me,
> So I boarded a boat for the brimstone sea;
> Maybe I'll be allowed to sit
> On the griddled floor of the bottomless pit;

But a jeering imp with horns on his face
Cried out as he forked me out of the place:
    Chorus:
It's Morgan's, it's Morgan's; the great financial gorgon;
Get off that spot, we're keeping it hot;
That seat is reserved for Morgan!"

The public seized with zest upon its new "personality." Morgan liked it not a bit. He withdrew into himself to an even more marked extent. He repulsed all overtures. An impecunious Wall Street man wrote to him during this period, requesting an invitation to witness the yacht races from the deck of the *Corsair*. Morgan replied:

"My dear Sir:
"Unfortunately, I have loaned the *Corsair* to my friend, Mr. Ledyard, for the yacht races. However, if you think you would care to go on the yacht of either Mr. Gould, Mr. Goelet, Colonel Astor, or any of the others that may be going down the bay, I will try to get an invitation for you; and will assure whoever may take you that they will have the honor of entertaining the cheekiest man I ever heard from.
                    (*signed*) "J. P. Morgan."

Overwhelming had been the response from America and Europe to Morgan's brief, significant circular inviting subscriptions to his steel syndicate. It was a tremendous demonstration of the asset value of one man's reputation. Checks and pledges poured in upon Morgan & Co. Extra clerks had to be engaged to handle a great volume of mail. Millionaires thronged Morgan's anteroom, begging as the highest favor the privilege of participating in the syndicate. The amount asked was $200,000,000. It was quickly subscribed. The list contained the names of the wealthiest men and institutions in the United States.

Three years earlier it had required several months for the United States Treasury to market $200,000,000 of United States bonds. Morgan's credit outmatched that of the Government.

Morgan's tremendous achievement created an aura of power never before acquired by an individual. On his European trip that spring he was greeted as the greatest man of his time. London speculators paid him the compliment of insuring his life, as if he had been contemplating a coronation. They felt that hundreds of millions of stock were composed of Morgan and water. Withdraw the Morgan stiffening, they reasoned, and the water would have trouble in standing alone. So Threadneedle Street took the extraordinary precaution of applying to Lloyd's for insurance on the Morgan life, paying premiums at the rate of thirty pounds on the thousand for three months.

That summer the King of England asked that Morgan be seated at his right at the American Ambassador's banquet. The German Emperor received him with as great consideration as that prescribed for a brother potentate. He dined, *à deux,* with the Kaiser. The latter brought up the subject of Socialism. Morgan looked at him blankly. "I pay no attention to such theories," he said with finality. Afterward he gave a brief impression of William II: "I have met the Kaiser and I like him."

Morgan had become the first financier of the world.

CHAPTER TWELVE

MORGAN'S MASTERPIECE—U. S. STEEL

AN UNPRECEDENTED BOOM PERIOD IN THE YEARS 1898-1901 brought to the fore the industrial promoter—a type no less greedy, no less adroit than his brethren of the wildcat railroad era. The new model get-rich-quick man operated on broader lines. He would invade a given industry, buy up a string of competing plants at inflated prices, combine them under a high-sounding name, and offer stock to the public. Overflowing with confidence and cash, the public gobbled up the securities—good, bad, and indifferent. In 1899 alone new industrial companies were incorporated with a total capitalization of $3,593,000,000. Of this $2,354,000,000 was common stock—simply "water" by frank confession of the promoters.

No field offered such lush possibilities for the speculative promoter as the iron and steel trade. A flood of prosperity had inundated this industry. New uses for fabricated materials in buildings, bridges, railroad construction, etc. fostered a worldwide demand for American steel and iron.

Perhaps the most venturesome operator in this field was John W. Gates, a stout, boastful individual whose readiness to plunge on any proposition won a glamorous nickname in which he gloried—Bet-a-Million Gates.

Gates would have been perfectly at home cracking the whip as ringmaster in a circus. Beginning his career as a poacher upon barbed wire patents, this Prince of Gamblers, "half-fakir, half-fanatic," rose to command a huge combination in the steel trade. In 1898 Gates combined seven wire factories in Illinois into the Consolidated Steel and Wire Company. A couple of months later he added seven more mills, christened his concern the American Steel and Wire Company of Illinois, and issued $24,000,000 stock.

Early in 1899, Gates formed the American Steel and Wire Company of New Jersey. The new combination paid $33,600,000 for the Illinois company's $24,000,000 stock, absorbed eleven additional wire plants and boosted its capitalization to the tidy total of $90,000,-000. Three years later, in a court action, Gates was asked what had become of $26,000,000 in stock that was not accounted for. "I don't know," he replied. Considerably more than half of the Gates $90,000,000 issue was common stock. Much of it had been bestowed as bonuses in the various deals; yet, in those flush days, it rose as high as $92 a share on the Stock Exchange.

Gates bought rods for his wire from the Illinois Steel Company and had worked his way into the management of this conservative, pioneer concern. The owners of Illinois Steel—Marshall Field and H. H. Porter of Chicago, Nathaniel Thayer of Boston, and others—were men of very different stamp from Gates. But the latter had proved so sharp a bargainer they felt it safer to have him with than against them. Besides, they had a balance wheel for Gates in their general counsel, Elbert H. Gary.

Although he had known Gates from boyhood and had been drawn into the growing steel and iron industry by the latter, Gary, too, was of different fibre from the swashbuckling promoter. Gary was a patient, able man of pious Methodist upbringing. He had never touched a card. His idea of a good time was a church supper or a Sunday School picnic. For eight years he had been a judge in DuPage County, Illinois. He was a tremendous worker and had become an expert upon every phase of the iron and steel business.

In 1898 Gary was asked to attend a meeting of the Illinois Steel Company board in New York to discuss his suggestion that Illinois Steel merge with the Minnesota Iron Company. The amalgamation was voted upon one proviso: that J. Pierpont Morgan would undertake the financing. Morgan agreed. For three months Gary worked in close touch with Morgan. The result was the organization of the Federal Steel Company. This was capitalized at $200,000,000—half common, half preferred.

Morgan added to the directorate D. O. Mills, Robert Bacon, his partner, H. H. Rogers of the Standard Oil, and others, but emphatically refused Gates a place. "I don't think property is safe in his hands," he said in his usual blunt fashion. Morgan, however, was to hear from Gates again. The flamboyant, poker-playing promoter was a tough customer and hard to down.

Morgan, though, had placed the priceless accolade of his approval upon Gary. He astonished the lawyer one

afternoon (this was late September, 1898) by inform-
ing him that he had been selected as president of Federal
Steel. "When can you take up your duties in New
York?" asked Morgan. "But, Mr. Morgan," protested
Gary, "I have a law practice in Chicago that brings me
in $75,000 a year. I don't want to leave it."

"Oh, that's all right," retorted Morgan, casually, "I'll
take care of that. You can name your own salary, choose
your own executive committee, select the directors if
you want to."

Gary begged for time. Morgan gave him twenty-four
hours. Next day Gary signed a three-year contract as
president of the Federal Steel Company. Thus began a
warm and unusual association. Gary's ideas on business
ethics, personal and social morality, and the like differed
widely from those of Morgan. Yet, with the exception
of two or three memorable clashes, Gary and Morgan
worked in harmony for fifteen years.

"Judge Gary is too good a man to oppose," Morgan
once told a friend. Often, when in one of his black,
sou'east moods, the financier would send one of his
juniors for Gary. "Senior wants to know why you
haven't been over," was the message. Gary would walk
over to the bank and he and Morgan would talk, sometimes for hours, about everything under the sun.

Under Gary's excellent management Federal Steel returned splendid profits. But it did not prove the
"rounded proposition" Gary had hoped for. In the face
of domestic competition, it was impossible to establish
European depots as Gary had planned.

In 1899 there came an amazing series of new mergers.

Gates, as we have seen, launched his American Steel &
Wire Company of New Jersey. The daring Moore
brothers, William H. and James, founders of Diamond
Match and National Biscuit, turned to iron and steel.
With Daniel G. Reid and others, the Moores snapped a
rubber band about 265 tin plate mills and formed the
Tin Plate Trust. Followed also the National Tube Company, which Morgan had been persuaded to finance;
the American Steel Hoop Company; the American
Sheet Steel Company; the National Steel Company; the
American Bridge Company. Partly, these mergers were
forced by the necessity for larger units in handling huge
contracts. Steel-making is an expensive art.

The public watched the dizzy course of the steel promoters with mingled feelings: awe and admiration, fear
and curiosity.

In a Fifth Avenue mansion, however, was a squat,
bearded little man who noted the movement with joy.
Spider-like, Andrew Carnegie lurked in his web and
wove schemes to turn the situation to his profit. Carnegie was the key to steel and iron trade problems, and
well he knew it.

For half a century, since his penniless parents had
brought him and his brother Tom to America from Dun-
fermline, Scotland, Carnegie had accustomed himself to
looking out for the main chance. In 1848, at thirteen, he
became a bobbin-boy in a Pittsburgh cotton mill at
$1.20 a week. Later he was a messenger boy, railroad
telegraph operator, finally secretary to Col. Thomas A.
Scott, general superintendent of the Pennsylvania Railroad in Pittsburgh, afterwards president. Carnegie prof-

ited by inside information and made paying investments. He went into iron in 1864. In 1875 he saw a Bessemer converter in blast and leaped to organize a company which built the Edgar Thomson Steel Works at Braddock, Pennsylvania.

Fortune smiled upon him from the very first. He obtained as manager the famous Captain Billy Jones whose success in turning out great quantities of steel founded the Carnegie fortune. Carnegie was a curious little person, eaten with ego—and ability. Sometimes he seemed to forget that he was neither Henry Bessemer, who discovered the process for making steel, nor William Kelly, who produced the first malleable iron when Carnegie was a youngster in short pants.

Carnegie was a financier pure and simple. He never experimented. He bought into going concerns—Homestead and Duquesne. Soon he had a monopoly in steel rails. He absorbed ore lands in the Lake Superior region and built railroads and ships. In 1889 Henry Clay Frick threw his fortunes in with Carnegie. Fifteen years younger than Carnegie, Frick, a thoughtful, reticent man of Swiss ancestry, had worked up from errand boy in a village store at Mount Pleasant, near Pittsburgh, to become the greatest coke-maker in the country. A few years later Carnegie combined all his undertakings into the great Carnegie Steel Company.

Carnegie had been raised in a rough school. He had no business morality. He was a cruel competitor, indulging in every devious device to gain an advantage.

From $7,000,000 in 1897, the Carnegie Steel Company's net profits had in 1900 risen to $40,000,000.

This did not dampen the little Scot's eagerness to retire. He knew he could get a top price on a rising market. He cherished an ambition to be known as the world's greatest philanthropist. He loved such resounding aphorisms as "he who dies rich, dies disgraced," and "I would prefer to have my niece marry an honest working man than a worthless duke!" However, those not sentimentally inclined noted the exquisite, Boswellian pleasure afforded to Carnegie when he hobnobbed with the great.

The Laird of Skibo knew that this was the time for him to cash in. But he was not one to sell out without extracting the last penny. He saw his chance when Morgan organized Federal Steel and when other mergers came tumbling along. Early in '99 he granted a ninety-day option to William H. Moore for $157,950,-000. The option expired and Carnegie pocketed a million-dollar forfeit. A little later he began to flirt with John D. Rockefeller. His price now had gone up to $250,000,000. This was too much for John D.

Now Carnegie began to work subtly upon Morgan. In relation to the new mergers he wrote his managers to preserve "armed neutrality," adding:

"If they decline to give us what we want, then there must be no bluff. We must accept the situation and prove that if it is fight they want, here we are 'always ready.' Here is a historic situation for the Managers to study—Richelieu's advice: 'First, all means to conciliate; failing that, all means to crush.' Shakespeare has it: 'First in your right hand carry gentle Peace'; but after Peace is gone the worst policy in the world is 'gentle war.' We should look with favor upon every

combination of every kind upon the part of our competitors;
the bigger they grow the more vulnerable they become. It is
with firms as with nations; 'scattered possessions' are not in it
with a solid, compact, concentrated force."

Early in 1900 Carnegie broke with Frick. The two
men were never *en rapport* temperamentally. Frick was
a bit of a dreamer, a scholar, an idealist in a way. Carnegie grated upon him. Their differences were carried
into the courts. Carnegie reorganized and made Charles
M. Schwab president of the Carnegie Steel Company.

Schwab, then but thirty-eight, was the apple of Carnegie's eye. Twenty years before he had been a laborer
in the Braddock works. When Carnegie first met him,
he was a jolly, good-natured boy attached to his father's
livery stable in Cresson Springs, Pennsylvania, where
Carnegie had a summer bungalow. Young Schwab had
a good voice and raised it joyfully when he brought the
horse and buggy around to the Carnegie cottage. "When
that boy of yours is ready for a job, send him to me,"
Carnegie told Schwab *père*.

Charlie Schwab developed into a man of fascinating
fervor, an exceptional salesman, and an extraordinarily
charming human being. Schwab was the sort of man
who would appeal to Morgan. Carnegie, craftily aware
of Morgan's personal dislike for himself, brought
Schwab to New York and set him to work upon Morgan and Gary.

At the same time Carnegie trumpeted throughout the
land a series of new projects that threw the steel and
iron industry into turmoil. He actually let contracts
for a $12,000,000 tube plant on Lake Erie to compete

with Morgan's National Tube Company. He announced that he would fight Gates by erecting a gigantic rod mill at Pittsburgh. He said he would bring his own raw materials from the Great Lakes by means of his own ships and his own railroad from Lake Erie to Pittsburgh. He even planned a road from Pittsburgh to the Atlantic to rival the Pennsylvania.

This was too much for Gates, the Moore brothers, and the other steel promoters. They realized that Carnegie meant business. Panic seized them. From every direction came appeals to Pierpont Morgan to buy out Carnegie and organize the steel trade into one indomitable unit. At first, Morgan believed the proposal too difficult. "I don't think I could raise the money," he told Gary when the latter urged the purchase of the Carnegie interests.

Such was the situation in December, 1900, when Morgan found himself at a private dinner seated next to Schwab. The latter was the only speaker. He stirred Morgan's imagination by painting the possibilities of manufacturing steel upon a larger scale than ever before. "For instance," Schwab pointed out, "there is in the United States no one plant making steel cars, exclusively. Instead of having one mill make ten, twenty, or fifty products, why not have one mill make one product, and that continuously?"

Schwab touched upon metallurgical, mechanical, transportation economies. His words bewitched Morgan. When the dinner was over, Morgan did not withdraw, as usual. Instead, he drew Schwab into a corner. They talked long and earnestly. A few days later there was a further conference in Morgan's office. "Get me an option upon the Carnegie properties," directed Morgan.

One may imagine the willingness with which Schwab carried Morgan's dictum to his mentor!

After a proper period had elapsed, Schwab stood again before Morgan. Mr. Carnegie, he said, would not grant a written option but had scribbled his price upon a piece of paper. "Here is the figure, Mr. Morgan." This was the price later accepted—equivalent in cash to more than $400,000,000 for the Carnegie Steel Co., lock, stock and barrel, majority and minority interests. Morgan stowed the slip in a pocket of his capacious vest and growled that Schwab would hear from him—later.

One Sunday morning, a fortnight afterward, Robert Bacon appeared in Judge Gary's apartment in the Hotel Plaza, bearing a detailed memorandum of the Carnegie proposition. "The Chief wants to know if you think this practical," explained Bacon.

Gary worked into the small hours upon a plan which he thought would justify the purchase, and presented his findings to Morgan in the morning. The Gary plan proposed an amalgamation not only of Carnegie and Federal Steel but of half a dozen other of the new combinations. This merger, as Gary visualized it, would control its own raw materials and its manufacturing and distributing facilities, and would be able to make and dispose of, most economically, all forms of finished steel for sale in this country and abroad.

Morgan absorbed the plan—in split-seconds. "All right," he splurted, "where shall we start?"

It was decided to make Federal Steel the nucleus. Within an hour or two Gary, chiefly by telephone, obtained the approval of the Federal directors. From Chicago Marshall Field expressed the general opinion: "I am in agreement with whatever Mr. Morgan and you decide."

Late in the afternoon of that memorable Monday, Morgan placed his hand upon Gary's shoulder and said: "Now, there's one thing I want understood: if I go into this you are to go with me, not only as my lawyer but as my friend—that is, you are to stand by me."

"For the next four weeks," writes Ida M. Tarbell, Gary's biographer, "the Morgan offices were the scene of as nearly exciting activities as was possible in that dignified and controlled quarter. Judge Gary set up his headquarters there. . . . Men came and went from morning until night and the newspapers were soon agog with curiosity. The public became anxious. Early in February it became necessary for Judge Gary . . . to make to the public some kind of announcement as to what was contemplated."

Gary's statement, made "solely on my own responsibility," told of the proposed merger. It disavowed any intention of creating a monopoly or in any way antagonizing any principle or policy of the law.

There were many exciting moments during these weeks of negotiations. Gates, as might have been expected, was the most recalcitrant of those invited into the combination. Morgan thought Gates' demands unreasonable. One noontime Morgan sent for Gary. The financier was flushed and irritable. "Gary," fumed

Morgan, "Gates, William Edenborn, and his other associates are in that room"—pointing—"and I can't settle
with them. I am through. You take it up. "

This is how Gary told the story:

" 'Mr. Morgan sent me in to trade with you,' I said to them
when I went in. 'Luckily, I know the wire game as well as
you do. You have been offered all your property is worth,
and it is all you are going to get.' We wrangled for several
hours, and gradually I was whittling away their points when,
about four o'clock in the afternoon, Mr. Morgan—whose
habit it was to go home at three—sent in word that he was
going home. I sent word back, 'Don't go—wait another half-
hour.' At the end of the half-hour, word came a second time
that he was leaving for home. I sent back the same word.
Along about five o'clock, when I found he was determined to
leave, I went in. 'Mr. Morgan,' I said, 'I want you to come
in and tell those men that the offer that you made will not be
changed, that they can take it or leave it, but that, if they
have not taken it in ten minutes, it will be withdrawn and the
Steel Corporation will build its own wire plant.'

" 'All right,' Mr. Morgan said. In a moment he came in—
big and fierce, his eyes like coals of fire. 'Gentlemen,' he said,
pounding the desk, 'I am going to leave this building in ten
minutes. If by that time you have not accepted our offer,
the matter will be closed. We will build our own wire plant.'
And he turned and left the room.

"John W. Gates scratched the top of his head and turning
to Edenborn said: 'Well, William, I don't know whether the
old man means that or not.'

" 'You can depend upon it he does,' I said.

" 'Then,' said Gates, 'I guess we will have to give up.'

"I sent for Mr. Morgan. 'The gentlemen have accepted
your proposition,' I told him when he came in.

" 'Is that right?' Mr. Morgan snapped.

" 'Yes,' they all said.

"Never have I seen Mr. Morgan more elated. 'Now,' he said, 'let's go home.' We went up on the Elevated to Fiftieth Street, where his old electric car met him. He was like a boy going home from a football game."

One day Morgan called in one of his own lawyers and Judge J. H. Reed, of Pittsburgh, Carnegie's chief counsel. "Do you know what I have done?" Morgan asked them, "I have sold myself short. I have agreed to take over the stock of all these companies and I have not got a scratch of the pen from Mr. Carnegie which would hold him or his estate if he died."

The lawyers dashed to Carnegie's house and explained the dilemma. Carnegie readily dictated a satisfactory document. "Of course," he said, "Pierpont ought to have a letter." Morgan grimaced when he heard that Carnegie had spoken of him as "Pierpont." He disliked the very shadow of the canny little Scot. A month or two later, when he found himself crossing the ocean with Carnegie, he did his best to avoid the latter. Carnegie, however, one day braced Morgan on deck. "Mr. Morgan," he said, "I sold out to you too cheaply. You'd have given me two million dollars more."

"Yes. I would have given you two million more," retorted Morgan, adding, as he hurried away, "if only to be rid of you."

The first Morgan circular announced the capital of the United States Steel Corporation as $850,000,000. A month later a second and final circular provided capital stock of $1,018,000,000 and bonds of $301,-000,000. Miss Tarbell gives us a fascinating explanation:

". . . The plans of the managers, large as they were, had grown larger. Judge Gary, particularly, was anxious about ores.

" 'We ought to have the Rockefeller ores.'

" 'We have got all we can attend do,' Morgan growled.

"Judge Gary told him what he thought.

" 'How are we going to get them?' Mr. Morgan asked.

" 'You are to talk to Mr. Rockefeller.'

" 'I would not think of it.'

" 'Why?'

" 'I don't like him.'

" 'Mr. Morgan,' said the Judge, 'when a business proposition of so great importance to the Steel Corporation is involved, would you let a personal prejudice interfere with its success?'

" 'I don't know,' he replied.

"The next morning, however, he came in excitedly, throwing up his arms in exultation and shouting to Judge Gary, 'I have done it!'

" 'Done what?'

" 'I have seen Rockefeller.'

" 'How did he treat you?'

" 'All right.'

" 'Did you get the ore lands?'

" 'No. I just told him that we ought to have them, and asked if he would not make a proposition. How much do you think we ought to pay?'

" 'I am not prepared to say. It would take me a week to figure out what I would consider a reasonable price.'

" 'Well, tell me offhand what you think we ought to pay.'

"The Judge worked for half an hour, and finally announced, 'There's an *outside* figure—so many millions.'

" 'To my surprise,' Judge Gary says in telling the story, 'Mr. Frick brought in a figure from Mr. Rockefeller a few days later—$5,000,000 more than my outside figure. "This is a prohibitive proposition," I said.

" ' "Judge Gary," exclaimed Mr. Morgan, "in a business proposition as great as this would you let a matter of $5,000,000 stand in the way of success?"

" ' "But I told you, Mr. Morgan, that mine was the outside."

" ' "Well, put it this way: would you let these properties go?"

" ' "No."

" ' "Well, write out an acceptance."

Carnegie Steel Company stock was purchased at $1,500 per share, paid in five per cent bonds secured by the stocks of all the amalgamated corporations. Carnegie bonds were exchanged at par for the same security. Controlling more than half of his companies, Carnegie received a personal payment of $217,720,000. His partners were bought out on somewhat less favorable terms. The other combinations, merged into one huge holding company, received Steel Corporation shares on a basis ranging from equal exchange to 125% of their former outstanding capital.

Morgan formed a bankers' syndicate of $200,000,000 to guarantee successful flotation of the stock. Actually, only $25,000,000 was required.

Then began the ballyhoo to sell stock. The Billion Dollar corporation caught the public's imagination.

Salesmen were sent into the tiniest towns; agents employed in every market abroad. On the New York Stock Exchange a horde of brokers, commanded by the celebrated manipulator "Jim" Keene created a semblance of tremendous activity. Within a month Steel Common advanced from 38 to 55 and the seven per cent Preferred from 82 to 101. Within a comparatively short time the $25,000,000 underwriting syndicate got its money back in cash, plus 200% in dividends.

The Steel deal initiated a period of wild speculation. Carnegie's young partners, made into multi-millionaires over-night, led the dance. There were forty of them, and some of them quite lost their heads, indulging in freaks of extravagance, buying yachts and divorces, hurling gold this way and that. The public generally joined the orgy. Prices went to the sky. The papers were chock-a-block with tales of sudden fortune that had come to waiters and barbers and clerks.

The Steel Trust—Morgan's great empire of commerce—began business on April 1, 1901. Its organization was modeled after that of Standard Oil. There were twenty-four directors, including (with the exception of E. H. Harriman) every name famous in the industrial annals of the period. Gary headed the all-powerful executive committee. Gary soon saw that his most difficult task lay in welding the human elements. Miss Tarbell tells us:

"There was a will both to speculation and to monopoly represented in the management. More than one of the gentlemen on that board had had the habit of joyfully participating

in great stock market raids. As for monopoly, the concern
which had created and operated the most nearly perfect
monopoly we have seen in the United States—the Standard
Oil Company—was represented by its strongest leaders,
Messieurs John D. Rockefeller, senior and junior, and H. H.
Rogers; and as for stifling competition, the greatest advocate
of that robust policy which ever operated, the Carnegie Company, was represented by Schwab, Frick, and Gayley. The
only one of the twenty-four gentlemen . . . who had openly
and repeatedly declared that the purpose of the concern was
in no way antagonistic to the public good was its chairman,
Judge Gary. But Judge Gary, we must remember, was Mr.
Morgan's chosen spokesman."

Gary soon found that he was in a nest of thieves.
These fellows played the game heartlessly. He had to
lecture them even upon primary ethics. The first nine
months of operation showed net earnings for the Steel
Corporation of $85,000,000. Gary immediately gave
the report to the newspapers. This outraged some of the
directors who wanted a chance to clean up on the stock
market. They were natural gamblers, fellows like H. H.
Rogers, Norman Ream and P. A. B. Widener, and they
even tossed heads-and-tails for the $20 gold pieces of
absentee associates. It was all very bewildering to Gary.
Morgan had made Schwab president of the Steel
Corporation. Reared in the rough Carnegie school,
Schwab worked constantly at cross-purposes with Gary.
Schwab had been accustomed to a free rein. Gaily he
frolicked in his new environment. Schwab's salary, the
papers said, was a million a year. Chairman Gary, when
asked, stated frankly that the Steel Corporation was

paying Schwab exactly one-tenth of this amount. Nevertheless, the buoyant, energetic Schwab continued to draw the headlines.

There were other points of conflict, no less sharply defined. When Gary came to New York he believed that the charges of immoralities and irregularities against Big Business were the mere mouthings of irresponsible demagogues. Sadly, through actual experience, he came to recognize that many of the men who controlled Big Business possessed the morality of alley cats.

Was Pierpont Morgan also a crook? Gary could not believe it. Yet, intangibly, he had begun to feel a withdrawal of Morgan's support. In his simple, direct manner he brought the matter to a focus. He went to the bank and told Morgan he thought his usefulness to the Steel Corporation was over. Morgan seemed shocked. Gary told of his troubles in his efforts to play fair with the public and to consider the good of the Corporation and the stockholders—not the personal advantages of individual directors and officers.

"I didn't know that you felt this way, Judge Gary," said Morgan. "Now, you remain where you are and, from this time on, when you want me to do anything or say anything, all you have to do is to tell me. You needn't explain. Just say, 'Do so and so' and I will do it."

Morgan kept his word.

The steel merger focused attention sharply upon the growth of the trusts. Everywhere thoughtful men were asking how far the concentration of power and wealth in a few hands was to be permitted to go. The plain people believed that Wall Street controlled the Government and scowled blackly at mention of such names as Morgan and Rockefeller. The people cried aloud for a champion. One was at hand in the person of the many-sided Theodore Roosevelt who, by the accident of assassination, had succeeded in the White House the conservative, Fabian-minded McKinley.

The new President, young, vigorous, eager to make a record, determined to show the kings of capital that they were not greater than government. He selected as the object of his first spectacular demonstration Pierpont Morgan, acknowledged master of the monopolists.

CHAPTER THIRTEEN

ROOSEVELT VERSUS MORGAN—NORTHERN
SECURITIES SUIT

LATE ON THE AFTERNOON OF WEDNESDAY, FEBRUARY 19, 1902, after the Stock Exchange had closed, news wires from Washington flashed a brief announcement of Philander C. Knox, attorney-general in President Roosevelt's cabinet. "The Government," it read in effect, "has decided to test the legality of the recent merger of the Northern Pacific and Great Northern railroad companies. Under the Sherman Anti-trust Act of 1890 a bill in equity will soon be filed in the Federal courts. The Government will demand the dissolution of the Northern Securities Company."

The Northern Securities Company was a gigantic holding concern engineered by Pierpont Morgan and James J. Hill to control the Northern Pacific, Great Northern and Chicago, Burlington & Quincy roads. It had been incorporated November 12, 1901, in New Jersey with a capital of $400,000,000—"a capital large enough," explained Morgan subsequently, "so that nobody could ever buy it." Morgan, Hill and their associates were determined to prevent for all time another such daring raid as E. H. Harriman had made upon Northern Pacific the preceding spring.

Until the dramatic announcement of Knox not the

slightest intimation had come that President Roosevelt, but five months in office, intended to launch the first of his historic measures to control the corporations. In fact, the President had confided his purpose only to the head of his law department.

Not since the assassination of President McKinley had Wall Street been given such a shock. Stocks dropped like lead. A cyclone of attack centred upon Roosevelt and Knox. The former was called a dangerous demagogue; the latter a little country lawyer who was swimming beyond his depth. These were the mildest of the epithets that poured from the moneyed interests and the predominating portion of the press. Roosevelt was accused of flouting the Supreme Court of the United States. Under an exactly parallel case in 1895, it was recalled, the high tribunal had decreed, by a vote of eight to one, that a corporation could acquire all the stock of other corporations through exchange of its securities for theirs. The precedent had been set in the so-called Knight case—an action brought against the Sugar Trust by the Cleveland administration.

Here and there the denunciations of the new President were varied by expressions of approval. While eminent lawyers, conservative newspapers, and most Leaders of Public Opinion were emptying their vials upon him, plentiful evidence came to Roosevelt that he had struck a responsive chord in the breasts of Abraham Lincoln's "plain people." Thousands of heartening messages poured into the White House from the crossroads. Bewildered, harassed, frightened by the economic monsters that had grown up among them, the people saw in Roosevelt the prophet of a new social creed. Soon the restless and combative man in the White House—practised in politics as in life—realized that his challenge to the trusts was approved by the masses.

At 23 Wall Street, however, the atmosphere was sulphurous. Morgan was almost apoplectic in his wrath. He summoned his lawyers. These eminent gentlemen assured him that Roosevelt had reached the limit of folly. There was no doubt, they said, that the courts would properly chastise the revolutionary Roosevelt and his obscure legal adviser Knox. Why, in the Knight case, the Supreme Court had held that exchange of stock between corporations was not "commerce" under the Sherman Act, even though such exchange created a monopoly in the necessaries of life.

Roosevelt knew this. But seven years had passed since the Knight decision. People were thinking on different lines. He believed he could force a more responsive interpretation of the Sherman law even from the traditionally hesitant Supreme Court. "It was necessary," he says in his autobiography, "to reverse the Knight case in the interest of the people against monopoly and privilege just as it had been necessary to reverse the Dred Scott case in the interest of the people against slavery and privilege."

While the excitement was at fever heat Morgan charged down to Washington and strode in upon Roosevelt and Knox. It was a dramatic meeting. Morgan could see in Roosevelt's purpose only an outrageous violation of vested rights. Angrily he berated Roosevelt for failure to give him warning. "That is just what we

did not want to do," replied Roosevelt, his jaw set, eyes
and teeth gleaming.

Morgan was in a high state of emotion. "If we have
done anything wrong," he exclaimed, "send your man
[referring to Knox] to my man [mentioning one of his
attorneys] and they can fix it up."

Roosevelt regarded the fuming financier—twenty
years his senior—in amazement. "That can't be done,"
he grated. To which Knox added: "We don't want to
fix it up. We want to stop it."

"Are you going to attack my other interests, the Steel
Corporation and the others?" demanded Morgan.

"Certainly not," replied the President, "unless we
find out that in any case they have done something that
we regard as wrong."

According to Joseph Bucklin Bishop, Roosevelt's
intimate friend and editor of his papers, Roosevelt
turned to Knox after Morgan had retired and remarked:
"That is a most illuminating illustration of the Wall
Street point of view. Mr. Morgan could not help regarding me as a big rival operator, who either intended to
ruin all his interests or else could be induced to come
to an agreement to ruin none."

Morgan, still sizzling with anger, returned to his hotel
and wrote a wrathful letter to Roosevelt. It was so intemperate in tone that one of the Morgan lawyers persuaded
him to destroy it. From now on Roosevelt became Morgan's pet dislike. Because of the complete distortion of
his own point of view, the financier could see nothing
good in Roosevelt. He detested the latter's theatricalism.
"The man's a lunatic," he once told a common friend

who sought to bring them together. "He is worse than a Socialist." In Morgan's ample vocabulary of invective there was no word more scornful than "Socialist."

Morgan looked forward eagerly to Roosevelt's return to private life. Indeed, in the summer of 1903, the undisputed king of finance was willing to join even his ancient foemen of the Standard Oil in grooming Marcus Alonzo Hanna for the Presidency. "I'd even vote the Democratic ticket to get that fellow out of the White House," he growled. "If he had his way we'd all do business with glass pockets."

Elbert H. Gary and Dr. W. S. Rainsford were among those who sought to temper Morgan's bitterness. "The time will come," Rainsford indignantly told Morgan on one occasion, "when you will get down on your knees and bless Providence for having given us Theodore Roosevelt as our President." If the vision of Morgan and of the small group of conquering men who controlled practically all the floating capital of the country had not been so myopic, cursory examination of Roosevelt's career would have warned them of a coming collision. Throughout his long experience in politics, beginning as an assemblyman in the New York State legislature, Roosevelt had shown that he was responsive to fresh currents in both social and political thought.

When he accidentally came into the Presidency on September 14, 1901, Morgan and the other great corporation promoters were somewhat perturbed. But his first annual message in December lulled them. The new executive advised "caution in dealing with corporations," because "to strike with ignorant violence at the interests of one set of men almost inevitably endangers the interests of all," and because "the mechanism of modern business is so delicate that extreme care must be taken not to interfere with it in a spirit of rashness or ignorance."

The captains of industry paid scant attention to other assertions in the same message: that "there are real and grave evils, one of the chief being overcapitalization"; that "combination and concentration should be, not prohibited, but supervised and within reasonable limits controlled," and that "corporations engaged in interstate commerce should be regulated if they are found to exercise a license working to the public injury."

From these thoughts grew Roosevelt's policies and the Northern Securities prosecution. "The case, in my opinion," writes Alexander Noyes, "was such that any and all available measures for protection of the public welfare would have been invoked by any government resolved on challenging the pretensions of the great promoters of the day. . . . In my judgment, the overthrow of the Northern Securities combination was the most positive achievement of the Roosevelt Administration in the field of corporation finance. . . . The promoters of the Northern Securities were traveling on a path of capital inflation which logically had no end except in eventual exhaustion of credit and general bankruptcy."

The Northern Securities Company has been described as "the most promising machinery ever contrived for a complete monopoly." The $400,000,000 merger inflamed the public, particularly in the Northwest, where people saw in it merely another scheme of the corpora-tions to extort additional revenue by throttling compe-tition. So bitter was the criticism that James J. Hill was moved to publish a signed statement in his *St. Paul Globe,* denying sinister intent and describing the genesis and purposes of the Northern Securities plan from his point of view:

"Several of the gentlemen who have long been interested in the Great Northern Railway and its predecessor, the St. Paul, Minneapolis & Manitoba Company, and who have al-ways been among its largest shareholders, but not the holders of a majority of its stock, whose ages are from seventy to eighty-six years, have desired to combine their individual holdings in corporate form, and in that way secure permanent protection for their interests and a continuation of the policy and management which had done so much for the develop-ment of the Northwest and the enhancement of their own property in the Northwest and elsewhere. Out of this desire has grown the Northern Securities Company.

"It became necessary (in order to prevent the Northern Pacific from passing under the control of the Union Pacific interests and with it the joint control of the Burlington) to pay off the seventy-five millions of Northern Pacific pre-ferred. The enormous amount of cash required for this pur-pose, from a comparatively small number of men, made it necessary for them to act together in a large and permanent manner through the medium of a corporation; and the North-ern Securities Company afforded them the means of accom-plishing this object without the necessity of creating a separate company to finance the transaction for the Northern Pacific. . . . The Northern Securities Company is organized to deal in high-class securities; to hold the same for the benefit of its shareholders, and to advance the interests of the corporations whose securities it owns. Its powers do not include the operation of railways, banking, or mining, or the buying and selling of securities or properties of others on commission; it is purely an investment company; and the object of its creation was simply to enable those who hold its stock to continue their respective interests in association together; to prevent such interests from being scattered by death or otherwise, and to provide against such attacks as had been made upon the Northern Pacific by a rival and competing interest."

Hill's emollient words did not still the clamor. Nevertheless, Northern Securities completed its plan of organization, accepting stock of both Great Northern and Northern Pacific and allotting its own shares in return. Harriman turned in his Northern Pacific stock and received some $82,500,000 in shares of the new holding company. Then Roosevelt threw his bomb.

Nice legal issues were involved in the suit which the Government filed in the United States Circuit Court for the district of Minnesota on March 10, 1902. The Government charged that the Northern Securities Company was "a virtual consolidation of two competing transcontinental lines," whereby not only would "monopoly of the interstate and foreign commerce, formerly carried on by them as competitors, be created," but, through use of the same machinery, "the entire railway systems of the country may be absorbed, merged, and consolidated."

In April, 1903, the lower court decided for the Government, holding that the merger "destroyed every motive for competition between the two roads engaged in interstate traffic, which were natural competitors for business." The Circuit Court brushed aside the plea that Northern Securities had been inspired by "wholly laudable and unselfish motives" and that it was "the initial and necessary step in the accomplishment of great designs." Even granting these contentions, the combination was illegal, the Court held, if it *had power* to "suppress competition between two or more parallel and competing lines of railroad engaged in interstate commerce"—whether the power had been so employed or not. Northern Securities was therefore enjoined from voting stock, acquiring additional stock, paying dividends, or exercising corporate control.

Eight thousand pages of records and briefs went to the Supreme Court of the United States for final review. On March 14, 1904, the high court found for the Government by the narrowest possible margin. The Court decreed that "necessarily, the constituent companies ceased, under such a combination, to be in active competition for trade and commerce," and that, independently of overt acts, "the existence of such a combination, and the power acquired by the holding company . . . constitute a menace to, and a restraint upon, that freedom of commerce which Congress intended to recognize and protect."

On this ground four justices decided for the Government and four against. The ninth member, Justice Brewer, dissented from the ultimate application of the principle but voted for dissolution. In his concurring opinion, Justice Brewer drew a surprising picture of the possibilities of further centralization of corporate control.

"If the parties interested in these two railroad companies," he said, "can, through the instrumentality of a holding corporation, place both under one control, then in like manner, as was conceded in the argument of one of the counsel for the appellants, could the control of all the railroad companies in the country be placed in a single corporation. The holders of $201,-000,000 of stock in the Northern Securities Company might organize another corporation to hold their stock in that company, and the new corporation, holding the majority of the stock in the Northern Securities Company, and acting in obedience to the wishes of a majority of its stockholders, would control the action of the Securities Company, and through it the action of the two railroad companies. And this process might be extended until a single corporation whose stock was owned by three or four parties would be in practical control of both roads; or, having before us the possibility of continuation, the control of the whole transportation system of the country."

Justice Holmes voted against the Government. He held that the Sherman Act did not prescribe the rule of "free competition among those engaged in interstate commerce," as the majority held. It merely forbade "restraint of trade or commerce." Justice Holmes asserted that the phrases "restraint of competition" and "restraint of trade" do not have the same meaning; that "restraint of trade," which has "a definite and well-established signification in the common law, means, and has always been understood to mean, a combination made by men engaged in a certain business for the purpose of keeping other men out of that business. . . . The objection to trusts was not the union of former competitors, but the sinister power exercised, or supposed to be exercised, by the combination, in keeping rivals out of the business. . . . It was the ferocious extreme of competition with others, not the cessation of competition among the partners, which was the evil feared. . . . Much trouble is caused by substituting other phrases, assumed to be equivalent, which are then argued from as if they were in the Act. The court below argued as if maintaining competition were the express purpose of the Act. The Act says nothing about competition."

The decision of the Supreme Court had an almost indescribable effect upon the public mind. The people did not grasp the legal technicalities. But they did grasp the fact that "Teddy" had licked Wall Street, and they rejoiced accordingly. Roosevelt was toasted as a popular idol and lifted many steps nearer the triumphant victory he was to win at the polls the following fall.

In the other camp there was a different reaction. The decision stunned Morgan and enraged the lords of High Finance. A director of the Steel Corporation introduced a resolution instructing Chairman Gary to make no more visits to the White House. Alone, almost, among the captains of industry, Gary saw what Roosevelt was aiming at and was in sympathy with him. He believed the Government had a perfect right to investigate and

supervise the corporations. Gary's point of view was so
unexpected that Roosevelt had taken him to his bosom
and often invited him to join those informal gatherings
at the White House that made the Roosevelt régime so
enjoyable to a variety of visitors.

Now, Gary turned white with anger and defended
Roosevelt—in the very teeth of the men Morgan had
placed upon the Steel board as representatives of vested
capital. They listened—"Pete" Widener, Rockefeller,
Jr., Frick, and the others. And, when the usually patient
Gary paused, H. H. Rogers of the Standard Oil (Rogers
of all men!) moved that the motion be tabled. "Gentlemen," Rogers addressed the bickering board, "Judge
Gary has handled this Corporation very well to date.
I believe that he should be his own judge as to what is
wise and necessary in the present situation."

The offending resolution was tabled.

Distribution of Northern Securities assets revived the
old quarrel between Morgan and Harriman. Morgan
decided to distribute Northern Securities stock pro rata
—giving each owner of one share of Northern Securities
$39.27 in Northern Pacific stock and $30.17 in Great
Northern. This did not at all please Harriman. He
wanted to get back just what he had put in—slightly
more than a majority of Northern Pacific stock; and
carried his contention into the courts. He was defeated
and forced to accept Great Northern as well as Northern
Pacific stock. Harriman felt that he had been gypped,
and grumbled. However, the unwelcome apportionment
proved a blessing in disguise. For, in an extraordinary
stock market boom a year or so later, he disposed of the

securities forced upon him at a net profit of about
$58,000,000. "Harriman's greatest achievement," re-
marked Thomas Woodlock, a railroad expert, "was to
get licked in a fight and to pull out of it with a colossal
fortune as the result."

Harriman's Union Pacific treasury—the $58,000,000
added to other windfalls—was now bursting with quick
assets, and Harriman was swift to take advantage of his
position. He launched a new campaign of expansion.
He invested more than $130,000,000 in the securities
of nine railroads extending from ocean to ocean and
from the Great Lakes to the Gulf. His influence became
powerful in a network of lines reaching every part of
the United States.

"These purchases had a hostile effect upon public
opinion," says Otto Kahn. "They lent color to the impression that Mr. Harriman was aiming at a gigantic
illegal monopoly of the railroad industry." This, possibly, was just what Harriman *was* aiming at. And,
assuredly, the avaricious little genius of the rails could
not afford to pause for so puny a consideration as public
opinion.

Meanwhile, Morgan was reaching further into the
railroad field—applying his own pruning process, elimi-
nating small railroads or absorbing them into his own
great systems. In April, 1902, Bad Boy John W. Gates
provoked a flurry that caused Morgan to shuffle into
realignment the railroads of the South. The Louisville
& Nashville had issued $5,000,000 worth of new stock.
A bear raid was promptly launched on the Exchange.
Gates and Edwin Hawley jumped in, bought majority

control and threatened to form a corner and squeeze the shorts. A less menacing situation was created, though it resembled the Northern Pacific panic of recent and sour memory.

Morgan took hold. He dispatched one of his partners to Gates to obtain an option on the Louisville & Nashville. The Morgan missionary routed Gates out of bed at the Waldorf-Astoria Hotel in New York at three o'clock in the morning. "All right," said Gates, rubbing his eyes, "you fellows can have the road. But you gotta pay me and my friends a bonus of $10,000,000."

Morgan stood for the hold-up.

He did not at all relish the idea of Gates' competing with his Southern Railway. "I do not wish to impugn any man's ability," Morgan afterwards told the Interstate Commerce Commission, "but I did not consider that Mr. Gates was a proper person to manage the Louisville & Nashville Railroad. He was a dangerous element in the railroad world. He represented a stock exchange pool. They were not looking after the transportation interests of the South in any way, shape, or manner. They were looking after the profit of the transaction itself."

With the Gates cloud evaporating, Morgan sailed for Europe. He needed a vacation. The past year had been the most strenuous of his crowded life. At times he felt twinges that the doctors thought might indicate approaching gout. He was sixty-five and he still lived as high and smoked as heavily as at thirty. Also, he was concerned over an infection of the face—a growth of several years—that showed most sharply in an enormous excrescence upon his nose. The disfigurement worried him. He had always worshipped beauty and virility. He liked to be surrounded by comely folk. A homely man had no chance of being selected a Morgan partner! The Street had a saying: "When the angels of God take unto themselves as wives the daughters of men—the result is Morgan partners!"

Morgan became intensely sensitive over the mystifying growth upon his nose. While in Europe, on this trip, he investigated and was treated, without appreciable result, by a Danish electric light "cure" which Queen Alexandra had been instrumental in having introduced into several London hospitals. The lights were used in treating both cancer and tuberculosis, and had been employed successfully in many cases of lupus, a malignant affection of the skin of the face.

While Morgan was in Europe, George W. Perkins wrestled with the Louisville & Nashville problem. Perkins was Morgan's latest recruit. Perkins was an able, self-made man—a former grocery clerk. "I began life sorting lemons," he once wrote a friend, in jocular mood. "I have been doing it ever since." He had been drawn into the firm of Morgan & Co. from the insurance field. He was a handy man to have about, thoroughly familiar with finance in general and insurance practices in particular. In placing their tremendous stock and bond issues Morgan and the other great promoters had not overlooked the huge reservoirs of capital in the coffers of the life insurance companies.

When he eliminated Gates from Louisville & Nashville, Morgan's first impulse had been to attach this road to his Southern Railway system through the medium of a Southern Securities Company. Roosevelt rearranged this scheme for him. For L. & N. and the Southern were plainly competitive, and, moreover, the South had been aroused against such alliances. But Louisville & Nashville was a prize and soon the Seaboard Air Line and the Atlantic Coast Line were actively bidding for it. In Morgan's absence, John Skelton Williams, president of the Seaboard, called upon Perkins and asked the privilege of buying in the L. & N.

"No," explained Perkins, frankly, "we won't sell to the Seaboard. In fact, we are not willing to sell to any system we can't control."

"You mean that you won't sell to the Atlantic Coast Line, either, unless you can control it?" asked Williams.

"I do mean it," replied Perkins.

Soon Perkins was in touch with Henry Walters of Baltimore, president of the Atlantic Coast Line—later to become Morgan's "Secretary of Railroads" in the nomenclature of the Street. Walters was a remarkable railroad operator. He and two associates owned the $10,500,000 holding company which controlled the Atlantic Coast Line.

Morgan, directing the matter mostly by cable, formed an alliance with Walters similar to his pact with Hill. In that spring of 1902, there began a magical massing of mileage that multiplied the size of the Atlantic Coast Line fivefold in a few months—from 2,100 to 11,000 miles. The Atlantic Coast Line absorbed the Plant system of roads as well as the Louisville & Nashville; and with the Southern purchased the "Monon" route into Chicago.

"This sudden building-up," writes John Moody, "was done by the now very general practice of taking stocks from the hands of the public and replacing them with bonds; that is, by buying stocks for the corporation with money raised by selling its bonds. The result was an astonishing step in the centralizing of railroad control. The Atlantic Coast Line Company was one of those extraordinary legal structures, the holding companies, which were being devised at that period to concentrate the control of railroad properties in a few hands. When the aggregation made under it by Morgan was complete, this corporation, with $10,500,000 of stock and $13,000,000 of debt certificates, controlled a majority of the $50,000,000 stock of the Atlantic Coast Line road; this, in turn, had its big issues of bonds, and also owned a majority of the Louisville & Nashville stock. This also had great bond issues. By this continuous splitting of stock into fractions and the issue of bonds, the control of $470,000,000 of stocks and bonds in public hands was placed in the $10,500,000 worth of stock of the Atlantic Coast Line Company. One share over half of this, $5,250,100, would control the great whole, a capital ninety times its own size."

By these methods, independent railroads were fast disappearing into the maw of the great systems. In the latter, Morgan was the common denominator and therefore the most powerful individual force among the Giants of the Rails—Hill, Harriman, Henry Walters, and Alexander J. Cassatt, chief of the Pennsylvania.

This was the picture at the close of 1902. But, after the dissolution of Northern Securities, Harriman rose like a rocket. The insatiable little man began a drive that brought him into New York. Armed with his huge Northern Securities profits (thrown into his lap, ironically enough, by Morgan) Harriman bought the Illinois Central; half of the Pennsylvania's forty per cent of the Baltimore & Ohio; great blocks of Atchison, Topeka & Sante Fé. He capped his exploits by edging into New York Central—Morgan's holy of holies. He secured eight per cent of the Central's stock. His associates—William Rockefeller and Rogers of the Standard Oil, Henry Frick and others—owned as much more. Their combined holdings were larger than those of either Morgan or the Vanderbilts. It was a bitter pill for Morgan when Harriman broke into the Central. But he did not oppose the purchase.

Harriman, Morgan had discovered, was as difficult to fight as a flea. He was here one moment, gone the next, a master of stock manipulation, a magnificent practical railroad operator, and fully imbued with the notion that Destiny fought on his side. In a few years Harriman piled up a fortune of almost $100,000,000 and drew uncomfortably close to Morgan's leadership of the inner circle of railroad monopolists.

By an apparently inevitable force, capital was converging into the hands of a few. "The wonder of the movement, the thing that flashed danger to the imagination of the public," writes John Moody, "was that this process was cumulative. It was not that ten or twenty or fifty men could get together in a room and devise an artificial holding company. . . . No body of men could do that. The fear came from the fact that here was an irresistible natural movement of railroad capital into one central mass; and that that mass was controlled as inevitably by a group of men whose number would continually grow smaller."

As 1902 drew to a close, Morgan and his allies were in possession of three of the four rich railroad domains of the country—the Northwest, the South, and the East. Coal, cotton, wheat, oil, steel, textiles, all paid them tribute. Morgan's prestige was at the peak. But there was a period of reaction ahead—a period which would force a scattering of capital and a broadening, somewhat, in the ownership of American enterprises.

This fateful era was ushered in by an industrial crisis in which Theodore Roosevelt again clashed with and defeated the Masters of Money.

CHAPTER FOURTEEN

DARK DAYS

IN THE AUTUMN OF 1902 THE COUNTRY FACED A FUEL
famine. Since spring a strike of 150,000 miners had
tied up the great anthracite coal regions of Pennsylvania. Riots had broken out. Twenty men had been
killed, much property destroyed. At times the trouble
seemed to approach civil war.

Under the capable leadership of John Mitchell the
miners—men of many races—stood firm for union
recognition and better wages and working conditions.
The operators had refused to treat with the men or
recognize in the slightest their right to collective bargaining. The chief of the operators was George F. Baer,
an able though violent man. Baer was president of the
Philadelphia & Reading Railway. In dealing with his
employees he sought to apply the principles of feudal-
ism, then being rapidly and happily swept away. "Hands
off" was his motto so far as any and all outside interference was concerned. His attitude had been suc-
cinctly expressed in July to a correspondent who wrote
beseeching him to compromise on humanitarian grounds.
"I beg you not to be discouraged," replied the leader of
the operators. "The rights and interest of the laboring
man will be protected and cared for—not by the labor
agitators but by the Christian men to whom God in His

infinite wisdom has given control of the property interests of the country."

Friends explained that Baer's words were ironic. If
so, it was an unfortunate time for irony. From then
on the peppery, bearded president of the Reading was
known as Divine Right Baer.

As summer swept into autumn flickerings of unrest
showed here and there. In several communities citizens
seized loaded coal-cars. It was certain the cold weather
would bring appalling suffering. Governors and mayors
issued warnings of possible fuel riots. President Roosevelt was urged to intervene. Roosevelt had noted the
growing tension with increasing concern. Although he
had no legal power he determined to force arbitration.

Most of the anthracite mines were owned by the coal-
carrying railroads, and J. P. Morgan, as nearly as any
one man, controlled the railroads. Morgan's feeling for
Roosevelt was certainly not friendly, yet the latter knew
that Morgan was the one medium whereby he could
force the obstinate operators into a parley. Accordingly, the last week in September, he summoned to
Oyster Bay that eminent political gumshoe artist, Senator Mark Hanna of Ohio.

Hanna had been McKinley's mentor and knew his
way about Wall Street. Roosevelt found him useful in
executing such confidential missions as the one which he
now proposed. Roosevelt asked Hanna to see Morgan
and seek the financier's influence in bringing about a
conference. Hanna's mission failed. Morgan was willing
to advise the operators to go into conference but refused to *order* them to do so. Hanna reported to Roose-

velt in a letter dated September 28, 1902: "Confidentially I saw Mr. Mitchell (the public knows nothing about that). I got from Mr. Morgan a proposition as to what he would do in the matter. And I got Mitchell to agree to accept it, if the *operators* would abide by the decision. I really felt encouraged—to think I was about to accomplish a settlement. I went to Philadelphia and saw Mr. Baer, and to my surprise he absolutely refused to entertain it. You can see how determined they are. It looks as if it was only to be settled when the miners are *starved* to it. And that may be weeks ahead, as they are getting liberal supplies from their fellow-workmen all over the country."

The following day Roosevelt sent a more imperative message to Morgan. This was carried by Elihu Root, Secretary of War in the Roosevelt cabinet. Roosevelt warned Morgan to advise the operators that he intended shortly to take radical action "in reference to their business unless they wake up." The ultimatum brought results.

Operators and miners met the President at the White House on October 3. It was an exciting conclave. "Only one man in the room was calm," Roosevelt remarked later. "It was not I. It was John Mitchell." The President appealed to both sides on patriotic grounds. The operators were deaf. They denounced the miners as anarchists. They shouted that the administration ought to sue the union for violating the Sherman Anti-Trust Act. The meeting broke up in disorder.

Now Roosevelt determined upon drastic measures. He would appoint an arbitration commission of his own. He wrote confidentially to Grover Cleveland and obtained the former President's consent to serve. Organizing a commission, however, would take time, and time was pressing. Thereupon Roosevelt decided upon a daring stratagem, one that he frankly confessed was unconstitutional. He describes it in his autobiography:

"The method of action upon which I had determined in the last resort was to get the Governor of Pennsylvania to ask me to keep order. Then I would put in the Army under the command of some first-rate general. I would instruct this general to keep absolute order, taking any steps whatever that were necessary to prevent interference by the strikers or their sympathizers with men who wanted to work. I would also instruct him to dispossess the operators and run the mines as a receiver until such time as the commission might make its report and until I, as President, might issue further orders in view of this report. I had to find a man who possessed the necessary good sense, judgment, and nerve to act in such event. He was ready to hand in the person of Major-General Scofield.

"I sent for him, telling him that if I had to make use of him it would be because the crisis was only less serious than that of the Civil War, that the action taken would be practically a war measure, and that if I sent him he must act in a purely military capacity under me as Commander-in-Chief, paying no heed to any authority, judicial or otherwise, except mine. He was a fine fellow—a most respectable-looking old boy, with side whiskers and a black skull cap, without any of the outward aspect of the conventional military dictator; but in both nerve and judgment he was all right, and he answered quietly that if I gave the order he would take possession of the mines, and would guarantee to open them and to run them without permitting any interference either by the owners or the strikers or anybody else, so long as I told him to stay. I then saw Senator Quay who, like every other responsible man in high position, was greatly wrought up over the condition of things. I told him that he need be under no alarm as to the problem not being solved, that I was going to make another effort to get the operators and miners to come together, but that I would solve the problem in any event and get coal; that, however, I did not wish to tell him anything of the details of my intention, but merely to have him arrange that whenever I gave the word the Governor of Pennsylvania should request me to intervene; that when this was done I would be responsible for all that followed and would guarantee that the coal famine would end forthwith. The Senator made no inquiry or comment and merely told me that he in his turn would guarantee that the Governor would request my intervention the minute I asked that the request be made.

"These negotiations were conducted with the utmost secrecy, General Scofield being the only man who knew exactly what my plan was, and Senator Quay, two members of my cabinet, and ex-President Cleveland and the other men whom I proposed to put on the commission, the only other men who knew that I had a plan. . . . I personally saved a good deal of trouble by being able to avoid this drastic action. At the time I should have been almost unanimously supported. With the famine upon them the people would not have tolerated any conduct that would have thwarted what I was doing."

Once the problem was solved, Roosevelt believed, his enemies "would have plucked up heart and begun a campaign against me." Rather naïvely he adds: "I doubt if they could have accomplished much anyway,

for the only effective remedy against me would have
been impeachment, and that they would not have ventured to try."

Morgan apparently suspected some such design of
the President. He had learned that Roosevelt was a man
of quick and decisive action. The operators suddenly
changed front and agreed to discuss arbitration. Secretary Root went to New York and cruised for hours
with Morgan on the *Corsair*. They drafted an agreement for a commission to be appointed by Roosevelt.
The operators signed the agreement with the single
modification that the arbitrators should be selected
from certain specified classes—an Army engineer, a
business man familiar with the coal trade, a judge of
the locality, a sociologist, etc. The miners, in turn, asked
that Bishop John L. Spalding of Illinois be appointed;
also that E. E. Clark, chief of the Order of Railway
Conductors, be given the place which called for a
"sociologist." Morgan sent his partners, Bacon and Perkins, to Washington for the final conference. Bacon
had been a classmate of Roosevelt at Harvard.

A lively account of the final agreement appears in a
letter Roosevelt wrote to his friend, Senator Lodge, on
October 17, 1902, and which appears in J. B. Bishop's
"Theodore Roosevelt and His Time":

"The crisis came at the last moment. Between the hours of
ten P. M. and 1 A. M. I had Bacon and Perkins on here, on
behalf of Morgan but really representing the operators.
Neither Morgan nor anyone else had been able to do much
with those wooden-headed gentry, and Bacon and Perkins
were literally almost crazy. Bacon in particular had become

so excited that I was quite concerned over his condition. The operators had limited me down by a full proviso to five different types of men, including 'an eminent sociologist.' This was a ridiculous proviso because I could have appointed bad men in any case and yet have been kept to its letter; and they ought to have given me a free hand. The miners, on the other hand, wanted me to appoint at least two extra members myself, or in some fashion to get Bishop Spalding (whom I myself wanted) and the labor union man on the commission. I regarded their contention as perfectly reasonable, and so informed Bacon and Perkins and the operators. The operators refused point-blank to have another man appointed, and Bacon and Perkins came on nearly wild to say that they had full power to treat on behalf of the operators, but that no extra man should be added. Finally it developed that what they meant was that no extra man should be added if he was a representative of organized labor; and argue as I could, nothing could make them change; although they grew more and more hysterical, and not merely admitted, but insisted, that the failure to agree meant probable violence and possible social war.

"It took me about two hours before I at last grasped the fact that the mighty brains of these captains of industry had formulated the theory that they would rather have anarchy than tweedledum, but if I would use the word tweedledee they would hail it as meaning peace. In other words that they had not the slightest objection to my appointing a labor man as an 'eminent sociologist' and adding Bishop Spalding on my own account, but they preferred to see the Red Commune come rather than to have me make Bishop Spalding or anyone else the 'eminent sociologist' and add the labor man. I instantly told them that I had not the slightest objection to doing an absurd thing when it was necessary to meet the objection of

an absurd mind on some vital point, and that I would cheer-
fully appoint my labor man as the 'eminent sociologist.' It
was almost impossible for me to appreciate the instant and
tremendous relief this gave them. They saw nothing offensive
in my language and nothing ridiculous in the proposition, and
Pierpont Morgan and Baer, when called up by telephone,
eagerly ratified the absurdity; and accordingly, at this utterly
unimportant price, we bid fair to come out of as dangerous
a situation as I ever dealt with."

The men went back to work and the commission began an exhaustive investigation, reporting to the President March 21, 1903. The principal findings were: ten
per cent increase in wages for the miners; equal treat-
ment for union and non-union labor; and appointment
of a permanent board of conciliation.

Both sides hailed the commission's verdict as a victory. It was really the public that won the victory.
Homes were heated that winter. Morgan and Baer had
learned that when the public jumps into the ring no
champion can stand up against it.

This was a sombre period for Morgan.

For the first time failure attended one of his great
schemes. Promotion of the International Mercantile
Marine proved a dismal fiasco. I. M. M. was a shipping
combination designed to knit into one operating unit
the leading American, British, and German steamship
lines, passenger and freight. Eight companies came in:
White Star, Atlantic Transport, International Naviga-
tion, American and Red Star, Mississippi & Dominion
Steamship Company, Dominion Line, Leyland Line,
and National Steamship Company. But the British Gov-

ernment, by hastily contrived subsidy, kept the Cunard Line out; and the German companies remained aloof.

Morgan's underwriting syndicate had agreed to make a preliminary payment of $25,000,000 in gold in London. Morgan expected to obtain this amount and much more from the sale of some of the $120,000,000 stock to American investors. The so-called "Rich Men's Panic" of 1903 knocked the scheme galley-west. Forcible feeding of securities had been worked to the limit, and the public could digest no more. Indeed, there was so much selling that the market was dragged down to new low levels. The depression was general. U. S. Steel preferred dropped from par to 49; the common from 50 to 8.

Judge Gary came over to the Bank and recommended that dividend payments be suspended on Steel common. Morgan argued against it for two days. Finally, he said, wearily: "All right, my dear boy. Do as you think best." It was a bitter blow. The Steel Corporation was the pride of his heart.

Morgan was able to meet the $25,000,000 I. M. M. payment by ransacking the country for agricultural bills of exchange; but his syndicate was compelled to take and carry the stock it had subscribed for. The steamship combination staggered along for years. It did not justify itself nor become a paying proposition until dowered with the artificial profits of the Great War.

Now came another episode that caused a mighty decrease in Morgan's prestige. The United States Shipbuilding Company, a strangely financed $50,000,000 combination, collapsed with an exposure of crookedness that seemed to affect not only the judgment but the moral integrity of the House of Morgan. The promoters of the Shipbuilding Trust, as it was dubbed, were Lewis Nixon and D. LeRoy Dresser, president of a newly formed trust company with a highfalutin' title —the Trust Company of the Republic. Neither Nixon nor Dresser was a practical financier. They drew into their scheme eight oddly assorted plants extending from Maine to California.

The new trust was already wobbling when Charles M. Schwab chanced to meet Nixon and Dresser at luncheon, and proposed that they include in their combination the Bethlehem Steel Company. Without Morgan's knowledge Schwab had bought the Bethlehem a few months before as a private speculation. He was then president of the Steel Corporation and in constant friction with the executive committee. Possibly fearing that the brilliant Schwab would use Bethlehem as a nucleus for a rival steel trade creation, Morgan served blunt notice that the Steel executive must get rid of Bethlehem. He gave him a year to find a purchaser, meanwhile himself taking custody of the company.

In their eagerness to add a substantial property to their collection of "cats and dogs," Nixon and Dresser signed a contract with Schwab that gave the latter control of their combination. Schwab received $30,000,-000 in U. S. Shipbuilding stocks and bonds, and voting power was conferred upon his bonds. In return for carrying Bethlehem for him and other services, Schwab allotted $5,000,000 worth of shipbuilding stock to Morgan & Company. This stock was pooled, together with that of the other insiders, and included in what was known as a "sell mine first" agreement. This was a device whereby stock houses pushed upon the public at advantageous prices the holdings of insiders. If an order came in for 1,000 shares of a pooled stock, a block of 500, say, would be purchased on the curb. The other 500 would be supplied from the shares of the pool, thus gradually "working off" on the public the heavy holdings of the insiders. As it happened, the "sell mine first" agreement was not signed by Morgan & Company. But, after the collapse of the shipbuilding scheme, the secret contract was revealed at receiver's hearings and was employed with sensational effect by the newspapers and the bear operators.

Morgan was accused of brutal callousness to the public interest and disregard of considerations other than those of personal profit. He impatiently brushed aside all suggestions that he defend himself.

After the steel merger Morgan had been placed on a pedestal. Not that the public worshipped him precisely as a hero, but people were awed by his achievements. Now there came a complete reversal of attitude. He was called a blunderer, a stock-waterer, a ruthless corsair. The muck-raking era was at hand. Crookedness and graft in high finance swept all other topics out of the headlines. Popular magazines and newspapers campaigned against the masters of capital. Plenty of ammunition was at hand. The great insurance scandal of 1905 alone seemed to justify the most intemperate charges of the muck-rakers.

It had long been suspected that Morgan, Harriman

and the other Goliaths of Gold had employed the funds of the life insurance companies in their great promotions. All the larger promoters and the chief bankers of Wall Street, it was noted, had gradually taken places upon the finance committees of the life insurance companies.

The Big Three insurance companies were the Equitable, the Mutual, and the New York Life. Morgan was identified closely with the latter. Its president, John A. McCall, was spoken of in the Street as a Morgan man. Though the quantity and calibre of their investments was limited by law, the insurance companies edged up on the statutes by organizing subsidiary trust companies. Through them the giant promoters were able to tap the parent funds. The early years of the century witnessed a mushroom growth of trust companies.

Quite by accident, light was cast upon the methods of the insurance companies. A quarrel broke out between James W. Alexander, president, and James Hazen Hyde, vice-president, of the Equitable Life. Equitable was a joint-stock institution with $413,000,000 in total resources; yet with a share capital of but $100,000. Young Hyde (he was but twenty-seven) had inherited $51,000 of the share capital from his father, founder of the company. As a result of the quarrel Equitable trustees appointed a committee to investigate Alexander's charges that Hyde was not a fit person to handle trust funds. Three months later the Frick committee submitted a report that threw a directors' meeting into turmoil and caused a sweeping inquiry by the New York State Legislature. The report asserted that Equitable officers had used the company's funds in subscribing to "underwritings" organized by themselves; that these funds were juggled through three subsidiary trust companies so that the parent company had been unable to use its great cash surpluses for its own legitimate investments.

With Charles Evans Hughes as counsel, the legislative committee, in the final months of 1905, bared the entire history of life insurance finance. It was a sordid story of the reckless use and waste of the policy-holders' money. There had been false bookkeeping, bribery, exorbitant salaries and nepotism, speculation in all manner of promotion—including U. S. Steel and U. S. Shipbuilding.

The Hughes investigation led to new and stringent laws. Also, it had an effect upon the popular mind that can hardly be measured. Though the fraudulent employment of insurance funds apparently had been stopped, the public's misgivings were not lessened by the sale for $2,500,000 of young Hyde's controlling stock to the notorious promoter, Thomas Fortune Ryan; nor by E. H. Harriman's demand upon Ryan for a half-interest in the purchase—"I will take half your stock. I don't know what it cost and I don't care." Control of the Equitable eventually came to Morgan. But that is another story.

In that frenzied period Morgan stood forth as the very symbol of money and power. Soon the pendulum of prosperity was to swing again in a favorable arc and he would return to his place as Boss of all the Bosses in Wall Street. But now he was generally execrated even by his own world—including many who had become enriched by linking destiny with him.

There was no outward indication, in those gloomy days, that Morgan was disturbed in the least by public scorn or desertion of fair-weather friends. At sixty-eight he was still erect and powerful. His smouldering eyes had lost none of their fierceness. His hair had whitened, but his moustache was almost untouched by frost. He was proud, haughty, repellent to all save those of his immediate circle.

He spent longer periods abroad, seeming to revel in the greater freedom of movement permitted in Europe. In European cities he would hire a shabby carriage or hack at random and have it follow him for hours. One afternoon in early July, 1905, an acquaintance saw him standing on a balcony of the Hôtel Bristol in Paris, shouting and whistling for his coachman. The Place Vendôme was crowded and turbulent, and the ancient driver was dozing and deaf. Morgan could not attract his attention. Bareheaded he rushed backward through the white-curtained door, reappeared with a bit of fruit and hurled it at the cabby. It landed neatly atop the latter's tall black hat. The coachman jerked himself into wakefulness, pulled at his reins, and soon Morgan was on his way.

In Rome a carriage and pair always awaited him. Each spring he lengthened his stay in Rome, invariably occupying the same suite of corner rooms in the Grand Hotel. In Italy's capital he frolicked and relaxed and enjoyed a certain freedom of social contact not permitted in New York. In Rome there were a few people for whom Morgan unlocked the inner doorways of his nature. One of these was Salvatore Cortesi, Rome correspondent of the Associated Press. Cortesi was one of the few newspapermen to whom Morgan gave full confidence. Their friendship began when Morgan returned to Italy the gorgeous gold-embroidered Ascoli Cope after he had learned that this famous former possession of Pope Nicholas IV had been stolen. Morgan had paid a large sum for the cope but would accept no financial recompense.

The Italian Government wanted to show its gratitude by presenting an appropriate medal bearing Morgan's likeness. Cortesi was asked to procure profile photographs of the financier. He wired a request to Morgan, who had arrived in Catania on the *Corsair*. A few days later he was summoned to the Grand Hotel where Morgan sat playing solitaire with a Pekinese dog curled at his side. Morgan paced the carpet, inhaling and exhaling great puffs of cigar smoke, while Cortesi explained the Government's urgent need of the photograph. He did not know Morgan's aversion to the camera. Cortesi's plea seemed to be having not the slightest effect, when suddenly Morgan halted him and said: "All right. When shall it be?"

"We might go straight away," suggested Cortesi.

"Let's go then."

They drove to a studio in the Via Nazionale and in a few minutes the pictures had been taken.

Morgan took a fancy to Cortesi and the latter saw him often during his yearly visits to Rome. Cortesi gives us a sketch, all too short, of the Morgan that Rome

knew in his book "My Thirty Years of Friendship."
There was the evening when he and Morgan went to the
Vatican to see Cardinal Merry del Val, then Papal Sec-
retary of State.

Merry del Val occupied the gorgeous Borgia apartment with its vaulted ceiling and famous frescoes by
Pinturicchio. The Secretary of State sent out word
that a meeting of cardinals would delay him a few
minutes. "Tell him not to mind," said Morgan. "I am
perfectly happy here. I only wish I could have a bed,
so that I could lie on my back and remain for hours
looking at this ceiling."

Morgan admired tremendously the ritualism and
splendid organization of the Roman Catholic Church.
He was anxious to meet Pope Pius X; and, in April,
1905, Cortesi arranged a private audience. The chap-
eron noted Morgan's increasing nervousness as they
passed the papal gendarmes and multi-colored Swiss
Guards and made their way through vast halls and
rooms covered with rich carpets and decorated with
tapestries and frescoes. Finally they were taken into
the Pope's private library. Cortesi describes the meeting delightfully:

"Pius X was standing before the open door, dressed entirely
in white, with white slippers and a white *zucchetto*, the only
note of color about his person being a heavy golden chain
around his neck, from which hung a gold pectoral cross. With
his usual sweet paternal smile he motioned us to sit close to
his desk, Mr. Morgan taking a chair directly in front of the
Pope, while I sat at his left between the two. On the desk was
a statue of Joan of Arc on horseback, an artistically carved

bronze inkstand, a crucifix, and a whole sheaf of papers and documents, some of which had been marked in blue pencil by the Pope.

"To my dismay, I noticed that Mr. Morgan's nervousness was matched by that of the Pontiff. Both of them were so embarrassed that they did not know how to begin the conversation. When the silence began to become painful I decided to apply extreme measures in order to save the situation. Taking my courage in both hands, I addressed the Pope in Italian.

" 'Does not Your Holiness think that it would please your visitor' (I purposely avoided mentioning names) 'if you were to tell him how much you appreciate his kindness in wishing to visit you and pay you his respects in person?'

" 'Oh yes, yes!' he exclaimed in Italian, as he could not speak any other language. 'Tell Mr. Morgan how much I appreciate his kindness in coming to visit me.'

"I translated the phrase to Mr. Morgan in English, and he though obviously pleased and relieved that Pius X had been the first to speak, was evidently at a loss for a reply. Again I came to the rescue of the two illustrious personages. Turning to Mr. Morgan, I suggested:

" 'Don't you think that you might tell the Holy Father how glad you are at making his personal acquaintance and how much you appreciate his kindness to you?'

"Mr. Morgan repeated what I had said to him almost word for word.

" 'Yes, yes,' he said, 'tell the Holy Father how glad I am to know him personally and how much I appreciate the kind greeting he has extended to me.'

"The ice had now been broken and, with a little more assistance to both sides, the conversation took its normal course. It lasted over half an hour."

In view of what actually occurred, the Pope's visitors often chuckled over accounts of the meeting that appeared in some newspapers. One journal had the Pope and Morgan strolling in the Vatican gardens, slapping each other on the back and exchanging snuff.

In Rome and elsewhere art-collecting had become an enthralling form of sport to Morgan. Under the supervision of Mrs. Mary McIlvaine, of London, a remarkable woman, and other advisers, the Morgan collections (massive as they were growing) took on definite plan. They represented almost every field of art endeavor since art and history had anything in common. That master mind worked in logical sequence in assembling his matchless examples of the various branches of the fine and applied arts—painting, sculpture, carving, engraving, ceramics, textiles, glass, furniture, jewelry, gold- and silversmiths' work, arms and armor, and the like, examples dating from antiquity to the present era. Whether ivories or illuminated manuscripts, porcelains or pottery, clocks or arms, paintings or miniatures, the collections were visual textbooks and authentic records of art's history from its very dawn.

In London, Morgan housed his treasures—gathered by numerous agents in every corner of Europe—in an art gallery adjoining his Prince's Gate mansion. In 1905 he completed a beautiful building, in the Italian Renaissance style, in East Thirty-sixth Street—the famous Morgan Library. Here he placed priceless books and manuscripts. He was happiest when he retired behind the bronze doors of this Aladdin's palace.

Spurred by great grain and cotton crops of 1905 and 1906, the country resumed its industrial boom on a greater scale than ever before. The Wall Street pot began to boil again. A frenzy of speculation broke out on 'Change. There was an enormous demand for capital not only in America but all over the world. Early in 1906 the rate for demand loans reached 125 per cent. Jacob Schiff solemnly warned the New York Chamber of Commerce that if currency conditions continued "you will have such a panic in this country as will make all previous panics look like child's play." Roosevelt, triumphantly reëlected in 1904, continued his campaign against "malefactors of great wealth." He prosecuted the Standard Oil and the Harriman lines. He forced through the Hepburn Law empowering the Interstate Commerce Commission to fix railroad rates.

Another financial hurricane was sweeping in. Morgan, who had hoped soon to retire, was carried into the very centre of it.

CHAPTER FIFTEEN

"SAVING THE COUNTRY" AGAIN—
PANIC OF 1907

IN SEPTEMBER, 1907, J. P. MORGAN RETURNED FROM a long holiday in Europe laden with treasures of art. Throughout the summer he had wandered about the Continent, gathering rare wood carvings, historic ceilings, treasures from the trappings of ancient palaces. A million dollars' worth of the lovely spoils of his voyage lay in yet unopened cases at the Metropolitan Museum of Art. Morgan had been elected president of the Museum in 1904 and was set upon making it the finest institution of its sort in existence. By now no government in the world could compete with the acquisitive American as an art-collector. "The only thing that can give any idea of Mr. Morgan in the art world," remarked the Metropolitan's curator, Sir Caspar Purdon Clarke, "is the word COLOSSAL, pronounced by an enthusiastic Austrian, for instance."

Morgan leased a house in Richmond, Virginia, and planned to cap the summer with a month of quiet enjoyment with the clergy of the Episcopal Convention, to which he was a lay delegate from St. George's Church, New York. The arms of financial battle were laid aside. Gracefully and easily Morgan was drifting toward the peaceful haven of old age. His son, J. P.

Jr., now a man of forty, was bearing many of the burdens that had been his father's. Young "Jack" Morgan,
as the Street called him, was now a partner. In London
and in New York the heir apparent had come with flying colors through the rigorous Morgan mill.

Suddenly the trumpets of battle brayed in Wall
Street; the hordes of panic swarmed against the bastions
of capital; and the financial world was seized with a
trembling madness that threatened to bring down the
banking system of the country into ruins, smash the
credit of the nation, and smirch its name. Wall Street
screamed hysterically for a leader. There was but one
who could fill the rôle. Once more Morgan buckled on
his shield and went into action.

During many teeming, turbulent days mighty financiers—men whose greed and ambition had largely built
the stupendous structure of concentrated wealth and
overstrained credit now threatened—clustered about
Morgan like frightened children. In a nameless be-
wilderment of fear, as in the presence of a convulsion
of Nature, these bold, brave barons of gold sank mutual
differences and laid their riches and power in the hands
of one man. Day after day the captains of finance, both
high and low, came trooping into Morgan's plain, se-
verely furnished office, stood before his small, flat desk,
and took their orders. Night after night the kings of
the Street met in the Morgan Library and reported to
the master.

During those days of panic Morgan was undisputed
monarch. Indeed, in all save name, he was dictator of
the United States. The Government itself did his bid-

ding without question. Morgan rose to the emergency magnificently, joyfully. The incense of homage, the feeling of power rejuvenated him. He was a centre of calm in the core of the storm. Eventually he damned the torrent of panic, turned it aside, and broke it into a thousand little streams to be met and conquered at leisure. And, of course, he watched his own interests with a paternal and protective eye.

Nothing in financial history compares, quite, with the sight of this strange, aloof man withdrawing from the dronings of a church convention, from the passionless company of clerics, to take command of the fierce, clashing money forces of Wall Street, gone crazy out of sheer fright—to become the protagonist and hero of the most cynical, treacherous, cruel, arrogant, and cowardly human elements in the world.

For a never-to-be-forgotten week the massed banks and trust companies placed themselves obediently in Morgan's hands. The vaults of the United States Treasury were flung open to him. It was in his power to say who should and who should not borrow money in Wall Street. In that time of terror his rough fiat brought stock gambling temporarily to an end; and routed gangs of adventurers who had followed Morgan's lead, but not his more sure methods, in all manner of promotions.

These promotions, Morgan's as well as the wild-catters', unquestionably were a causative element of the panic. They had aroused a gambling spirit fierce and general beyond comparison in history. Also, there was a world-wide straining upon credit due to recent disasters and to the Russo-Japanese war. Then, too, there was the continued, almost sportive, trust-busting activities of the Roosevelt administration. Earlier in the year Morgan had sat in the gay riot of a Gridiron Club dinner in Washington with averted face, chewing an unlighted cigar, while President Roosevelt attacked him for his opposition to the Railway Rate Bill and other measures. At the climax of his speech Roosevelt strode toward Morgan, thrust a clenched fist in the financier's face, and shouted a warning to the rich men of America of the peril of resisting the new order of things. "And if you don't let us do these things," exclaimed Roosevelt, referring to administration moves for curbing the corporations, "those who come after us will rise and bring you to ruin!"

No one who observed the gray-haired banker as he frowned, drew down the corners of his mouth and stared straight before him, while the brilliant and flushed audience watched the orator, could doubt the suffering inflicted upon Morgan. He shook his head many times as he went away from the city where once he had been the trusted adviser of Presidents, the close friend and confidant of Cleveland and McKinley.

In February, 1907, the stock market began to crumble. The money market tightened. To secure $20,-000,000 for a railroad he was building in Virginia, H. H. Rogers, of the Standard Oil, was forced to endorse the notes personally. Came another dip known as the "March Panic" or "Silent Panic." However, high money rates drew gold from Europe and a crisis was averted for the time being.

Increasing financial disturbances caused tremendous

pressure to be brought upon President Roosevelt to modify his program. Furious assaults were made upon Roosevelt. Lifelong friends turned against him. With railroad earnings falling alarmingly, Morgan swallowed his pride and called at the White House on March 12. Afterwards he broke his rule of a lifetime and gave a statement to the press. He said he had "suggested to the President that it would be greatly to the public interest if he would see the railway presidents and confer with them as to what steps might be taken to allay the public anxiety now threatening to obstruct railway investment and combination, and especially to allay public anxiety as to the relations between the railways and the Government. The President had said that he would be glad to see them with this end in view."

Roosevelt, however, declined to issue a formal invitation, and matters dragged. On March 28 we find an exchange of letters between Roosevelt and Jacob H. Schiff. Roosevelt wrote:

"It is difficult for me to understand why there should be this belief in Wall Street that I am a wild-eyed revolutionist. I cannot condone wrong, but I certainly do not intend to do aught save what is beneficial to the man of means who acts fairly and squarely. When I see you I will explain at length why I do not think it advantageous from any standpoint for me to ask any railroad man to call upon me. I can only say to you, as I have already said to Mr. Morgan when he suggested that he would like to have certain of them call upon me (a suggestion which they refused to adopt, by the way), that it would be a pleasure to me to see any of them at any time. Sooner or later I think they will realize that in their opposition to me in the last few years they have been utterly mistaken, even from the standpoint of their own interests; and that nothing better for them could be devised than the laws I have striven and am striving to have enacted."

Schiff's letter was lengthy and adroit. The next generation, he wrote, would be better and happier because of Roosevelt's having been President, but the present generation would have to go through much suffering because of Roosevelt's "stern and uncompromising attitude in important questions and because of the manner in which changes in economic conditions . . . are forced upon the country and upon the interests involved." Schiff added:

"Mr. Morgan—the big man he is—has perhaps acted somewhat impulsively, but I can readily understand what was in his mind when he recently suggested that a few representative railroad men hold a conference with you. If instead of Mr. Morgan, who after all represents a class against which, unfortunately, great prejudice now exists, you as the head of the American people, in whom the people properly and fortunately have every confidence, will propose that the Interstate Commerce Commission, as the representative body of the Government, and the representatives of the railroads, chosen in such manner as the railroad interests may themselves determine, come together with a view of arriving at a solution of the difficult problems involved, I cannot but believe that the good which will result will be immeasurable."

The meeting never materialized.

The summer passed with growing uneasiness. The city of New York failed to find a market for its bonds. The huge Westinghouse Electric Company failed. The

New York street railway combination went into receivership. Charles W. Morse's attempted consolidation of Atlantic coast shipping collapsed.

Morse, whose morals were even more sebaceous than those prevailing in the period, was the inventor of "chain-banking." This was a simple and audacious scheme of employing stock of one enterprise as collateral on which to borrow money for the purchase of another. Morse and a group of associated gamblers were pouring funds under their control in the Mercantile National Bank, the Knickerbocker Trust Company and other depositories into all sorts of harebrained schemes.

Men of Morse's make-up found a lush field of operation in the trust companies. Each trust company did about as it pleased, since it was independent of national laws and not a member of the Clearing House. The Federal law required the fifty-three national banks of the N. Y. Clearing House to keep twenty-five per cent of their deposits on hand in cash. The trust companies, fifty in New York alone, were answerable only to the state, which to a practical extent permitted them to lend or invest ninety-five per cent of their funds. By 1907 the trust companies had forced the solid but low-interest-paying national banks into second place as depositories.

Market prices began to fall as wary capitalists withdrew their money. Slowly the whole fabric of stock and bond values seemed to crumble. It was evident that many were turning their investments into cash, and hoarding the cash. Within a few months, almost $300,-

000,000 actually disappeared from circulation. By a slow, inexorable draining process five billion dollars of values were wiped from stock exchange prices.

Roosevelt declared that great law-breaking million-aires had combined to crush him by producing hard times. Wall Street replied that the President had destroyed confidence in securities by wholesale denunciation of corporations. Others held that revelations of crookedness in mighty corporate enterprises—such as the life insurance companies, the Union Pacific system, the rapid transit companies of New York—had terrified the investing public of the whole world.

The climax came in mid-October.

A great gambling pool had attempted to corner the market in United Copper stock. Some one in the pool sold out secretly, and the corner, involving many millions of dollars, was smashed. The ruin produced by this disaster compelled Otto Heintze & Co., a firm of brokers, to suspend. Otto Heintze's brother, F. Augustus, was a speculative western adventurer who had acquired control of the Mercantile National Bank and was its president. Associated with him were Morse and Orlando F. and E. R. Thomas. In addition to the Mercantile National, the Heintze-Morse-Thomas chain included the New Amsterdam Bank, the Bank of North America and the Knickerbocker Trust Company.

On Wednesday, October 16, the Mercantile National applied for help to the other banks of the Clearing House. The Clearing House Committee announced that the Mercantile National would be given aid pending investigation. The bank was found to be deeply involved in the copper gambling; furthermore Heintze had permitted loans on all sorts of questionable securities. It was soon evident that other banks in the Heintze-Morse-Thomas chain were also involved. A special meeting of the Clearing House Committee was called.

In a gorgeous chamber adorned with the portraits of Washington and Hamilton, the leaders of the national banking system met, denounced as piracy the new method of using bank funds, and resolved that not another dollar should be given to assist the crippled institutions until Morse, Heintze, the Thomases, and all their associates and confederates should retire. In the arched hall of the Clearing House, between sombre mahogany wainscoting, sat the leading bankers of New York: Stillman, of the National City; Snyder, of the National Bank of Commerce; Baker, of the First National; Hepburn, of the Chase National; Simmons, of the Fourth National; Clarke, of the American Exchange National.

In a big, leather-cushioned chair in the corner sat Pierpont Morgan, the only private banker in the room.

Heintze and his associates surrendered and resigned.

The worst seemed to be over. But the drama was only beginning.

By the end of the week, the Clearing House investigation disclosed an alarming state of affairs in the Knickerbocker Trust Company, largest institution of the Heintze-Morse chain. Charles T. Barney, later to send a bullet through his body and die in the arms of his long-estranged wife, was president of the Knickerbocker. He was an intimate friend of Morse; and, without the knowledge of his executive committee, had loaned millions of the Knickerbocker's money to Morse.

Barney was deposed at once and A. Foster Higgins elected president.

On Monday, October 21, Higgins called together the executive committee. The tone of the meeting was hopeful. The directors could not believe that the Clearing House would precipitate a panic by permitting failure of a bank with 17,000 depositors and deposit liabilities of $35,000,000.

Suddenly the telephone rang.

Word came that the National Bank of Commerce had refused to continue clearing checks for the Knickerbocker. The directors were dazed. Was not the great Bank of Commerce largely controlled by Morgan and Thomas F. Ryan? Did these gigantic manipulators dare provoke a panic that might imperil even their own fortunes?

A meeting of the full board of directors was hastily called for that evening at Sherry's. This fashionable restaurant, thronged with diners, was an unfortunate choice. For waiters and outsiders went unheeded in and out of the private dining-room; and soon rumors of the Knickerbocker's terrible plight flowed all over New York. One by one men slipped into the Night and Day Bank, not far away on Fifth Avenue, and drew checks against the Knickerbocker.

The sun was still low next morning when a long line formed at the door of the trust company, at Fifth Avenue and Thirty-fourth Street. A messenger from the Night and Day Bank was first in line. He bore a thick portfolio. Millions of dollars were withdrawn in two hours. The vaults were soon empty. Amid scenes of furious anger, with men and women struggling desperately at the doors and squads of police fighting to maintain order, the Knickerbocker suspended business.

Early that morning President Higgins and two directors had gone to the home of Morgan's son-in-law, Herbert L. Satterlee, where the financier was staying, and begged for help. Morgan shook his head. "I can't go on being everybody's goat," he said. "I have got to stop somewhere."

That seemed to let hell loose in New York.

Next morning (this was Wednesday, October 23) haggard and terrified depositors confronted the cashiers of almost every trust company. Panic spread. The National Bank of America went down. Terror swept the Street and began to flow in widening waves over the country. Runs such as had never been witnessed, and were to last a fortnight, began on the Trust Company of America and the Lincoln Trust. Secretary of the Treasury Cortelyou hurried to New York.

Late that night Morgan, Stillman, Hepburn, Baker, Perkins, and other financiers, who had been conferring in Morgan's library, went to Secretary Cortelyou's room in the Manhattan Hotel. "Gentlemen," said the Treasury head, "the Government can deal only with private financial interests when they are united. The Government can offer relief only through the national banks. If it can deal with the situation as a whole, the Treasury can and will help."

The conditions were those of actual battle and no

time could be lost in debate. Some general must be chosen to decide hour by hour where the Government's millions, to be deposited in the national banks, should be distributed. Friends and foes must agree for the time being to obey one voice of command. All turned to one man.

Next morning Pierpont Morgan was in a position, virtually, to make or break almost any financial institution in New York.

Morgan reigned in his office. Across the street in one direction was the white marble Stock Exchange, its soul craven, its eyes and ears strained for some signal from the master. Across the street in another direction, behind the bronze figure of Washington and the stately pillars of the Sub-Treasury, was the Secretary of the Treasury, ordering the deposit of millions—with George Perkins dashing to and fro between his chief and Cortelyou. In its austere council room, the Clearing House committee met continuously, working out Morgan's plans.

Newsboys screamed out disaster and flaunted thrilling headlines in the faces of bewildered people. A great crowd stood in front of the Sub-Treasury, talking excitedly and moving like stirred water at every rumor from the room where Cortelyou was scattering the national moneys in response to Morgan's quick, sharp advice.

Morgan stuck to his desk or walked about among the money captains summoned to his office: Stillman, shrewd, cold, secret (an irrepressible City Bank wit once called him "Sunny Jim"!) bringing to Morgan's service the tremendous resources of Standard Oil and its allies, running into hundreds of millions; Baker, of the First National, who for almost two generations had gazed stolidly from his office into the graveyard where Alexander Hamilton, author of the national system of finance, slept under a white stone, forgotten by passing crowds; Harriman, Morgan's ancient foeman, pale, spectacled, anxious; Henry Frick, cool, low-voiced, helpful; Ryan, icy-eyed, rugged, with color not so ruddy as usual.

Thursday, October 24, was a day of terror on the Stock Exchange. All sales stopped. No money could be borrowed. Interest rates leaped to 150%. The great central heart of Wall Street ceased to beat. Morgan instantly summoned his lieutenants, bankers. They came running. In a few minutes Morgan had raised a pool of $25,000,000 to be loaned at ten per cent under rigid supervision. Wall Street broke into cheers. At the doors of the Stock Exchange, a group of excited brokers stood looking across at Morgan's office and singing in chorus.

Ironic thoughts must have passed through Morgan's mind as he listened to the serenade. The same profane voices that so lately had cursed and scorned him now raised in hymns of praise and patriotism!

Morgan sent down the street to his private humidor for box after box of cigars. He smoked interminably long black cigars and passed them out to all who came in, his eyes snapping fire, his under lip thrust out. Heavy jaws clenched upon his cigar, hands clasped behind his back, he silently watched crazy messengers running in

and out of the Stock Exchange, the black crowd sway-
ing murmurously, the troops of mounted police wheel-
ing and charging here and there to keep an appearance
of order and authority in the maddened neighborhood.

Overnight Morgan became a towering, heroic figure.
There was something elemental in this dogged, scornful man's appearance in his old age (he was six months
past seventy) after years of unanswered criticism; in
this crisis he gathered strength and courage from the
weakness and timidity of others, while the leagued wealth
of a nation called on him for leadership, and immense
systems of banks and trust companies, stock exchanges,
multitudes of brokers listened humbly, gratefully for
his word and depended for salvation upon his judgment
and force.

To the public at large Morgan had always seemed
merely a thick-necked, red-faced, horribly rich rogue
who mitigated his championship of Wall Street crookedness by royal generosities as a philanthropist and patron
of art. Now, though, even his most vituperant journalistic
critics lauded him as a statesman.

Commanding men, forging great events, Morgan was
in his glory.

Those who were with him in those days of tension
will never forget that burly figure, steady and slow-
pacing; the massive, bulging forehead overhanging deep-
set eyes; the heavy, fleshy nose, grim mouth and square
fighting chin; the gruff voice and indescribable manner—one moment all reason and kindness, the next
harsh and domineering as he swept everything into
obedience before his will.

"I am afraid we can't help with any more money, our reserves are so low," faltered one eminent trust company president.

"What!" cried Morgan, swinging his fist like a hammer and crunching his jaws until the muscles stood out rigid. "Do you realize what you are saying? Tomorrow you may have no reserves at all."

By the end of the week nine banking institutions in Greater New York had closed their doors and "men had died from excitement or from terror or by their own hand." Bank runs continued for weeks. The full force of the panic beat against the Trust Company of America and the Lincoln Trust. Day after day, Secretary Cortelyou went to the Sub-Treasury, passed on the securities offered by the banks, and directed the deposits of the Treasury funds. Under Morgan's direction these funds were in turn deposited in the threatened trust companies.

On November 6 it was announced that the older trust companies had organized a committee to help the weaker companies. A tale of drama lies behind this decision. Morgan believed that some of the smaller trust companies should be permitted to go to the wall. He regarded them as financial freebooters. Complaints had been made that Morgan had withheld relief from some trust companies, particularly the hard-pressed Trust Company of America. President Oakleigh Thorne had been bluntly repulsed when he asked for more aid.

The matter of forming a protective committee came up at one of the night meetings in the Morgan Library. "It was not the custom of the master of the Library to be present during the general plans which preceded actual decisions," says Anna Robeson Burr, James Stillman's biographer. "In a small adjoining room, he sat with his cigar, the patience-cards spread before him. If a picture caught his eye that hung a thought askew, he rose to straighten it. When the time came to lay results before him, he would stroll in, tall, heavy, powerful, and, standing on the hearth-rug, state his will. . . . Sometimes a sheet of paper would be handed him, on which each man present had set down either his resources or his needs. Glancing at this, he was likely to tear it up and go back to his patience-cards without a word. All then was to do over again. . . . It was late when the question of the trust companies came up. Morgan was perfectly frank about them. 'Why should I get into this?' he asked. 'My affairs are all in order. I've done enough. I won't take all this on unless'—he ended, with a gesture which the others perfectly understood to mean, *'unless I get what I want out of it.'* " Morgan and his friends always got what they wanted— no matter what the situation.

Morgan looked about the circle and asked opinions. The replies were non-committal—until he came to Stillman. Of this hitherto hidden history, Mrs. Burr writes:

"They say there was a long pause before James Stillman spoke; a heavy pause in which the room seemed to fill with thought. When he began, his words had all the intensity of his nature, added to the force of his intellectual conviction. At that moment he saw very far. Not only must he overbear the great power against him but he must convince them all. True, some of these men agreed with him, yet he was under no illusions as to their support. If Morgan held out, not only his partners but all present would flock to his side—they must.

"On the other hand, Stillman held an important strategic position. Of the whole group, he was the one who possessed at that moment immense reserves of actual gold, and everyone in the room knew that only gold talked. Even Morgan that night had not the cash resources which were held by the President of the City Bank. During all those hours, he had said nothing about what he was going to do. . . . What was he going to do? Those men heard him and realized that battle was joined between the two constructive forces of their world.

"It was a struggle. Perhaps for the most important hours of his life James Stillman was the rallying-point, for it was not his desire to overcome Morgan, but rather to carry him along so that they could continue to work together. Above all, he must prevent his antagonist from taking up a definite position from which pride might not allow him to retreat. That would have been fatal.

"The contest lasted until dawn. Frick stayed on and one or two others; certain men came and went. These merely waited, waited in anxiety, hardly knowing for what. They heard Morgan's deep and rumbling voice, answered by that lighter one. Some of them still remember a mind supple and strong, clear and persuasive, quieting undue heat, guiding impulse softly till it fell into line with reason, adroit, vigilant, incredibly tactful, incredibly patient.

"When James Stillman went home (probably to a day of headache and blackened toast and tea), he had carried every point and, in the old phrase, virtue had gone out of him."

Then, there was the night when $30,000,000 was supplied to the City Treasury. The city needed this amount to pay its school teachers and for other pressing purposes. Morgan asked the Mayor, Comptroller, and Chamberlain of New York to meet him in his Library in the evening. It was nine o'clock when Morgan arrived in the resplendent room where the three officials were waiting with Stillman, Baker, Perkins, and Francis Lynde Stetson, Morgan's lawyer.

Morgan had been working since daybreak, almost without food. As he entered the room he bowed to the group, went over to his table desk, laid his cigar down, and, reaching for pen and paper, covered three large sheets in a firm, clear hand. Then he handed the sheets to the others for inspection. He had written the terms upon which $30,000,000 of municipal bonds would be taken through the banks. So precise were the conditions, so deep and full the knowledge of the city's legal powers, so comprehensive the safeguarding of the banks, that neither the city officials, the bankers, nor even the sharp lawyer could suggest a word to be added or taken away. The transaction was concluded at once.

Morgan saw nothing incongruous in assembling the forces that stayed the panic in the company of a placid Madonna of Raphael or a delicate statuette by Donatello. There were two of Donatello's statuettes in Morgan's favorite corner. He was intensely fond of them, saying they reminded him of his own children.

This man, very embodiment of titanic force, would lay aside the most pressing matter to play with his grandchildren or caress his favorite dog. Each Christmas Eve, he gathered his growing grandchildren about him and read aloud the story of *Old Scrooge* and *Tiny Tim* from the original manuscript of "A Christmas Carol."

The great financier laughed and cried with the children over Dickens' simple and affecting little goblin tale. Of all the riches in the Library, the children's particular treasure was the sheets of yellowing paper in the well-known scratchy hand of Dickens.

During the height of the panic Morgan drove daily to Roosevelt Hospital where Mrs. W. S. Rainsford, wife of his former rector, lay gravely ill; and waited until permitted to enter the sick-room and place roses at the patient's bedside. On the afternoon of one of the critical all-night sessions Morgan presided over a long meeting at the Metropolitan Museum. Only after the routine was over did he casually remark that he had to hurry home to attend to a business transaction.

On the second Sunday after the panic began, the greatest conference of all began in Morgan's Library late in the afternoon. The master of the place had no eyes for the costly beauty and grandeur of his surroundings —the marvelous tapestries, sculptured angels and madonnas, the famous ceiling brought from an Italian palace, the stretches of books whose very bindings were the subjects of many volumes. On this occasion Wall Street's one indomitable power wrestled and commanded until five o'clock in the morning.

In that stupendous night the control of the vast Tennessee Coal, Iron and Railroad Company passed to the United States Steel Corporation.

Tennessee Coal and Iron was one of the chief competitors of the Steel Corporation. It owned enormous iron and coal deposits. Morgan was convinced that its purchase would help stay the panic—and also be a stroke

of good business for the greater corporation. Another
motive also swayed him. His closest associate, Baker, had
a brother-in-law, Schley, of the large brokerage firm of
Moore & Schley. This firm was in trouble. It had pledged
more than $6,000,000 of T. C. & I. among the banks;
and was hourly expected to break.

Lewis Cass Ledyard, a lawyer and one of Morgan's
chums of the New York Yacht Club, told the financier
of Moore & Schley's plight. The firm could be saved,
Ledyard thought, only through purchase of T. C. & I.
by U. S. Steel. The banks would accept Steel securities
as collateral but spurned T. C. & I. Morgan summoned
Gary, Frick, and other members of the Steel Corporation
finance committee. They opposed the purchase, but
yielded finally. However, Gary told Morgan: "Before
we go ahead with this, we must consult President Roosevelt."

"What has he to do with it?" demanded Morgan.

"If we do this without consulting the administration," persisted Gary, "a bill in equity might stop the
sale, and in that case more harm than good would be
done. He cannot say that we may or may not purchase,
but we ought to know his attitude since he has a general
direction of the law department of the United States."

"All right," assented Morgan, "you and Frick hustle
to Washington at once. Have a special train if necessary."

Gary and Frick were at the White House early the
following morning. Calling Elihu Root into consulta-
tion, Roosevelt gave left-handed consent to the deal.
He told the Steel men that, while he would make no

binding agreement or promise, he would not advise against the proposed purchase. "I was dealing with a panic and a situation," Roosevelt explained later, "where not merely twenty-four hours, but one hour might cause widespread disaster to the public."

When the Sunday night conference broke up on the morning of November 4, 1907, daylight was glinting the bronze doors of the Library. "Tired?" asked a bank president as Morgan brushed past a statue in the vestibule and sniffed the keen morning air. "Haven't time," he answered gruffly.

"I stayed there until five o'clock in the morning with Mr. Morgan," recalled Ledyard. "Then he told me to go home and get some sleep and come back by half-past eight as he expected to hear from Washington by long distance 'phone. I went home but I couldn't sleep. So I got a cup of coffee and a bath and came back. Mr. Morgan said he had had a fine sleep and a good breakfast and felt very well."

Morgan emerged from the panic of 1907 with prestige enhanced immeasurably. He was once again the idol of his world. There was also a startling, if temporary, change in the public attitude. The panic had produced some excellent reporting. The magazines and news-papers, so lately humming with hymns of hate, now teemed with articles lauding the Stalwart and Patriotic Old War Horse of Finance—the man who had Saved the Country.

The old war horse seemed as scornful of praise as he had been of abuse. But the keen scent of action was in his nostrils. He gave over thoughts of retirement.

CHAPTER SIXTEEN

PIERPONTIFEX MAXIMUS

PANICS ARE LIKE GREAT BATTLES. WHEN THEY ARE over, the wounded must be succored, the dead buried, and new lines formed.

The panic of 1907 marked the end of an era. The masters of capital realized that they must radically reconstruct their methods, if not their morals. The great banking groups must smooth out rivalries and knit into closer communion control of money and credit. "Safe" men must forever rule the kingdom of gold.

Morgan became the natural leader in the formation of one vast and harmonious money machine.

The single formidable obstreperous element was E. H. Harriman. Undaunted by assaults of the Government, shocked into only momentary sobriety by the panic, Harriman planned an individual banking power greater than that of either Morgan or the National City Bank. The indomitable little man dreamed of a world railroad empire. His restless eyes had turned to the Orient. He would build a railroad system in Asia, connect with the Siberian Railway in Russia, and eventually work through to the capitals of Europe. Lines of steamships in the Pacific and the Atlantic would enable him to span the earth.

Harriman most likely would have rewritten railroad

and financial history in the next five years had his colossal scheme not been halted by a greater power. His frail body could not stand the strain. He fell ill and died in the fall of 1909. His race was far from run. He was the only man in Wall Street big enough, bold enough, brave enough to stand up against Morgan.

Within three months Morgan, George F. Baker, and their associates had purchased Harriman's controlling interest in the great Guaranty Trust Company, with its $100,000,000 assets; and Harriman's holdings in the huge Mutual Life Insurance Company. Morgan also bought from Thomas F. Ryan control of the Equitable Life with its tainted history and assets now grown to more than $500,000,000. The Mutual, the Equitable, and the New York Life—the Big Three—were now in the hands of the Morgan group. The Morton and the Fifth Avenue Trust companies were merged into the Guaranty. Morgan now dominated the trust company field. He had taken over the rapidly expanding Bankers' Trust Company several years before. The financier's insurance holdings gave him, in addition, a more substantial interest in the National Bank of Commerce.

James Stillman, president of the National City Bank, entered the Morgan group, as an individual associate, shortly after the panic. This tended to soften and finally eradicate rivalry between Morgan and the Standard Oil.

Gradually Morgan & Company began to abandon its activities as a huge promotion house and take on more essentially the character of a great bank. New men were coming to the front. Times were changing. The younger

Morgan partners—Henry P. Davison, a former school teacher, Thomas W. Lamont, once a newspaper reporter, and others—were men of different stripe from the rough-and-tumble financiers of the old school. The brilliant Davison soon became Morgan's chief reliance, quickly pushing into the background George W. Perkins and hastening the latter's retirement.

"These newer men in Wall Street," writes John Moody, "were not the products of the old time, when experience was gained by building up and welding together the parts of the vast modern industrial and banking machine. They had not been educated in the hard and struggling school for mastery through which Morgan and Frick and Harriman and Rockefeller had come. When they arrived, they found the financial machine already in motion; their work was to perfect it and keep it well oiled. Consequently, with the arrival of the new and younger school of financiers, a less spectacular season set in for Wall Street. Money power increased; intercorporate relationships were maintained; but few further steps were taken in elaborating or developing the system."

Indeed, there was need of harmony and maintenance of peaceful "intercorporate relationships" among the masters of capital. The wave of adulation heaped upon Morgan for Saving the Country in 1907 quickly subsided. The public mind veered sharply. Big business was held responsible for the disaster. Demands for further regulation multiplied. Every conceivable panacea was proposed. Criticism thickened about the leaders of industry. The American people, to paraphrase Matthew Arnold, fell into one of their "periodical fits of morality."

The popular magazines, then at the height of their courage, renewed attacks. Congress echoed the public aversion to the methods of High Finance. Roosevelt swung his Big Stick even more vigorously. Standard Oil, Tobacco, and many other trusts were practically under indictment when Roosevelt turned the reins over to his successor, William Howard Taft, in 1909.

Thus far the greatest combination of all, Morgan's U. S. Steel Corporation, had escaped prosecution. This was due primarily to the suave diplomacy of Elbert H. Gary. Often, in those trying times, Morgan had reason to bless his choice of Gary as chairman of the Steel Corporation. "I don't know what I'd do without Gary," Morgan told a friend, feelingly. "The Judge can have anything within my power to give."

Morgan meant what he said. Early in 1909 Gary cabled Morgan at Aix-les-Bains that the finance committee wanted to cut wages. Frick and P. A. B. Widener, then in Nice together, had cabled that they favored the proposed reduction. Gary opposed. Revival of business was in sight, he thought. He asked for Morgan's support. Morgan promptly wired Frick and Widener to meet him in Paris. Within forty-eight hours a cablegram came sustaining Gary. It was signed "Morgan, Frick, Widener." Of course, it proved all-powerful. And Gary was correct in his prevision of improved conditions.

George Perkins, a member of the Steel finance committee, later paid glowing tribute to the psychological effect of Gary's stand. "I recall an interesting conversation with George W. Perkins at his house at dinner," narrated Bradford Merrill, a noted New York publisher, "about the value of the services of certain executives to certain corporations. It was a man's dinner with only five or six persons present. I think it was Senator Beveridge of Indiana who asked Mr. Perkins how many men were really worth the salaries of from $100,000 to $250,000 a year which great corporations were then paying to their chief executives. Mr. Perkins recalled a single decision by Chairman Gary, made against great opposition, which Perkins said was, in his opinion, worth one hundred times all the salary that the Steel Corporation would ever pay Gary in his lifetime." This was the decision concerning wages.

On another occasion Gary reinstated an official over the protests of the presidents of the subsidiary companies. The latter threatened to resign in a body if the finance committee backed Gary. The matter was taken to Morgan. "Tell them," said Morgan, banging his fist upon the table, "that their resignations will be accepted."

Gradually Gary whipped his ruthless associates into line. "It is probable that the spirits of the Steel men," writes Ida M. Tarbell, Gary's biographer, "had been so chastened by the after-effects of the panic of 1907 that they were peculiarly receptive to the evangelistic fervor of Gary's appeals to steadiness and to decent and friendly competition, however vigorous that competition might be. They had yielded to his advice to their own surprise, and in 1909, when things began to revive, they were almost buoyantly exultant over their virtue. 'Who would have thought we could have been so decent?' was the gist of their talks at luncheons and dinners! They had come to love one another like brothers. It was Gary who had converted them to this policy, and in October of 1909 a large number of his competitors showed their appreciation by giving him what I think is one of the most remarkable dinners in our business annals—remarkable because of its sincerity as well as the kind of thing it celebrated."

Morgan attended this love feast and bashfully blurted out a few words of appreciation, with one hand on Gary's shoulder, the other on his chair. But not all Gary's diplomacy could drown public demand for prosecution of the Steel Corporation. People everywhere were aroused over the evils of the seven-day week and the brutal twenty-four hour shift every fortnight. Though the seven-day week had been partly abolished in 1907, it still existed in some departments. Ridicule greeted the corporation's defense that the men *wanted* to work seven days in order to secure extra money.

Enlightened citizens of all degrees denounced the corporation's labor policy as barbaric. Samuel Gompers, president of the American Federation of Labor, called upon Attorney General Wickersham to dissolve the corporation. There was bitter criticism of the social relations between Gary and Wickersham. It was openly charged that the Government was shielding the Steel Trust. A section of the press demanded Wickersham's impeachment.

Early in 1911 Congress appointed a committee of investigation under the chairmanship of Representative

Augustus Stanley, of Kentucky. Gary sought to stem the rising tide through a surprising statement to the committee:

"I realize as fully, I think, as this committee that it is very important to consider how the people shall be protected against imposition or oppression as the possible result of great aggregations of capital, whether in the possession of corporations or individuals. I believe that is a very important question, and personally I believe that the Sherman Act does not meet and will never fully prevent that. I believe we must come to enforced publicity and governmental control, even as to prices, and, so far as I am concerned, speaking for our company, so far as I have the right, I would be very glad if we had some place where we could go, to a responsible governmental authority, and say to them, 'Here are our facts and figures, here is our property, here our cost of production; now you tell us what we have the right to do and what prices we have the right to charge.' I know this is a very extreme view, and I know that the railroads objected to it for a long time; but whether the mere standpoint of making the most money is concerned or not, whether it is the wise thing, I believe it is the necessary thing, and it seems to me corporations have no right to disregard these public questions and these public interests."

Congressman Martin W. Littleton, of the committee, asked Gary:

"Your idea, then, is that coöperation is bound to take the place of competition and that coöperation requires strict governmental supervision?"

"That is a very good statement," commented Gary.

Morgan's steel viceroy made another statement that

surprised the committee. This concerned Morgan's power. "I believe," said Gary, "any man of Mr. Morgan's wealth and strength of character and courage can do a great deal of harm in banking circles as well as a great deal of good. I believe that with power and privilege there is necessarily involved responsibility and obligation. That applies to the individual or the corporation and also applies to the Government. I do not think I would be frank and sincere with this committee if I should say that Mr. Morgan, under such circumstances, could not do a great deal of harm if he had the disposition to do so. That is true of other individuals, and that is one of the reasons why I say that this country, if it keeps up with other countries, in view of our great wealth and growing wealth, has got to come to the position, in my judgment, where there is coöperation between the Government and the individual."

In May of 1911, the United States Supreme Court ordered the dissolution of the Standard Oil and the Tobacco Trust. This crystallized charges that the administration was favoring the Steel Corporation. One evening in early summer Gary and Wickersham chanced to be seated next to each other at a public dinner. The Attorney General said: "I have something on my mind which I think I ought to tell you. There is such excitement over the Stanley investigation, such hostility to the Steel Corporation, so many charges that the administration is favoring it, that we believe that we must proceed to a searching examination."

"Do you mean a suit?" asked Gary.

"Yes," replied Wickersham.

"I am overwhelmed," said Gary. "This is so different from what I have believed to be your view of our corporation. But you must make your own decision."

Morgan purpled with rage when he learned that his pet combination was to be sued. He pressed buttons and summoned his lawyers. At least one eminent attorney suggested that efforts be made to settle the case without a trial. Morgan spurned the suggestion. "No, let them go ahead," he grated. The Government filed its petition October 26, 1911, praying that eight of the subsidiaries as well as the Steel Corporation itself be held "unlawful monopolies" and dissolved. The case was tried in New Jersey before four Federal circuit judges.

Beginning in May, 1912, testimony was taken at intervals for over two years. The record filled thirty volumes and there were four thousand pages of Government and Corporation exhibits. Gary spent a week on the stand. Four hundred and two witnesses were called, including Theodore Roosevelt and many characters in the Tennessee Coal & Iron drama.

Interrupted by the war, the case dragged until 1919, when the Supreme Court decided against the Government by a vote of six to three. Morgan did not live to witness the triumph. Friends bantered Gary, asking when they encountered him: "How is the good trust this morning?" When Mark Twain first met Gary, he remarked: "I know you. You are the good corporation." "Mr. Clemens," retorted Gary, "the time will come when you and every one else will see that there is a difference in corporations."

Among the Old Guard of finance Morgan, alone almost, retained active control of his great affairs. One by one ancient associates and ancient foemen dropped out. George F. Baker still carried on. But James Stillman retired and went to France to scatter bonbons among the children. John D. Rockefeller basked in the sun, handing out dimes and platitudes. William Rockefeller was no longer an active promoter. Henry H. Rogers was dead. Harriman was gone. Alexander J. Cassatt, the great Pennsylvania Railroad chieftain, had passed away.

Morgan himself was beginning to feel the inexorable inroads of age. Those in daily contact with him—his family; Charles King, his secretary; Phillips, his valet—noticed a gradual lessening of that tremendous vitality, a perceptible slowing up of the financier's inner "spring." Morgan began to place greater responsibility upon his younger partners. More and more he turned for his anodynes to religion and art and travel. His nature responded to the greater freedom and stateliness of life abroad. As he aged he mellowed somewhat.

One humid June morning, James Stillman found Morgan alone eating strawberries in his London garden. "What brought you to see me, Stillman?" Morgan asked after a bit of talk. "Oh," replied Stillman, "I thought you might be lonely." Morgan leaped from his chair, ran around the table—and kissed Stillman on the cheek! "I was very much amused," remarked Stillman, relating the anecdote.

"And what did you do then?"

"We ate up all the rest of the strawberries!"

Again, Morgan and Stillman stood before a beautiful tapestry in Rome. "I suppose I oughtn't to buy it," said Stillman, "but it's a great temptation." Morgan laughed gaily and quoted Wilde (perhaps unconsciously): "Always resist everything, Stillman, except temptation!"

In Rome Morgan was looked upon as an honorary citizen. When in 1911 Italy celebrated the fiftieth anniversary of her unification, Morgan was offered the honorary presidency of the Foreign Committee of the Turin Exhibition. Deputy Teofilo Rossi, the vermouth manufacturer of Turin, was so anxious to forestall the Rome committee that he rushed into Morgan's rooms in the Grand Hotel, Rome, a day ahead of an appointment that Salvatore Cortesi had arranged for him. "Entering suddenly and without being announced," says Mr. Cortesi, "he was confronted by an old gentleman who was putting on his shoes. One he already had on and the other he was holding in his hand. Deputy Rossi produced his visiting card and presented it with a flourish to the man he supposed to be Morgan's secretary. The old gentleman rose, still clutching a shoe with one hand and said: 'I am Mr. Morgan.' The Deputy apologized profusely for intruding, all the while warmly shaking the shoeless hand. It was in this attitude that Mr. Morgan listened to a high-sounding address in Italian. He did not understand a word of what was being declaimed at him."

Each year now Morgan included Egypt in his travels. The mystic silence of the Pyramids appealed to him subtly. He made his first trip across the desert to visit a Metropolitan Museum archæological expedition in the

[288]

Great Oasis of the Sahara. With his widowed sister, Mrs. Burns, and his daughter, Mrs. Hamilton, he journeyed from Cairo up the Nile in the beautiful dahabiyeh *Arabia*. Their guide was a young Englishman who later gave this vivid vignette of Morgan:

"I had been directed to take charge of Mr. Morgan and his party in the special train he had ordered for the six-hour journey across the desert. At the station he came up to me and in a jovial manner asked me how I did. This introductory (How do you do?) was almost the only words he said to me. For the rest of the six hours he scarcely uttered a syllable, with the exception of two terse questions about the desert.

"Throughout the entire journey he appeared to be plunged in the deepest thought; he sat, immersed in the profoundest contemplation, in the wicker-work armchair in the little saloon. This mood of silent thoughtfulness was the more surprising to me, because the journey is so full of interest that the ordinary traveler asks numberless questions along the route. After leaving the Valley of the Nile the line enters a long and desolate ravine having immense cliff-like walls of grey limestone, and finally climbs to the weird plateau of the Libyan Desert. Mr. Morgan was left entirely to himself during this journey; no one attempted to draw his attention to anything. Every now and then he would write out a cable message, which was sent off to the main line by telegraph from one of the little huts or stations on the line. An excellent luncheon was set before him, but all he took was an egg and a piece of bread, and as soon as the egg and bread were finished he plunged into thought again. His only distraction was smoking big cigars, and he must have got through a large number of them on this journey."

Everywhere he went Morgan added to his collections. A work of art, a piece of exquisite music kindled in him extraordinary emotion. The man of steel and iron became putty before the brush of Raphael, the melody of Mozart. In collecting, as in business, Morgan got what he went after. He vexed the souls of amateurs whose purses were more slender, and excited the envy of museum directors whose government grants were insufficient to compete with his large resources. His interests as a collector were wide and he ransacked the world through agents everywhere. Some focused their attention upon ancient art, mediæval art, watches, snuff-boxes, miniatures; others upon paintings, drawings, tapestries, furniture, Chinese porcelains, armor, manuscripts, and association books. Excavators dug into the ruins of ancient lands for him. Scholars poured over his Coptic writings. Others searched the earth for rare Bibles.

His house at Prince's Gate was a museum in itself. There was his famous Fragonard Room. There were his collections of miniatures and many of his choicest pictures. The Victoria and Albert Museum, popularly called the South Kensington, in London, had the benefit of extensive loan collections from him for many years. His miniatures assembled the beauties and princes of two centuries: Charles the Second, Charles the First as a youth, Louis the Fourteenth on horseback, Madame de Montespan, Madame de Pompadour, Marie Antoinette, the Duchess of Devonshire, George the Fourth as Prince Regent; scores of others. The oldest miniature was a portrait of Mary, Queen of Scots. The painter was unknown, but the portrait bore the initials of a former owner, Charles the First.

The Morgan illuminated manuscripts surpassed any collection ever brought together, wonderful examples of antique ornamentation and handwriting in English, German, Dutch, Spanish, French and Italian. There was the Huntingfield Psalter, a manuscript on vellum, containing ninety-two miniatures of scenes from the Bible and the lives of the saints. This was executed at Mendham Priory toward the end of the twelfth century. There was the Bourbon Book of Hours, done in 1485; and another Book of Hours, of Flemish workmanship, bound for Mary Stuart at the time of her marriage. Morgan owned the celebrated Gutenberg Bible and the Psalter of 1459, "the most valuable books in the world." He possessed magnificent pieces of old English plate: a Tudor bowl made in London when Shakespeare was alive; a set of "Apostle" spoons, dating from the reign of Henry the Eighth; a cup and cover made for James the First from silver of the great seal of Ireland; a massive siver tankard presented by Queen Mary to Simon Janszen, a Dutch master, for safely conveying her husband, William III, across to The Hague in 1691; a huge, tri-paneled silver vase depicting the finding of Romulus and Remus, Mettus Curtius leaping into the pit, and Æneas carrying his father, Anchises, from the burning city of Troy.

The building Morgan loved best was his white marble Library in New York. Here the light fell softly through a central double skylight of glass so transparent that the blue of the sky was seen as through the empty air.

Around the octagon of the skylight were painted the Muses of Art, Science, Literature, and Philosophy.

On shelving of Circassian walnut were stored books and manuscripts rich and rare beyond description. The mere enumeration of these required a thick catalogue; and to tell adequately the story of these treasures many volumes would be needed. To mention but a few of thousands of original manuscripts, Morgan had, under glass and in fireproof cases and vaults, the manuscript of Milton's "Paradise Lost," of Keats' "Endymion," Shelley's notebook, Pope's "Essay on Man," Lord Byron's "Don Juan," "The Corsair" and "Marino Faliero"; Burns' "Auld Lang Syne," "Mary Morrison," "Comin' Thro' the Rye," "Tam O'Shanter," "The Cotter's Saturday Night"; the manuscript of a poem by Swift describing Stella at Wood Park; of Scott's "Waverley," "Ivanhoe," "Anne of Gierstein," "Old Mortality," "Guy Mannering," "The Lady of the Lake," and Scott's own journal. Most of the famous novelists and essayists of English literature in the nineteenth century were represented—George Eliot, Anthony Trollope, Charles Reade, the Brontës, Macaulay, Carlyle, Ruskin. The collection also contained the finest assemblage of manuscripts and letters of American authors and statesmen—Poe, Whitman, Hawthorne, Thoreau, Washington, Adams, Franklin, Jefferson, Lincoln.

Bourbon though he was, Morgan was passionately interested in Lincolniana. Once he offered $50,000 for a single manuscript sheet in Lincoln's hand. The offer was refused by Mrs. John Hay. The priceless paper contained the Gettysburg Address. However, Morgan possessed many of the rarest Lincoln items. One was a long poem called "The Bear Hunt"—a narration in crude but telling rhyme of an incident Lincoln witnessed when a young backwoodsman in Kentucky. After a bear had been tracked and slain, a small cur leaped from nowhere, took his place with the bleeding, panting hunting dogs, and yelped proudly as though he had won the victory all by himself. In his engaging volume of collected miscellanea, "Lanes of Memory," George S. Hellman, who aided in forming the Morgan collection of manuscripts, writes that "The Bear Hunt" was offered to Morgan at two prices.

"Acceptance of the first price," says Mr. Hellman, "would have placed him in possession of the manuscript itself, with the right of publication reserved; the second and higher price left the manuscript entirely at Mr. Morgan's disposal. He was willing to pay considerably more to have it on the latter terms. . . . This point of privacy in possession is stressed because it was so characteristic. It was a regrettable element in Mr. Morgan's nature as a collector."

On one of the darkest days of the 1907 panic, Hellman went to the Morgan Library with a group of unusual letters written by Lincoln to the men who were to succeed him in the White House, Andrew Johnson and Ulysses S. Grant. Miss Belle Greene, the Morgan librarian, told the visitor that Morgan had decided to make no purchases for a year.

"In spite of this discouraging news [writes Mr. Hellman] I asked to see Mr. Morgan and a few moments later had entered his large room, where I found him alone. I had hardly crossed the threshold when, on seeing me, he said: 'I am not buying anything at all now.' 'I'm not trying to sell anything,' I replied, 'I'm giving something away.' 'What do you mean?' 'I think, Mr. Morgan, that after you have looked at these Lincoln letters, and heard the price, you will agree with me that they are a gift.'

"The letters were indeed superb. Lincoln's recommendations and instructions to Johnson and Grant had to do with some of the most significant events, both military and executive, of the Civil War period, and Mr. Morgan after looking over their contents was quick to realize their importance and their rarity. When he heard the price—less than four figures for the entire collection—he said: 'Yes, that's very reasonable.'

"Then there was a moment of silence, for between him and his acquisition of the manuscripts remained his unwillingness to purchase new treasures at this time of public stress. Finally he cut the Gordian knot: 'I'll take them; but I won't pay for them for a year.' "

Morgan had supreme confidence in his own judgment. A noted art dealer once showed the financier a small but exquisite Vermeer.

"Who is Vermeer?" asked Morgan.

"This question [narrates Hellman] would seem astounding if it were made today; but it was made many years ago, when there were probably not four paintings by this artist in all America, and his name was practically unknown in the circles of American art collectors. . . . Mr. Morgan's question was one that might have been asked by many lovers of paintings, unless they were students of Dutch art. The dealer briefly told Mr. Morgan a few facts concerning the Dutch painter, who, coming after Rembrandt, had achieved such perfection in the use of his brush that he still remains the last word from the point of view of finished detailed beauty. He added the, commercially speaking, important information that Vermeers were almost unobtainable by private collectors, only some twenty-eight examples of his art being recorded in the private and public collections of Europe.

"Whereupon Mr. Morgan again looked at the picture carefully and asked the price. The price was a hundred thousand dollars. 'I'll take it,' said Mr. Morgan. The whole affair took only a few moments; here was a collector who was willing to pay this large sum for a picture by an artist of whose existence he had not been aware a quarter of an hour earlier. No one but Mr. Morgan could have done this. He did it because his eye told him that he was in the presence of a consummate work of art, and his quickly working mind recognized that, as there were extant so few paintings by this master, the price was moderate. Within a few years Mr. Morgan could, had he so desired, have sold his Vermeer at a very large advance to Mr. P. A. B. Widener, and that at least a quarter of a million dollars could be obtained for it today there is no doubt."

The same quality of abrupt decision distinguished Morgan's charities. He gave away enormous sums, yet without set plan, and generally specified that his name should not be attached to the benefaction in any public way. Often his manner in making gifts was so repellent as to chill the recipients. While an officer of the New York Life—long before he became a Morgan partner—George Perkins asked Morgan to subscribe toward a fund for saving the Palisades. Morgan listened a moment impatiently, then asked brusquely: "How much do you need?"

"One hundred and twenty-five thousand dollars," replied Perkins.

"Well, you go and see Rockefeller and Stillman and some others. See what they'll give. Then you can come back to me and I'll see what I can do."

"But, Mr. Morgan," Perkins ventured, "I had hoped you would lead the subscription list. Then it would be easy for me to get the rest."

"Oh, well," said Morgan indifferently, "put me down for the whole amount." And he turned to his desk as though the incident were closed, as indeed it was.

In the same off-hand way, he gave millions to museums, churches, colleges. He gave a million-dollar plot for a lying-in hospital in New York, then built and financed the institution. He gave hundreds of thousands at a time (a total of almost $5,000,000) to the Cathedral of St. John the Divine, a million to Harvard Medical School, half a million to the Trades Training School, another half-million to the Loomis Sanitarium, a hundred thousand to the Y. M. C. A., the same amount for a public library at Holyoke, Massachusetts, a new parish house and rectory for St. George's, a collection of gems to the Museum of Natural History in Paris, a collection of Burns manuscripts to the Liverpool Library, an isolation pavilion at Aix-les-Bains, and so on.

He also had a long list of private pensioners on both sides of the water. No one knew the names, or the circumstances, except himself.

In the public imagination Morgan had now become almost a legendary figure—a vast, overshadowing Octopus whose colossal power, sensed if not seen or directly felt, reached everywhere.

It remained for a committee of Congress—the Pujo Committee to Investigate the Concentration of Control of Money and Credit—to translate the story into cold figures. Incidentally, it is worthy of note that the resolution creating the committee was introduced in Congress by the father of Colonel Charles A. Lindbergh, who was later to marry the daughter of a Morgan partner! The Pujo committee had the aid of an experienced staff of attorneys and accountants headed by Samuel Untermyer, of New York. Untermyer was a wily lawyer, schooled in both criminal and civil practice, whose inordinate vanity and fondness for exhibitional tactics marred, but could not conceal, striking ability. Morgan had no love for Untermyer. The latter, also, was a fancier of collies and had once aroused Morgan's choler by outbidding him for some prize dogs. Such things weighed with Morgan.

Under the direction of Untermyer, the Pujo Committee showed that a definite community of interest had been established between Morgan & Co., the First National, and the National City Bank. Figures made plain the enormous power of these groups in banking resources, transportation systems, producing and trading corporations, great public utilities. Firm members or directors of the three institutions, it was disclosed, together held 341 directorships in 112 corporations having aggregate resources or capitalization of no less than $22,245,000,000. The committee asserted that competition had practically been blotted out in underwriting securities; also that, as a matter of "banking ethics," the large banking houses did not seek to take customers away from each other.

The tumbling cascade of facts stirred people tremendously. Overwhelming demand arose for the masters of the Money Trust to make some defense. Untermyer sent subpoena servers into Wall Street in squads. Followed an astonishing spectacle. The committee's agents found themselves blocked at every turn. Some of the masters of capital discovered suddenly that business called them to Europe; others, of whom William Rockefeller was one, went actually into hiding, dodging the chase like common pickpockets. The newspapers joined gleefully in the hunt. The public enjoyed the sport. However, one by one, the great capitalists were cornered and placed on the stand. Reluctantly joining the parade, George F. Baker testified that in his opinion concentrated control of banking resources and credit had gone far enough; that the peril would be great if ambitious and not over-scrupulous men should get into places of power; and that the safety of the existing system lay in the personnel of the men in control.

"Do you think that is a comfortable situation for a great country to be in?" Baker was asked.

"Not entirely," he replied, slowly and after a period of thought.

But the committee, and the country, were gunning for one other, the most powerful of the money lords —Pierpont Morgan.

Word had gone forth that Untermyer intended to drag from Morgan his innermost "trade secrets." Morgan held the impression that Untermyer was prejudiced and had a deep personal feeling against him. The matter preyed upon his mind until he was in an extremely nervous condition. "I'll go to jail rather than discuss my private affairs," the financier told friends. Morgan detested Untermyer's methods. He hated being "placed on exhibition." He was in his seventy-sixth year, and the iron constitution that had carried him so far was beginning to break. Now and then a spasm of "jumpiness" seized him that resulted in sleepless nights and attacks of indigestion.

However, the great centralizer felt that he had his life's work to uphold, his whole social and economic philosophy to defend. And so, flanked by a battery of lawyers and friends, he went to Washington.

Once on the stand, his fears proved groundless. The fire-eating Untermyer treated him tenderly. Morgan testified briefly on December 18, 1912, and at length the following day. He declared bluntly that "all the banks in Christendom" could not form a Money Trust; and that no man nor group of men could ever obtain a monopoly of credit or coin. He defended his conduct of great corporations through voting trusts. Everything he had ever done had been for the protection of property. When a man abuses his power, he loses it. The ability to obtain credit is "largely a matter of personality."

His numerous amalgamations, he asserted, came about because they were necessary. He dealt with "things as they exist," adding: "If it is good business for the interests of the country to do it, I do it."

"But, Mr. Morgan," purred Untermyer, "is not a man likely quite subconsciously to imagine that things are for the interest of the country when they are good business?"

"No, sir."

"You think that you are able to judge and impartially differentiate, where your own interests are concerned, just as clearly as though you had no interest at stake, do you?"

"Exactly, sir."

Counsel went at length into Morgan's purchase of the Equitable Life from Ryan and the Harriman estate. The par value of the stock that Morgan bought was $51,000, the total capital of the company being $100,-000. The dividends on the stock were limited to seven per cent, or a total of $3,570 a year.

Q. And you paid how much for that stock?

A. Somewhere in the neighborhood of $2,500,000 or $3,000,000; I do not know the amount.

Q. It yields a return of about one-eighth or one-ninth of one per cent a year?

A. I believe so.

Q. You may explain, if you care to, Mr. Morgan, why you bought stock that could yield you only one-eighth or one-ninth of one per cent?

A. Because I thought it was a desirable thing for the situation to do that.

No amount of questioning could elicit any more illuminating response. The witness would not admit that control of the Equitable's vast assets had anything to do with the matter.

Another exchange revealed the personal, almost naïve, Morgan code. The financier bluntly declared that a man he did not trust could not get money from him on "all the bonds in Christendom." On the contrary, "I have known a man come into my office and I have given him a check for a million dollars and I knew that he had not a cent in the world."

Q. There were not many of them?

A. Yes, a good many.

Q. Commercial credits are based upon the possession of money or property?

A. No, sir; the first thing is character.

Q. Before money or property?

A. Before money or anything else. Money cannot buy it.

Q. So that a man with character, without anything at all behind it, can get all the credit he wants and a man with the property cannot get it?

A. That is very often the case.

Q. But that is the rule of business?

A. That is the rule of business, sir.

During the entire examination the financier was in the best of humor and on several occasions gave evidence of deriving considerable amusement out of his experience. At the conclusion, he shook hands with all the members of the committee and several of the corps of assistants and secretaries, including one of the doorkeepers and a Capitol policeman.

Despite the unexpected ease of his ordeal, Morgan left Washington a weary man—how weary, none but he knew.

CHAPTER SEVENTEEN

CURTAIN

ON JANUARY 6, 1913, MORGAN SAT IN REVERY BEFORE the fire in his room at the western end of the Library. He was sailing next day for the Mediterranean and Egypt—a health quest ordered by his physicians. He had been unable to rebound from the mental and physical strain of the Pujo inquiry. In spite of his seeming sprightliness and easy carriage, Morgan's associates perceived that he came from the committee hearing a different man from the one who had gone to Washington.

Colonel George Harvey was announced. Harvey was editor of *Harper's Weekly* and a pioneer supporter of Woodrow Wilson who had been elected to the Presidency two months before. Harvey assured Morgan that his assertion that character was the basis of credit had made a favorable impression upon the country. "I hope so," remarked the financier. "I hated to go to Washington, but I am glad I went. Perhaps people know me better now."

The talk turned upon President-elect Wilson's advanced political views. Morgan regarded with apprehension Wilson's plans for corporation and financial legislation, but said he did not doubt the sincerity and the patriotism of either Mr. Wilson or his future Secretary of State, William J. Bryan. Morgan told of a man in London who had sought to win favor with him by speaking contemptuously of Bryan. Though he had always opposed Bryan, Morgan defended the Commoner as a loyal American. Harvey was moved to quote Scott's lines:

> Breathes there a man with soul so dead,
> Who never to himself hath said:
> "This is my own, my native land!"

Morgan asked Harvey to give the rest of the poem, which he did.

"Half a minute is a long time," recalled Colonel Harvey later, "but for fully that period Mr. Morgan sat perfectly still. Then he repeated as if soliloquizing: 'Who never to himself hath said: "this is my own, my native land,"' and rising with difficulty from his chair, for he seemed quite feeble, he said, with emphasis: 'When you see Mr. Wilson tell him for me that if there should ever come a time when he thinks any influence or resources that I have can be used for the country, they are wholly at his disposal.'"

Harvey left and Morgan again sat musing before the fire.

Later in the afternoon Judge Gary dropped in. After a long talk he started several times to go, but Morgan called him back, evidently reluctant to say goodby. Gary had seen Morgan declining physically for a year. The previous summer, at the Morgan country place in England—Dover House—Morgan had been called to the house from the garden, where the two were sitting. Gary noticed the financier's unaccustomed slowness in mounting the steps. Now, when the time came to withdraw, Gary gripped his host's hand and said: "Come back to us well and strong, Mr. Morgan." The master of the Library, with a look of indescribable sadness and a shake of his great head, replied: "I don't know. I may never come back."

Morgan knew that he was not to come back. He felt the approach of a magnificent darkness soon to close upon him; and calmly he set about preparing for the end.

The Sunday before he sailed he drove as usual to St. George's Church. He greeted everyone and stood out, almost in the aisle, beating time with his book, singing with strong voice and moist eyes his favorite hymn: "Blest Be the Tie That Binds."

Only three days before starting on the ocean journey from which he was not to return, he executed his will. The document began with the striking and extraordinary utterance of faith which we have already quoted. At the same time he prepared a memorandum for his funeral service. He placed this in a sealed envelope addressed to the Rev. Dr. Karl Reiland, rector of St. George's. Morgan prescribed a service of extreme simplicity, identical with the rites observed for his father. There was to be no eulogy, no address of any kind. Three hymns—"Lead, Kindly Light," "Asleep in Jesus," and the recessional "For All the Saints Who from Their Labors Rest"—were to be sung with the regular service of the Episcopal church. The financier asked that the Bishops of New York, Connecticut, and Massachusetts officiate at his funeral; also that Henry Burleigh, Negro baritone at St. George's, sing "Calvary" as a solo. Burleigh's voice was one of Morgan's delights.

The year before, he had transferred all of his art treasures in England to America. The effect, practically, was to shift the art centre of the world. Morgan had hoped some day to see all of his collections assembled together. It was not to be. He thought of leaving his great altarpiece by Raphael in the National Gallery in London, to which he had loaned it for many years. He made inquiry, however, as to the death duties which would have to be paid in case he died leaving this picture in England. When he ascertained, authoritatively, that the amount would be over $325,000, he concluded not to be generous to England at so great a cost.

Morgan's decision to remove his treasures to America caused wailing and moaning throughout England. "I make the transfer with great reluctance," he explained, "deeply appreciating the constant kindness and courtesies received and the appreciation shown by everyone in England. But, being an American citizen, there was no other way for me to avoid double duties by both the American and English authorities."

When he sailed from New York for Egypt on January 7 Morgan was a sick man. No physician was with him, but he was accompanied by his daughter, Mrs. Herbert L. Satterlee, and by the Count and Countess Jean La Grèze—the latter a daughter of Charles Steele, a Morgan partner.

The steamship on which he sailed, the *Adriatic*, grounded on a mudbank near Governor's Island for a few hours, but the rest of the trip was uneventful. Morgan reached Monte Carlo on January 22. After touching at Naples he visited the ruins of Pompeii. Then he went to Alexandria, reaching Cairo on February 7. Shortly afterwards he started up the Nile. Rumors that his health was greatly impaired were sent out from Cairo. It was said that he suffered from indigestion and that the trip had failed to benefit him.

The party returned to Cairo in ten days. It was apparent at once that Morgan was in a very serious condition. The utmost precautions were taken regarding his food. Fresh eggs and butter were sent to him from his Cragston farm at Highland Falls. On February 25, Herbert L. Satterlee, Morgan's son-in-law, joined the party in Cairo. Professor Giuseppe Bastianelli, the most celebrated specialist in Italy, was already in attendance upon the financier. Professor Bastianelli issued a bulletin which said that Morgan's condition was good and that the patient seemed to improve.

A few days later Morgan expressed a desire to see the ruins of the Temple of Karnak at Luxor. He wanted to drive around the ruins. A guard refused permission. There were protests, but the guard said that none could be wheeled around unless he went in an invalid's chair. This Morgan declined to do and returned to Cairo. His pride would not permit him to use a wheel chair. Besides, news that he was unable to walk would have been cabled to America, with possible bad effect upon the stock market.

Morgan was obliged, also, to forgo contemplated visits to the Khedive of Egypt and to Lord Kitchener. However, he was able to take part in the annual merry-making at Heliopolis, where he was pelted with flowers by American tourists and seemed to enjoy the experience. Every step, though, was now an effort and Morgan knew, if did none other, that his time was short. Looking out over the domes and minarets of the mosques, amid the mementoes of the ages, Morgan longed for Rome. He wanted his expiring knell to sound, if sound it must, in the Eternal City, not in a stronghold of the Moslem.

And so Morgan turned his weary eyes toward Italy. He arrived in Naples on March 13 and went immediately to Rome, where his old suite in the Grand Hotel had been made ready for him. There he received no visitors. He put in much of his time reading or playing solitaire. Others had joined his party now—Mrs. Lucy Lee, a cousin, Helen Hamilton, a granddaughter, Mrs. John Hulbert, and Dr. George A. Dixon, of New York. "Mr. Morgan's illness is due to overwork," insisted Herbert Satterlee. "He has no organic disease."

Morgan denied himself to all callers. He was put on a diet of chopped meat and barley soup. His physicians endeavored to reduce the number of his daily cigars. Up to Easter he seemed to be mending.

An acute change came on Easter Sunday. Morgan drove to the American Protestant Episcopal Church and walked with difficulty to the pew reserved for him. In the middle of the service he became ill and was assisted from the church. He did not leave his room again. He grew worse and much of the time was unconscious. His throat muscles refused to function and he could not swallow. Liquid nourishment was provided by injection. He could not talk, but his dominating, depthful eyes spoke for him.

On Thursday, March 27, he sank into a comatose state from which he did not arouse, except for fleeting periods. On Sunday night the doctors discovered that he was not assimilating his food. Then they knew that death was only a few days off. The sick man suffered no pain but simply wasted away; he literally starved to death. During Sunday night heart stimulants were administered without effect, and salt-water injections were tried.

The end came at five minutes past noon on Monday, March 31.

Mr. and Mrs. Satterlee and Miss Hamilton were in the room, besides three physicians and four nurses. There were no last words, no final gesture, as this tremendous personality left a world whose course he had so largely directed. For hours before death, the stricken man gave no sign, except that once or twice he seemed to smile in recognition of those about him. Once he extended his right arm across his breast, but the arm fell back at his side as if the effort were too much.

At the entrance to the Morgan suite stood the financier's faithful Italian courier, Antonio Pace. He wept frequently, but brushed back the tears when anyone approached.

News of the great financier's passing was not given to the public for three hours. Meanwhile there had been an exchange of cipher cables between Rome and New York. A detailed medical report was cabled to Morgan's son in New York. It was not made public. Widespread rumors that death had been caused by an organic disease of long duration were met on April 2 by formal report, signed by the attending physicians:

"When Mr. Morgan left New York he was a very tired man physically and mentally. His digestion and nutrition were impaired. It was hoped that his usual trip to Egypt would be of great benefit, giving him rest and building up his nervous strength, especially as he had no organic disease. His appetite failed, however, and consequently his strength and weight did not improve.

"Mr. Morgan contracted a severe cold while in Egypt, which further weakened him. A state of mental depression and feebleness developed. He arrived at Cairo in a very rundown condition, but during three weeks in Cairo he improved mentally and physically, his powers of concentration and memory showing no impairment. The trip to Rome did not fatigue him, and he continued to gain slowly for ten days.

"A week before his death his strength began to fail. He was put to bed on Wednesday afternoon, March 26. He became delirious, and extreme exhaustion followed. This continued until Sunday evening when he passed into a state of coma. He died at 12.05 P. M. on Monday.

(*signed*) "GIUSEPPE BASTIANELLI
"M. ALLAN STARR
"GEORGE A. DIXON."

While the great of the earth flooded the family with condolences, the body was brought on a special train to Havre; and from Havre to America on the liner *France*. A week later Morgan rested once more in his wonderful treasure-house in New York. Hundreds of friends

passed the bier. Upon the masterful countenance was
an expression of serenity seldom present in life. Large-
eyed and solemn, the financier's grandchildren were
taken to the beautiful rooms where he had romped and
played with them so often.

On the day of the funeral, April 14, the Stock Exchange closed for half a day, flags were at half-mast
upon hundreds of buildings, memorial meetings were
held in Paris and in Westminster Abbey. Commanding
figures in finance, art, and politics thronged St. George's,
while thousands pressed against police lines. Around
the chancel were banked magnificent floral tributes
from kings, emperors, governments. The coffin was
piled high with delicate Jacqueminot roses, Morgan's
favorite flower.

A special train sped to Hartford over Morgan's
favorite railroad. It was the hundredth anniversary of
the birth of Morgan's father, three days before his own
seventy-sixth anniversary. The modest cottage on
Asylum Street where Junius and Juliet Morgan had
first set up housekeeping was draped with black and
white streamers, crossed and re-crossed. Pip Morgan's
birthplace was now a boarding and lodging house with
two small shops on the ground floor.

Hartford paused to pay last respects to its famous
son. Business houses were closed, with drawn window
blinds, as were the city schools and the offices of munic-
ipal and state governments. Thousands stood with
bared heads as the cortège moved from the railroad
station to Cedar Hill cemetery. At intervals of twenty
seconds the great city fire bell tolled seventy-six peals.

The chimes of Christ Church played "Abide With Me," "Blest Be the Tie That Binds," "Just As I Am," "Lead, Kindly Light," "Nearer, My God, to Thee," "The Rock of Ages," and "Asleep in Jesus."

Morgan was laid at rest beside his parents and his paternal grandparents.

As in the case of so many men of large wealth, Morgan's fortune had been exaggerated. He left a net taxable estate of $68,384,680. The direct bequests totaled somewhat less than $20,000,000. J. P. Morgan, Jr., was residuary legatee. To him, also, was willed $3,000,000 outright. Trust funds of the same amount were established for each of the three daughters, Mrs. Satterlee, Mrs. William Pierson Hamilton, and Miss Anne Tracy Morgan. The widow was given an annuity of $100,000, $1,000,000 outright, and the use for life of city and country homes in this country. One million dollars each was left to the two sons-in-law.

The income of $500,000 was provided for the support of St. George's Church, as well as $100,000 to the Diocesan Convention for a mission in New York. An annuity of $25,000 was left to Dr. James W. Markoe, director of the Hospital of the Lying-In Institution; and the son was directed to continue, if necessary, Morgan's yearly donation of $100,000 to the Institution. Every servant, practically every employee in both England and America, was remembered.

Complete discretion was given the son in the disposition of the art treasures. Article 32 of the will read:

"I have been greatly interested for many years in gathering my collections of paintings, miniatures, porcelains, and other works of art, and it has been my desire and intention to make some suitable disposition of them or of such portions of them as I might determine, which would render them permanently available for the instruction and pleasure of the American people. Lack of the necessary time to devote to it has as yet prevented my carrying this purpose into effect.

"Unless I shall accomplish it, or make some disposition of these collections, in my lifetime, they will pass to my son, John Pierpont Morgan, Jr., or to his son, Junius Spencer Morgan, Jr., under the foregoing clauses of this will whereby I dispose of my residuary estate. Should either my said son or my said grandson thus succeed to the ownership of these collections, I hope he will be able, in such manner as he shall think best, to make a permanent disposition of them or of such portions of them as he may determine, which will be a substantial carrying out of the intentions which I have thus cherished. It would be agreeable to me to have 'The Morgan Memorial' which forms a portion of the property of the Wadsworth Atheneum at Hartford, Connecticut, utilized to effectuate a part of this purpose."

The collections were appraised at but $20,000,000 for taxation purposes—an estimate admittedly far below their value. For instance, the famous room of Fragonard's unique and beautiful panels cost Morgan $325,000. They were sold by Morgan's son to Henry C. Frick for $1,250,000 and became the most striking adornment of Frick's magnificent residence at Fifth Avenue and Seventeenth Street, former site of the Lenox Library.

Failure of the city of New York to provide a wing

at the Metropolitan Museum of Art prevented the
Morgan collections from being intact and forever available to the public. Morgan's son was bitterly criticized
for selling the Fragonards and other rarities. The son
once told a friend that he was forced to dispose of these
because of the alarming shrinkage in the estate after
payment of various death and transfer taxes.

Even under the swift and sudden detachment of
death, men could dimly perceive Morgan's great career
as a whole; could recognize in him the controlling figure
in an amazing half-century movement of the forces of
civilization. "We were fundamentally opposed," said
Theodore Roosevelt, "but I was struck by his very great
power and his truthfulness. Any kind of meanness and
smallness were alike wholly alien to his nature." Said
Lord Northcliffe: "Had he been born to country life
in England a century ago he might have become a great
squire, a sort of Coke of Norfolk, but a good deal more
Tory than that progressive landowner. He had all the
obstinacy, tenacity, and bulldog courage that we at-
tribute to the old Tory Squire."

Today, in a real sense, we are trying to live down the
Morgan methods. We shall never have another Morgan.
A better banking system has made another Pierpont
Morgan no longer indispensable in time of panic. Better
corporation laws, backed by more enlightened public
sentiment, have made another Morgan impossible in the
field of industry.

The Alexander of American finance appeared in the
single hour which had room for him and his methods.